# Abortion Politics in
## North America

# Abortion Politics in North America

## Melissa Haussman

LYNNE
RIENNER
PUBLISHERS

BOULDER
LONDON

Published in the United States of America in 2005 by
Lynne Rienner Publishers, Inc.
1800 30th Street, Boulder, Colorado 80301
www.rienner.com

and in the United Kingdom by
Lynne Rienner Publishers, Inc.
3 Henrietta Street, Covent Garden, London WC2E 8LU

**Library of Congress Cataloging-in-Publication Data**
Haussman, Melissa, 1959–
   Abortion politics in North America / Melissa Haussman.
      p.   cm.
   Includes bibliographical references and index.
   ISBN 1-58826-336-3 (hardcover : alk. paper)
   1. Abortion—Political aspects—United States.   2. Abortion—Political
aspects—Canada.   3. Abortion—Political aspects—Mexico.   I. Title.
   HV767.5.U5H38 2005
   363.46'097—dc22

                                                        2004026064

**British Cataloguing in Publication Data**
A Cataloguing in Publication record for this book
is available from the British Library.


Printed and bound in the United States of America

The paper used in this publication meets the requirements
of the American National Standard for Permanence of
Paper for Printed Library Materials Z39.48-1992.

5   4   3   2   1

*For Linda*

# Contents

# Acknowledgments

As with most books, *Abortion Politics in North America* was neither formulated nor conducted in an influence-free environment. Therefore, I wish to name certain individuals along the way who have helped me to hone this work.

First is Mary Clancy, former member of Parliament (Canada, 1988–1997) and consul general of the Canadian Consulate General to New England from 1997 to 2002. She was always available to toss ideas around and to give me her insights on events taking place in the Canadian Parliament at the crucial time when the subject of reintroducing a national abortion law was discussed. Another person in the Canadian government's representative network in the United States, Daniel Abele, the academic relations director in the Canadian Embassy in Washington, D.C., was always extremely helpful and encouraging regarding grant and research opportunities.

Others continually fighting to keep reproductive choice a reality in North America, who provided me with information, files, and networking opportunities, include Jane Koster of the Childbirth by Choice Trust in Toronto and director Marilyn Wilson and her extremely knowledgeable and active staff at the Canadian Abortion Rights Action League, Ottawa. I owe huge thanks also to Joyce Arthur of the Pro-Choice Canada Network, who maintains invaluable information and resource files. Additional thanks go to those who made themselves available for interviews and/or participated in various meetings, including Ellen Wiebe of Vancouver, British Columbia, and Maureen Paul of Boston. Thanks also to numerous contacts at the National Abortion and Reproductive Rights Action League in Massachusetts and Washington,

D.C., and the staff at the National Abortion Federation in Washington. Other extremely invaluable resources have included the staffs and publications from the Center for Reproductive Law and Policy, New York; the UN Development Fund for Women; and Mexfam in Mexico City and Tijuana/San Diego. I also benefited greatly from the work of Catholics for a Free Choice in the United States.

Within the scholarly community, my work on the Canadian abortion issue, which led me to develop this book, was fostered by the Research Network on Gender and the State (RNGS), codirected by Dorothy McBride Stetson, Department of Political Science, Florida Atlantic University, Boca Raton; and Amy Mazur, Department of Political Science, Washington State University, Pullman. Others who were of particular help within RNGS are Birgit Sauer, University of Vienna, Women's Policy Institute (my codirector on the RNGS "hot issue" network); Joyce Outshoorn and Jantine Oldersma, University of Leiden, the Netherlands; and my Canadian "team director," Kathy Teghtsoonian, University of Victoria, British Columbia. Scholarly colleagues in the United States who have been particularly helpful are fellow travelers in the area of comparative abortion policy studies, including Donley Studlar, Department of Political Science, West Virginia University; Ray Tatalovich, Department of Political Science, Loyola University, Chicago; Mildred Schwartz, emerita professor of political science, New York University (NYU); Judy Baer, Department of Politics, Texas A&M University; and Joyce Gelb, Department of Political Science, NYU. I have also been helped by numerous conversations with my friend and colleague in North American politics, Jeffrey Ayres, Department of Political Science, St. Michael's College, Colchester, Vermont.

My thanks also go to my partner, the Reverend Linda Privitera, who has watched as much change happen within the Worldwide Anglican Communion as I have witnessed in abortion rights in North America over the past five years. She has remained an incredibly good sport about all the travel and financial demands put upon us as I completed this project. Thanks also to good friends Michael and Jane Doherty in Vancouver, British Columbia, who have hosted me during numerous research and conference trips and who also work for justice in Canada. Others in this category include the Reverend Garth Bulmer, his wife Kathleen, and the Reverend Sharon Schollar, all of St. John's Anglican Church, Ottawa, a progressive outpost in a shrinking constellation.

For their continued tolerance, good humor, and most especially their support, financial and otherwise, I thank the College of Arts and Sciences at Suffolk University (including former dean, Michael Ronayne, and current dean, Kenneth Greenberg) and my colleagues in the Government Department. In particular, I thank Agnes Bain, John Berg, Judy Dushku, and Sebastian Royo for their unfailing support and good jokes. Thank you also to Lynne Rienner of Lynne Rienner Publishers and two important editors there, Leanne Anderson and Karen Williams.

# 1

# Exploring the
# Policy Paradox of Abortion

The reality of current access to abortion services in Canada, the United States, and Mexico is located in a gap formed between legal declarations of rights and the extent of health services provisions. In Canada and the United States, abortion is legal at the national level. In Mexico, abortion remains a part of the Mexican national criminal code and thus is illegal. However, there is subnational (and sub rosa) access to abortion services in Mexico in private facilities for those who can pay. In Canada, access to abortion services has been in decline since the early 1990s due to shrinking health-care services, numbers of providers, and some legal constraints that typically cover facilities' funding. In the United States, most of the constraints exist in a sharper format because although first-trimester abortions remain legal under the 1973 *Roe v. Wade* decision, the parameters for legal action against facilities are wider than in Canada. For example, such parameters include twenty-four-hour waiting periods and "conscience clauses" exempting pro-life medical personnel from performing abortions. The numbers of abortion providers in the United States have also decreased because of extremist attacks on facilities and personnel.

*Abortion Politics in North America* explains the historic and current variations in abortion access among Canada, the United States, and Mexico by looking first to the different structures of federalism found in each country, including which constitutional powers are given to which levels of government. The explanation encompasses the political opportunities for both sides of the abortion question within these federal structures. Another part of the explanation is found in identifying the ways in which federal divisions in these countries have camouflaged a lack of political will on the abortion question, at times leading the pro-choice and pro-life movements within them to lobby a different level of government. Therefore, variations in the constitutional forms and political interpretations of federalism comprise the main explanatory factor for abortion policy differences across these three political systems. What will also be seen is that both the United States and Canada had relatively brief periods of federal political will to get involved in the abortion question and to mandate conditions of access. This period spanned from 1973 until the 1980s in the United States and from 1969 until 1988 in Canada. What is also true is that, since the 1980s, these two federal governments have withdrawn from being the main policymaking level and referee on abortion and have turned these functions over to the states and provinces, respectively. This is likely the result of intense pro-life lobbying and attacks as anything else. The outcome for women in these countries has not been positive. Conversely, Mexico has never gone through the stage of federal will to oversee a relatively consistent set of rules for abortion access. Thus, women remain caught in a strange scenario in which abortion is almost always illegal but readily accessible for a price. In this climate, there is no guarantee to a safe, much less an inexpensive, abortion.

In Mexico, federalism has traditionally been defined mainly as a top-down affair with the bulk of power vested in the president. This has begun to change, however, since the fall of the Institutional Revolutionary Party (PRI) and the election of the National Action Party (PAN) president, Vicente Fox, in 2000. Canada has been at the opposite end of the spectrum, having the most decentralized federation since the 1940s through granting of increased financial powers to the provinces, the subnational units. Yet the provinces are constitutionally limited in the health-care field, denying abortion opponents the opportunities to pass restrictions such as those seen in the United States. While the United States falls between Mexico (a traditionally pro-national federal structure) and Canada (a pro-subnational structure), it is arguably the most porous of the three polities in having fifty state governments open to lobbying by social movements. This may be compared with the thirty-one Mexican states and ten Canadian provinces.

It is important to relate historic and current differences in the interpretation of constitutional powers under federalism in the three countries to social movement organizing. In the United States, 87 percent of counties have no abortion provider. In the smallest Canadian province of Prince Edward Island, no abortions have been officially performed since the early 1980s. While abortion is nationally illegal in Mexico, data from the United Nations (UN) indicate that nearly a quarter of Mexican women of childbearing age have had an abortion.[1] The unfortunate truth of all three countries, based on federal models, is that where a woman lives within them largely determines her access to abortion services. The geographical inequities are often compounded by fiscal ones, so that if a woman must travel to have an abortion and does not have the money, she faces an insurmountable barrier.

Canada, the United States, and Mexico have been linked in the world's largest free trade agreement, the North American Free Trade Agreement (NAFTA), since 1994; therefore, it is logical to study these nations together. It is also true that the United States and Canada have viewed each other as their number one trading partner and ally since the nineteenth century. Culturally, many works describe Canada and the United States as similar, although there are important differences to note as well, particularly in Canada's support for bilingualism and multiculturalism. This study of political frameworks and movements across North America is also important at this time because the largest and best-funded pro-choice and pro-life movements in the world are based in the United States, are active in Canada and Mexico, and regularly confront each other at UN conferences.

This chapter describes the factors contributing to the policy paradox of national constitutional legality of abortion (or illegality in Mexico) versus subnational access to it. First, the different structures of the three political systems are shown, including relevant wide-scale changes in Canada and Mexico. Second, the nature of interest-group and social movement access to each political system are described. Finally, a review of the legal status of abortion in the three countries is provided along with why political elites seem to tolerate a vast gap between the federal reality of abortion in the United States and Canada and decreasing access to it subnationally; this equation is reversed for Mexico.

## The United States

### Political Structure

The U.S. political structure has often been described as porous and containing multiple power centers based on its separation-of-powers framework at both the national and state level. U.S. legislators at both the national and state level function with a large degree of independence from party constraint upon voting, unlike their counterparts found in parliamentary democracies. Recognized theorists of federalism have pointed to the U.S. system as one of having "fifty policy laboratories," where states can, in effect, try out different policy options to be either copied or improved upon by other states or the national government.[2] Some activists in social movement organizations have accused Congress of not having had the political will to resolve the abortion question, yet in some instances Congress cannot do so because criminal law formulation is shared with state legislatures. In contrast, pro-life activists have decried the increased judicialization of abortion policy while having been highly successful participants in it.[3]

One of the baselines of disaggregating power under the U.S. Constitution was the separation of powers thesis elucidated by James Madison in "Federalist No. 51" of *The Federalist Papers*. Asserting in this paper and in another, "Federalist No. 10," that the "greatest cause of evil in [U.S.] society is faction," which he attributed to "various and unequal distribution of property," he proposed to remedy this by the checks and balances and separation of powers system ultimately enshrined in the Constitution. While many believed that the Federalists wished to make Congress (as the "people's representative") the preeminent branch, the final outcome was one of three coequal branches. This system included sharing of some similar powers but reservation of other unique ones across the three branches. Madison advocated this so as to "first allow the government to control the governed, and in the next place oblige it to control itself." Since the Constitution's implementation, debate has taken place within the United States as to whether Madison's scheme of "fighting faction with faction" has really worked. Pluralist political scientists generally hold that the Madisonian scheme has worked over time, avoiding a concentration of power by one social segment in one governmental branch. The response from the critical theorists has been that "the choir sings with a decidedly upper-class accent" in the seemingly egalitarian United States.[4] Thus, critical theorists have believed that the government has a decided predisposition to favor the interests of the rich and powerful. This became a more marked trend in the late twentieth-century period of escalating corporate campaign contributions.

## Social Movement Organization Access

The large amounts of money needed to run for national political office in the United States, unmatched anywhere else in the world, has meant that well-funded groups tend to gain more consistent access to policymakers. Groups lacking monetary clout must be able to portray themselves as moderates and open to compromise to gain access to the legislative halls of power. Yet one lever of access that has been available to "outsider" groups off and on throughout history is the Supreme Court, often described as the most active—and activist—in the world.

U.S. policymakers most often describe themselves as mainstream, protecting the tenets of liberal (elected) democracy with two middle-of-the-road parties. It is not surprising that, more often than not, the social movement groups having most success on a policy question upon its introduction tend toward the mainstream. Within the constellation of abortion policy, the groups having the most access throughout the first one hundred years of abortion regulation, from the late nineteenth century through *Roe v. Wade* in 1973, were those that could be described as typically moderate. They included doctors and lawyers through the 1960s and then, with the founding of the U.S. second-wave women's movement in the 1960s, the liberal mainstream groups within the women's movement. Since the late 1970s, the constellation has changed on the pro-life side to include groups that could only be described as terrorist, those which condone killing doctors and destroying clinics and their personnel. Within the more mainstream pro-life organizations, which believe in electoral and litigation strategies, their strategy has moved successfully to devolve decisionmaking on U.S. abortion policy to the states. This devolution began by 1980 but was most clearly expressed in the 1989 *Webster v. Reproductive Health Services* decision; since this time, it may be said that pro-life forces have been more successful at chipping away at U.S. constitutional law protecting abortion and that pro-choice forces have been moved into a rearguard action, trying to defend the existing right to privacy as enshrined in *Roe*.

## Legal Status of Abortion

Abortion policy, probably because of its controversy, was largely untouched by U.S. policymakers until the second half of the nine-

teenth century. Many experts have attributed the shifts toward crimi-
nalization across the states to the medical profession's desire to
assert control over all facets of reproduction.[5] Common law, based
on the British framework, was and is a major source of family law,
which itself is a good-sized component of the states' powers. Until
the mid-nineteenth century, women could make the decision about
whether to abort a fetus before "quickening" (without the means
being specified, usually either self-induced or with the help of a midwife), but the laws changed significantly after that time. All states
then changed their laws to permit abortion only where, in the doctor's opinion, continuing the pregnancy endangered the mother's
life.[6] Not only was the abortion decision shifted from the woman to
the doctor, it drove midwives out of providing abortion services and
gave physicians discretion as to whether to provide the services or
not. While the numbers of physicians performing the services were
not great, the latitude embedded in the new laws could cover a variety of situations.

For the twentieth century, a patchwork of state laws governed the
constitutional and access questions for abortion. In the early 1970s, a
challenge to Texas law, accepted by the U.S. Supreme Court, brought
about the "nationalizing moment" in abortion policy, which began
with the 1973 *Roe v. Wade* decision. The nationalized policy moment
in our history on abortion policy has been the shortest of any, lasting
a mere sixteen years. This short period of nationally directed policy,
falling in between centuries and decades of state-led policy, illustrates national politicians' tolerance for ambiguity on this most fundamental legal question and the most fundamental right to privacy as
enshrined in various Supreme Court decisions.

Within the climate of national political ambiguity that has
regained supremacy since the 1980s, the pro-life movement has
acted successfully to restrict abortion access at the state level. Eleven
states are currently on record as being ready to eliminate abortion
access if *Roe* is overturned. Twenty-eight states are listed as being at
risk for abortion-access reduction either through legislative or gubernatorial initiatives. Forty-five states now have conscience clauses
that cover either medical personnel or institutions opposed to abortion.[7] Twenty-eight states and the District of Columbia currently follow the restrictions set forth in the Hyde Amendment, which pro-
hibits all federal Medicaid funds for abortion except for
endangerment to women's health or in rape or incest cases. Twenty-

one states fund abortions, to varying degrees, beyond the Hyde restrictions.[8] Similarly, thirty-one states have banned "partial-birth" (officially referred to as dilation and extraction, or D&X, in the medical literature) or other abortion procedures, although the National Abortion Federation (NAF) states that at least twenty of them lack the constitutional woman's health exemption as articulated in the 2000 Supreme Court case *Stenberg v. Carhart*.[9]

The current status of abortion access in the United States is more tenuous than most people realize. Recent figures from NARAL Pro-Choice America show that 49 percent of U.S. pregnancies are currently unintended, including 30 percent of those within marriage. And with 86 percent of counties having no identified abortion provider, access to services can be difficult. The majority of abortions in the United States are sought within the first trimester—88 percent within the first twelve weeks, going up to 90 percent within the first twenty weeks of pregnancy.[10]

In January 2003, the Alan Guttmacher Institute, one of the most reputable and well-known independent providers of statistics on U.S. and global contraception, reproductive rights, and abortion policies, released a report stating that the U.S. abortion rate had dropped to its lowest level in twenty-nine years. This was explained mainly by factors such as increased contraception use and access to emergency contraception. Another factor given was the declining infrastructure for abortion provision. The national picture of access to abortion now appears polarized, with the abortion rate having decreased in thirty-five states during the period under study since 1973 and increasing in fifteen. The states with minimal access restrictions find themselves more heavily used. Bearing out this picture is that, in the same time period, the Guttmacher report stated that "the number of providers declined in 38 states and rose in nine."[11] Of the three countries discussed in this book, the United States leans toward the polarized spectrum of access.

## Canada

### Political Structure

Despite its often stodgy, traditionalist portrayal in world media, Canada has been a cutting-edge polity in its political structure. It is considered the first country to have combined a Westminster (British-based) majoritarian parliamentary system with federalism, in which subnational government units have distinct powers. Having worked in various ways to integrate its settlers of native, French, and English origins in various "compact theories" from the 1700s onward, Canada as such was formed through the *British North America Act* of 1867. Newfoundland, the last province to join Canada, was tied to Britain until 1949; similarly, a new territory, Nunavut (literally "Our Land" in the language of the native Inuit peoples) was carved from eastern Arctic territory at the end of the twentieth century.

With reference to the party system, the two main parties that have historically controlled the national government have been the Conservatives, more linked to the British tradition, and the Liberals, who appeal to francophone and anglophone voters. Canadian parties have undergone realignments at certain times. One western protest party of the left, the New Democratic Party, has maintained seats in the federal Parliament since its creation from the previous Cooperative Commonwealth Federation (CCF) in the 1960s. Other more recent factionally created parties have been the socially conservative Reform Party of the western provinces, which recently merged with some social conservatives from the national Conservative Party, forming the National Alliance, which currently holds official opposition party status in the House of Commons. On the other end of the spectrum is the pro-Quebec separatist, pro–French language Bloc Québécois, which emerged in the early 1990s from the wings of former Conservatives from Quebec. Since 1993, Bloc Québécois and the Reform Party (as previously called) traded places with each other as the official opposition, as they represented the majority of the previous Conservative Party.

Another important factor is how the Canadian Parliament works. The House of Commons, the major lawmaking body, is popularly elected, theoretically representing each province based on population, although somewhat overweighted in favor of Quebec and Ontario. The reverse is said to be true for the appointed Senate, where certain regions with lower populations (notably Atlantic Canada) are often viewed as disproportionately favored to the exclusion of provinces west of Ontario. Indeed, that is the source of much of the Alliance Party's current discontent. As a nonelected chamber, the Senate's role has traditionally been to consider individually based bills, known as Private Member Bills, and to acqui-esce to the will of the popularly elected House. The Senate's role in Canadian abortion politics in the early 1990s was highly unusual, as will be seen. Two final relevant factors at this point include first that traditionally the Canadian House of Commons has operated as "the most party-disciplined legislature in the world," surpassing even the British House of Commons.[12] This has framed traditional expectations for party members' behavior on all sides of the aisle, but it also changed somewhat along with the Senate's role in the abortion legislation debate of the late 1980s through the early 1990s.

## Social Movement Organization Access

The nature of civil society actors' access to political power in Canada is quite different from those in the other two countries, given the dif-ferences in political structure and culture. Since the 1980s, the Canadian House of Commons has become increasingly executive centered. The prime minister (PM) and his/her executive agencies plus the prime minister's office and Privy Council Office, which has more of a liaison responsibility between the PM and the Privy Councillors (past and present Cabinet ministers), have become the main political actors on shepherding legislation through the legisla-tive pathways. Most legislation in the Canadian system is govern-ment sponsored, and there are only rare opportunities to amend government-sponsored legislation.

In terms of civil society group access to the government, the Canadian system would likely best be described as falling in between the continuum of the Mexican system as historically the most closed to civil society influence and the United States as the most open. The Canadian system shares with the other two counterparts the idea that getting access to the executive branch (including highest levels of the bureaucracy) is important when trying to initiate legislation. Traditionally, of the three countries, Canada has placed the highest importance on having a neutral civil service below the level of politi-cal appointees. If a group wished to influence forthcoming govern-mental legislation on a matter (such as abortion), they would have to gain access to either a politically appointed member of the minister's department (such as at the deputy ministerial level) or to the minister herself.

In this political system, civil society members are often limited to being in reactive mode when the government has formally tabled legislation and therefore must combine tactics such as lobbying individual House members (in both government and opposition) with wide-scale publicity-drawing actions, for example, sitting in the gallery during House debates, marching on Parliament Hill, and getting into the newspapers and onto TV. Only those groups that seem moderate and open to compromise have gained the extraordinary degree of access needed to affect legislation before the government party introduces it to the House of Commons. Throughout most of its history, the Canadian political system has been marked by its degree of closure to interest-group access, for high-level bureaucrats and Cabinet ministers are difficult to sway. Again, the comparison with the Mexican system must be kept in mind, for the Canadian closed system has functioned within a commitment to democracy, whereas that has not always been the case with Mexico (hence, Canada's middle position on the structure-of-access spectrum). Finally, campaign contribution access to members of Parliament (MPs) in the Canadian system is simply not as available as in the United States, because Canadian elections are conducted within the environment of spending limits and public financing. Private contributions, when they occur, are much more likely to go to the national or provincial party committee than to an individual candidate.

Moving from civil society in general to the women's movement in particular, the Canadian one, like its U.S. counterpart, has been found mostly in the liberal, rights-based branch. These groups usually have emphasized working within the existing political and legal systems, placing pressure on legislators and effecting coalitions with powerful insiders, such as physicians.

### Legal Status of Abortion

In the late 1960s, under newly elected Liberal Party prime minister Pierre Trudeau, Canada began an omnibus revision of its federal criminal code.[13] One of the many amendments enacted included the decriminalization of abortion. The issue was brought to the forefront both by policymakers, especially those in the third-party opposition ranks, as well as the Canadian Medical Association (CMA) working with the Canadian Bar Association. By 1966, the CMA had developed an internal mandate to work to decriminalize abortion.[14]

The main part of the reform included specifying a limited set of conditions under which abortion would be considered legal and, therefore, not a criminal offense for either the woman or the doctor. This was a significant shift from the system in place over the previous one hundred years, where a physician could be decertified, fined, and imprisoned (as in the United States until 1973), and a woman could be prosecuted. The umbrella under which legal abortions could be performed in Canada from 1967 onward required abortions to be performed in qualified hospitals, and agreement was required from three doctors from the hospital constituting a "therapeutic abortion committee" (TAC), none of whom could be the one actually performing the abortion. The TAC was required to approve the abortion on the grounds offered by the World Health Organization, that withholding the procedure would damage a woman's health or end her life.

The omnibus reform only set up the structure within which legal abortions could be performed. Many have stated that this reflected the unofficial reality that had been present for years, similar to that in the U.S.[15] The reform contained no mandate that hospitals become accredited to perform abortions, nor did it require that hospitals implement TACs. While officially reported abortion rates climbed across Canada into the 1970s, abortion facilities were limited mainly to the urban areas of British Columbia, Ontario, and Quebec.

In 1988, the legal regime that had governed Canadian abortion provision since 1967 was overturned in the *Morgentaler v. The Queen* decision (decriminalizing abortion) issued by the Supreme Court of Canada. Since that time, there have been virtually no controlling federal laws on the subject of abortion, save that it be performed by a qualified physician. This has meant that the bulk of pro-choice organizing has concerned ways in which to keep abortion facilities fully funded by the federal and provincial governments to keep facilities open and doctors performing abortions. The main recourse available to pro-life activists then has been either on the symbolic or terrorist ends of the spectrum, as provincial legislatures have no constitutional authority to pass the sorts of restrictions available to U.S. state legislatures. Symbolic protests have occurred outside of clinics, on Parliament Hill in Ottawa, and in the courts, where several have tried unsuccessfully to have the definition of "life" altered to begin at conception. Terrorist attacks have included acid attacks on clinics, burning of clinics, and wounding of Canadian doctors. One such prominent attack on British Columbia physician Garson Romalis was conducted by James Kopp, killer of U.S. physician Barnett Slepian.

## Mexico

### Political Structure

While Mexico is technically a federation, it is the most top-heavy of the three countries under review, as the national constitution supersedes any state or district legislation not in accordance with it. One observer has characterized Mexico as a "nominally federalist system," with nearly absolute power concentrated in the president's hands.[16] The Mexican president, with his appointed party council, designates his successor, until 2000 assumed to be in the PRI. The new president then chooses his Cabinet and advisers. While technically the Senate must approve high judicial and military appointments, this is in practice a formality because usually all or nearly all of them are from the president's party. It has been noted, also, that "the Supreme Court rarely makes the news, since most legal cases are solved outside the court system."[17] This holds true for women's abortion access. The president as the center of the system dates back to the early 1930s, prior to which the national legislature, Congress, had more bases of autonomy. With the rise of the PRI, however, the power shifted to the executive, where it has remained.

From its founding in 1929 through 2000 when it lost the presidential election, the PRI was not only the majority party at the federal level, it was viewed as the apparatus of national governance in Mexico. As noted by one scholar, "As the tool of a highly vertical and centralized power structure, its job is to mobilize the population behind the president."[18] Similarly, the party was described as "a vote-getting machine with few ideological principles other than holding on to state power."[19] To many observers, the intertwining of the national state and the PRI in Mexico was a near-total result. Future reforms to the Mexican state could only come by weakening PRI power, which seemed laughable to many. Similarly, only internal changes to the PRI could ever be forecast to make the party function more democratically.

One change that began to be apparent in the 1980s was the separation of the executive—the PRI president and close advisers in his

Cabinet—from the rest of the party apparatus. These "technocrats," as they are commonly known, usually come from wealthy families and obtained their educations at Ivy League universities. This began to distance those who ran the Cabinet departments along technocratic and increasingly neoliberal lines from the "dinosaurios," or party hacks solely concerned with maintaining power.

The other change that has led to new party control of the presidency since 2000 has been the increased mobilization of civil society as a reaction to PRI excesses, as well as new avenues for the expression of opposition. It can be traced both to the rise of technocrats and drastic shifts in Mexico's economic fortunes as it joined the global economy. PRI president Carlos Salinas de Gortari, from 1988 to 1994, was known as the technocrat and privatizing advocate par excellence. His policies included "sharply reducing public spending, modernizing Mexico's communications infrastructure, privatizing most public enterprises, internationalizing banking, liberalized trade, and encouraging foreign investment."[20] Although this made Mexico look like an extremely attractive plum for outside investment, these changes lead to a drop in real wages and a dramatic increase in poverty for the majority of Mexican citizenry. While in 1993 Mexico was included in the "first world" economic system by becoming a signatory to NAFTA, which mainly opened Mexico to foreign investment, "more than 50 percent of its citizens were living below the poverty line, and about 30 percent in absolute poverty."[21]

Cuauhtemoc Cardenas, son of a founder of the PRI, broke away from the PRI by creating a new political party in 1988, the Partido de la Revolucion Democratica (Party of the Democratic Revolution, PRD). This party became attractive to social movement groups newly mobilized in the 1980s, particularly concentrated in and around the Federal District (DF), basically Mexico City. The splinter PRD has mainly drawn votes from urban dwellers or in some instances poor rural ones such as in Chiapas. In terms of the pre-existing national parties, the PRI and the National Action Party (PAN), it is the former that has lost far more of its voting strength to the PRD. The PAN's Christian Democratic basis could not work with a party officially interested in abortion reform and other reforms disagreeable to the Catholic Church, so it, in turn, has been less affected. The PAN was first helped by the PRI's internal split mainly at the subnational level, for prior to the 1980s the PRI had never allowed a subnational election in which the PAN won to stand as the official result.

By 1989, due to the size of the win, the PRI officially recognized the PAN gubernatorial victory in the northern state of Baja California, "the first time an opposition candidate had been allowed to win a statehouse since PRI was formed" (in 1929).[22] These wins were followed by PRD control of the state of Chiapas and Mexico City after the 1997 election.[23] The increasingly vital social movement presence has helped to keep the expanded spectrum of party competition going, and in 1997 the PAN won majority control of the national House of Deputies and the presidency under Vicente Fox in 2000.

### Social Movement Organization Access

Social movement access is in the same interesting state as the political structure, because the decoupling of the PRI and national state control has broadened available space in both the party system and state institutions. Until the 1980s and in some cases the 1990s, social movement groups only existed officially through cooptation into the PRI through a corporatist structure. While movements could claim to have representation in the party structure, the chief beneficiary was always the PRI-dominated state. The corporatist structure worked mainly to allow the PRI state to maintain top-down control of the biggest social sectors, including farmers, laborers, and peasants. The disintegration of the PRI's control beginning in the middle 1980s must be viewed as occurring in tandem with the rise of social movement opportunities for organizing and their resulting presence in public life. Consequently, the vital social movement presence fed opposition parties, mainly the splinter PRD, which drew heavily from the PRI. The result was that the PAN won majority control of the national House of Deputies in 1997 and at the presidential level in 2000.

The appearance of new social movement groups in the 1980s was in response to many factors. They included women's activities in response to the devastating 1985 earthquake in Mexico City, particularly in the face of state inaction. Another newly empowered sector covered what has been called the "professional middle class," including public sector employees, middle-class and poor urban dwellers, and students. Part of civil society's transformation was enabled by changes involving "a more educated civil society . . . much more mobilized at the local level." These newly mobilized also had access to new technology such as the Internet and a decentralized telecommunications network that previously had been privately controlled by a PRI-allied firm.[24]

## Legal Status of Abortion

The Mexican government added abortion to its federal criminal code in 1931.[25] Although states are assigned the jurisdiction of regulating how health services are delivered, including reproductive services, they have very little leeway on this, as "states may not pass laws which contravene the federal constitution."[26] Each of the thirty-one states, as well as the DF of Mexico City, shares the exception to the national prohibition that women who are raped may petition the state's attorney general to permit an abortion.[27]

In the case of abortions not meeting the state's designated criteria, women who either begin an abortion procedure or consent to it are subject to a prison term of one to five years. The national code decrees that while it is illegal to begin an abortion procedure, a woman who goes to a hospital may be treated (i.e., the procedure may be completed). Thus, while treated, she may also be charged, leading to the fact that many women choose not to go to hospitals if an abortion procedure goes wrong. An exception to the national law provides that "a woman of good reputation and has hidden her pregnancy" can have the term of imprisonment reduced to six months to a year.[28] Imprisonment of women is extremely rare, but it has happened. More often, she simply pays approximately U.S.$100 to avoid prosecution.[29] Knowledgeable organizations put the annual figure at anywhere between 0.5 million and 1.5 million procedures per year. This is the highest rate of any Latin American country. Given the unofficial availability of abortion to those who can pay the fee, it is perhaps not surprising that illegal abortion is the third largest cause of pregnant women's death in Mexico.[30]

The role of physicians in this framework is ambiguous. Obviously, many physicians in Mexico are performing abortions illegally for those who can pay the fee. Only physicians are allowed to perform an abortion, as was decreed in 1976 by the Federal Ministry for Public Health.[31] On one hand, physicians are in an odd situation, in not being able to contest publicly for federal reform. On the other hand, some have served on boards of family-planning organizations that support both abortion provision and abortion law reform in

Mexico. There is evidence that the topic of abortion is becoming more publicly contested by women's and other social movement groups, even under the PAN (Christian Democratic) government.

## Social Movement Concepts
## of Pro- and Anti-Choice Tactics

One very helpful social movement concept for this analysis is that of "transnational advocacy networks," developed by Margaret Keck and Kathryn Sikkink.[32] Keck and Sikkink's work points up the fluid and changing nature of advocacy networks. Such networks of social movement organizations continually create their identities through discourse with internal and external actors. The process in which "actors and interests are constituted in interaction" is shown in the ways that the North American pro-choice and pro-life movements have shown evidence of strategic learning from each other. Following from the notion that social movement identities and strategies are constituted through interactions is Keck and Sikkink's point that "transnational advocacy networks must be understood as political spaces, in which differently situated actors negotiate . . . the (social, cultural and political) meanings of their enterprise."[33]

Another well-known social movement theory that has contributed to our understanding of how and when social movement organizations emerge and gain success is Tarrow's "political opportunity structure." Sidney Tarrow has found that social movement organizations will be aided when the state is open to their demands, when powerful allies are available, alignments in either state or society shift, and/or divisions are present among elites.[34] An example regarding abortion politics in the United States is that for anti-choice activists the opportunity structure within the Republican Party opened up after Ronald Reagan's presidential nomination. This involved pro-life organizations' gaining entrée into the national platform-writing process, producing their long-desired "human life amendment" in the Republican platform, beginning in 1984. Here in *Abortion Politics in North America,* the political opportunity structure is examined both over time within each country and cross-nationally, to ascertain when it opened to help each side of the abortion issue.

Keck and Sikkink believe that there are three strategic options for transnational advocacy networks. The first is symbolic politics, whereby "activists frame issues by identifying and providing convincing explanations for powerful symbolic events, which in turn become catalysts for the growth of networks."[35] The use of symbolic politics is central to the domestic and transnational pro- and anti-choice movements in North America. Another available strategy is that of "leverage politics," where network activists pressure institutions, "either by financial or moral means . . . affect public opinion via the media . . . and aid in mobilizing their own members."[36] Through leverage politics to implicate a powerful institution, a weak group may be able to gain important allies with whom it can influence the state. The presence of helpful allies is also central to Tarrow's theoretical structure.

Leverage politics may take two forms, according to Keck and Sikkink. The first, material leverage, can involve money in campaigns, or votes in international organizations, such as UN votes for economic sanctions on countries to exert human rights change. The second type, moral leverage, can involve the "mobilization of shame." U.S.-based examples include threats by mass membership organizations—such as the National Rifle Association or the American Association of Retired People, to take the largest—to withhold votes from members of Congress, or even to actively campaign against them. Another option in this vein would "hold the behavior of target actors up to the light of international scrutiny."[37] Both pro- and anti-choice movements in the United States have become increasingly fond of using the electoral method of morality politics. One example is that of the Susan B. Anthony List (a pro-life organization) helping to elect many conservative Republican women as U.S. House members in 1994. The third type of advocacy network strategy is the use of accountability politics, which seems to be almost indistinguishable from the concept of moral leverage. Accountability strategies involve holding governments accountable for their actions, usually through the threat of mobilization against them if they don't do what the group wants.

With regard to the potential for success of their identified strategies, Keck and Sikkink state that transnational social movement networks have organized most effectively on two sets of issues: "issues involving bodily harm to vulnerable individuals" and "issues involving legal equality of opportunity."[38] This is fascinating for the scope of this book, because it fits perfectly the rhetoric of both the anti- and pro-choice movements, showing why this conflict will likely be omnipresent. It also shows why these conflicts, which many feel are domestic only, have increasingly been used successfully in organizing transnational activism. This has been true, for example, when the Vatican tries to tell globally southern women that radical women of the global north only want to involve other women in their own radical causes rather than being genuinely interested in helping all with issues of reproductive control. Conversely, Planned Parenthood International and the International Women's Health Coalition (IWHC), for instance, have been extremely active in countering the Vatican's arguments.

## Economic Forces upon the Political Opportunity Structure

The United States, Canada, and Mexico have each seen their national budgets cut back since the early 1990s under the neoliberal philosophy. The parts of the budgets usually the hardest hit are those relating to social policy, such as education and health care. In the three North American countries under study, the adoption of the neoliberal doctrine involved a shift to a leaner model of government service delivery premised upon private-sector practices, such as efficiency and cost accounting. However, the sources of the shifts to neoliberalism were a bit different for Canada and the United States, as developed countries, compared to the Mexican shift under some force from the more industrialized world. Many believe that free trade as contained in NAFTA in 1994 caused neoliberal policies in these three countries. While revisions to sectoral trade policies have indeed had some effects, they are clearly not the lone or largest causal agent in countries' governance model shifts since the 1980s. For example, the United States and Canada were integrated as each other's number one trading partners in the 1940s, cemented by free trade in 1965 for the most significant trading sector between the United States and Canada, that of the automotive industry. While Canada and the United States ultimately recognized their integration formally in the precursor agreement to NAFTA, the Canada-U.S. Free Trade Agreement of 1989, each government had also been working, although unsuccessfully, to trim its national budget deficits throughout the 1980s. Mexico not only had the same lack of success regarding the deficit, but it was subject to oil price crashes on the global market and then a self-induced currency devaluation crisis in the early 1990s, just prior to NAFTA's implementation.

Thus, these three North American countries have witnessed trajectories since the early 1980s that are largely parallel but sometimes intertwine. The first involves the signing of free trade agreements, and the second involves the domestic politics of budget cutting. Unfortunately for those facing lack of resources and, thus, most dependent on the welfare state (often women, who are much more likely in these countries to live in poverty than men across their life spans), the parts of the budget most often deemed expendable and inflationary have been precisely those that keep women and children lifted above poverty. In the name of improving "efficiency," all three North American governments generally reduced their public-sector outlay between 1990 and 2000. For example, the governments in the United States and Mexico reduced government outlays as a percentage of gross domestic product (GDP) by about 10 percent, and in Canada it was reduced slightly more, by about 12 percent.[39] In Mexico and Canada during that time, percentage of overall budget spending on health declined; the largest decline was in Canada. It did not decline in the United States because the private administration of the health sector in effect underwrites its glaring inefficiencies and thus retains it as a high ticket item within the GDP.

## The Structure of This Book

Chapters 2–4 cover the creation of abortion as a political problem in the United States, Canada, and Mexico, detailing how the laws regarding abortion have changed over time and what social movements on both sides of the issue have been able to do. Chapter 5 takes the main domestic social movement actors identified in Chapters 2–4, including Planned Parenthood, the National Abortion Federation, IWHC, Catholics for a Free Choice, and various denominational organizations on the pro-choice side, and Human Life International, Human Life International–Canada, Pro-Vida, and the Vatican as main actors on the anti-choice side and describes their actions at recent UN conferences. It will be shown that as UN conference structures have evolved to take increasing account of non-governmental organizations' input, and by doing so in the name of democratization, it also provided further opportunities for polarization and wasting of precious dialogue time at the conferences.

Throughout these chapters, the shifts across federal sites with regard to policy control over abortion—for example, from subnational to national or vice versa—will be discussed. The social movement theories relating to political opportunity structure changes and developing transnational advocacy networks are relied upon to explain how and why the policy debates and control shifted back and forth within these three countries constructed along federal lines. The theories will also present ways to explain social movement learning from one side to another and how this learning may be present in a later period in the country, for instance, how right-to-life-strategists in the United States and Canada learned from the first periods of subnational control to bring back abortion policy to subnational control after the 1980s. It will also be shown how this learning has been analogous to transnational networks' organizing at UN conferences, where pro-life forces have tried to argue, mostly unsuccessfully, for returning control of women's health policy generally and reproductive control specifically to the national level. Where relevant, party changes in government are discussed.

Chapter 6, the concluding chapter, will pull together the insights presented throughout this discussion as to the highly fluctuating and overtly political nature of abortion rights and access and how the only guarantee that they continue to be defined in a woman-friendly manner is constant vigilance by women governmental representatives and in NGOs. It will offer both heartening and discouraging news about the degrees to which the pro-choice and pro-life sides have learned strategies from each other and will speculate about the future of reproductive rights at UN conferences. It will also prognosticate about the likely convergence or divergence in abortion rights within North America, particularly with respect to devolutionary trends.

## Notes

1. United Nations, *Abortion Policies: A Global Review,* vol. 2, *Gabon to Norway* (New York: United Nations, Department of Economic and Social Affairs, Population Division, 2001), 137.
2. David Truman, *The Governmental Process: Political Interests and Public Opinion* (Westport, Conn.: Greenwood, 1951, 1971, 1981); Daniel

Elazar, ed., *Federalism and Political Integration* (Lanham, Md.: University Press of America, 1984).

   3. Karen O'Connor, *Women's Organizations' Use of the Courts* (Lexington, Mass.: Lexington Books, 1980).

   4. E. E. Schattschneider, *The Semisovereign People: A Realist's View of Democracy in America* (New York: Holt, Rinehart and Winston, 1960); he responded to the pluralists, among them Robert Dahl, *Who Governs?* (New Haven, Conn.: Yale University Press, 1961).

   5. For example, Dorothy McBride Stetson, "Abortion Politics: Public Policy in Cross-Cultural Perspective," in Marianne Githens and Dorothy McBride Stetson, eds., *Abortion Politics: Public Policy in Cross-Cultural Perspective* (New York: Routledge, 1996), 104; and Rosalind Pollack Petchesky, *Abortion and Women's Choice: The State, Sexuality, and Reproductive Freedom* (Boston: Northeastern University Press, 1985), 78.

   6. Stetson, "Abortion Politics," 104.

   7. All figures were taken from the NARAL Pro-Choice America website, www.naral.org. Two sections were accessed: "Fact Sheets: Access to Abortion" and "State Legislation." All figures were listed on the website as of 1/31/02.

   8. NARAL fact sheet, "Medicaid: Discriminatory Funding for Abortion," www.naral.org, 1/15/04.

   9. NAF (National Abortion Federation) website, www.naf.org, accessed 1/19/04.

   10. NARAL website, www.naral.org, accessed 1/19/04.

   11. IPPF (International Planned Parenthood Federation), *News,* 1/14/03, citing *The Guttmacher Report on Public Policy,* www.ippf.org.

   12. Sylvia Bashevkin, *Women on the Defensive: Living Through Conservative Times* (Toronto: University of Toronto Press, 2003).

   13. Raymond Tatlovich, *The Politics of Abortion in the United States and Canada: A Comparative Study* (Armonk, N.Y.: M.E. Sharpe, 1997).

   14. Ibid., 33–34.

   15. Gail Kellough, *Aborting Law: An Exploration of the Politics of Motherhood and Medicine* (Toronto: University of Toronto Press, 1996), 78; Melissa Haussman, "Of Rights and Power: Canada's Federal Abortion Policy, 1969–1991," in Dorothy McBride Stetson, ed., *Abortion Politics, Women's Movements, and the Democratic State* (Oxford, UK: Oxford University Press, 2001), 68.

   16. Tom Barry, ed., *Mexico: A Country Guide* (Albuquerque, N.M.: Inter-Hemispheric Education Resource Center, 1992), 14.

   17. Ibid., 15–16.

   18. Ibid., 15.

   19. Ibid.

   20. Ibid., 281.

   21. Ibid., 281–282.

   22. Ibid., 38–39.

   23. Ibid., 38–40.

   24. Ibid., 285–286.

   25. United Nations, *Abortion Policies,* 136–137.

26. Tom Barry, *Mexico*, 3–14; Center for Reproductive Law and Policy (CRLP) and Grupo de Informacion en Reproduccion Elegida (Group for Information of Reproductive Choice, GIRE), "Women's Reproductive Rights in Mexico: A Shadow Report" (New York: December 1997), 9.

27. United Nations, *Abortion Policies,* 136.

28. Ibid.

29. CRLP/GIRE, "Women's Reproductive Rights in Mexico," 11; Lucero M. Gonzalez, "La penalizacion del aborto en Mexico," *Mujeres y Politica* (Universidad Autonoma Metropolitana, Xochimilco, Mexico), No. 1 (Autumn 1992): 55, n. 109.

30. United Nations, *Abortion Policies,* 134–138; CRLP/GIRE, *Women of the World: Issues and Policies Affecting Their Reproductive Lives, Latin America, and the Caribbean,* 1st ed. (New York: CRLP, November 1997), 145–158.

31. United Nations, *Abortion Policies,* 136.

32. Margaret E. Keck and Kathryn Sikkink, *Advocates Beyond Borders: Advocacy Networks in International Politics* (Ithaca: Cornell University Press, 1998).

33. Ibid., 3. Keck and Sikkink cite in n. 6 the work of Martha Finnemore, *National Interests in International Society* (Ithaca: Cornell University Press, 1996); and they cite in n. 5, regarding the meaning of "norms," "which may operate like rules that define the identity of an actor," the work of Peter Katzenstein, ed., *The Culture of National Security: Norms and Identity in World Politics* (New York: Columbia University Press, 1996).

34. Sidney Tarrow, "States and Opportunities: The Political Structuring of Social Movements," in Doug McAdam, John D. McCarthy, and Mayer Zald, eds., *Comparative Perspectives on Social Movements* (New York: Cambridge University Press, 1996), 41–61, esp. 54.

35. As discussed in Keck and Sikkink, *Advocates Beyond Borders,* 7.

36. Ibid., 23–25.

37. Ibid., 24.

38. Ibid., 27.

39. Donald Kettl, *The Global Management Revolution* (Washington, D.C.: Brookings Institution, 2000), 53.

# 2

# Establishing and Contesting
# Abortion Rights in
# the United States

In describing the history of abortion-law change in the United States and identifying the social movement organizations most responsible for it, this chapter splits U.S. history into three parts. The first part was when abortion was subnationally controlled, from the late nineteenth century until the *Roe v. Wade* decision in 1973. The second period covered the shortest time frame, from the 1973 decision until the Supreme Court's decision in the 1989 *Webster* case that certain state regulations could be upheld. Many people correctly viewed this decision as a demonstration of the strength of the right-to-life movement, which had been organizing over the previous decade. It also showed the Court—having been shaped by appointments under President Ronald Reagan, such as Justice Sandra Day O'Connor and Chief Justice William Rehnquist—as willing to accept pro-life arguments. The final period of the legal and social movement history on abortion in the United States has been conducted in a devolved federalist setting, starting from the time of Reagan's presidency. This includes both increasing legal maneuvering room for pro-life activists and state legislatures, as well as funding cuts to states that have primary responsibility for administering health care. Although this third period started under the Reagan administration, for abortion history purposes it is dated from 1989.

## Period One: Subnational Control of
## Abortion Policy and Public Contestation, 1860–1973

The first two centuries of U.S. history were ones where women who wished to interrupt pregnancies did so, typically in the first trimester, by self-inducement or reliance on a midwife to provide a remedy. As Kristen Luker has noted, what "minimal regulations did exist" prior to the nineteenth century were based on English common law, which held that abortion could be regulated after "quickening" (fetal movement), assumed to be somewhere within the second trimester (between the fourth and six months).[1]

Doctors in the United States were in the midst of a drive to professionalize their organization during the nineteenth century. The founding of the American Medical Association (AMA) in 1847 and its resulting national network of doctors was of strategic significance in helping doctors to further involve themselves in the arena where definitions were made of allowable procedures and practitioners. Following the key tenets of Sidney Tarrow's political opportunity structure, we would describe doctors during this time as having access to the state, particularly state legislatures, on the basis of being professionals. We also draw from Tarrow's political instability factor because Luker views the general pace of social and economic change beginning in the second half of the nineteenth century as a prod to physicians' actions to regulate women's access to abortion.[2] The relevant changes included a population shift from mainly rural and agrarian areas to mostly urban and industrial centers, with an accompanying 50 percent drop in the birth rate to an average of four children born to a woman in 1900, compared with a seven-child average in 1800.[3]

Regarding the concepts introduced in Margaret Keck and Kathryn Sikkink's theory, physicians were particularly able to use the politics of moral leverage and accountability. This involved, in essence, working with legislators as fellow elites, barring any other potentially interested participants from the lobbying process. The "morality" of their strategy was found in their appeals to set up a network to "police the profession," for by the mid-nineteenth century all sorts of practitioners, ranging from quacks to faith healers, were offering remedies of dubious origin and value in a pre–U.S. Food and Drug Administration (FDA) world.[4] As feminist scholars have noted, the profession's organizing was also done to provide a way to reduce the role of midwives, on whom many women depended. In part, the AMA members seem to have been alarmed about potential patient loss due to both lowered birth rates and nonmedically trained personnel.[5]

Although most doctors were not opposed to performing abortions, a vocal group was, and it showed particularly strong organizing skills vis-à-vis the AMA. For example in 1859, twelve years after its formation, the AMA passed a resolution "condemning induced abortion and urging state legislatures to forbid it."[6] Leslie Reagan details particular nodes of organizing within the AMA's Section on Obstetrics and Gynecology, where between 1893 and 1911, four section chairs addressed "the need for suppression of abortion in their annual speeches to the sections."[7] Some of these physicians claimed that it was their "Christian duty" to have abortions stopped.[8] While anti-abortion doctors worked diligently to inform their fellow practitioners and the public about the evils of abortion, they did not have much of an impact on the profession as a whole. Despite organizing success through the Chicago Medical Society and a Committee on Criminal Abortion it formed in 1904, these physicians concluded that they had no hopes of converting a majority of Americans to their view.[9] Most Americans tended to view a fetus prior to quickening as nonviable, views that certainly followed English and U.S. common law.[10]

Many ironies were present in the doctors' requests for state governments to regulate abortion. One that was pointed out by some was that doctors usually shied away from wanting the government to tell them how to practice, so this new lobbying focus seemed inconsistent. Another conflict, still present today, is that when lines were drawn as to which types of abortions could and could not be performed, each side of the debate was open to charges of waffling. Whether the line was drawn at the time of gestation or (more commonly during the nineteenth century) with proof that physical or mental harm would result to a woman if she were denied permission for an abortion, the result would be that "some women would get the procedure and some wouldn't," and for the opposite side, "some fetuses were worth saving while others weren't."[11] In particular, the paradox about having to draw lines and allowing some abortions while not allowing others is one that policymakers, physicians, and activists freely admit, and it persists into the twenty-first century. The question of regulating physicians' practices and, more directly, doctors' ability to regulate abortion provision, was handled by all states passing some form of restriction by 1900.[12] State laws were worded to prohibit not only abortion by "poisoning" but also by use of instruments, prohibiting the performance of abortion on young women under sixteen years of age, and allowing for fining, imprisonment, and delicensing of doctors who ignored these provisions.[13] The escape clause by which doctors could still perform abortions was to "preserve the woman's life." Legal scholar Laurence Tribe notes that forty states passed anti-abortion statutes within twenty years, testifying to the efficacy of the doctors' lobby. As most statutes included all types of abortifacients as illegal, they typically defined the regulatory framework as in effect from conception onward.[14]

For doctors, activism in the coalition usually resulted from one of three catalysts. The first was a belief that abortion was wrong; second was a desire to see gynecologists and obstetricians occupy the professional field and regulate abortion practitioners. Related to the second catalyst but expressed differently was the Progressive movement, beginning at the end of the nineteenth century, generally described at its height from 1890 to 1920, where doctors became a crucial part of the discourse. As described by Reagan, the physicians' campaign to restrict abortion and contraception information "took the form of a classic Progressive Era reform movement," where elements of "the native-born, white middle-class, identified a problem, investigated and documented its extent in 'objective' reports, and mobilized to promote a state-sponsored solution."[15] Similarly, the "problem" of pregnancy and abortion was generally thought to exist in the "neighborhoods of the 'other,' among the city's immigrant masses."[16] The doctors' leading role in this discourse was to claim that midwives, particularly the immigrant ones, many of whom were illegal, were giving contraceptive information and performing abortions without a license. At the same time, this argument raised the specter of unqualified immigrants invading women's reproductive systems and the need for professional gatekeeping as to who could dispense this type of medicine. This spurious campaign was joined by "nurses, female reformers, and journalists."[17] Even as stories of incompetent physicians surfaced, where upper-class white women were killed by mistake during abortion surgery, the public impression of an illiterate, immigrant woman, likely similar to the "witches" of the seventeenth century, was formed. As Reagan notes, the typical image of an "abortionist," a negative term, was constructed from precisely these women during the "Progressive" era.

Women doctors participated in this campaign, too, probably for many of the same professional protection desires as their male colleagues, as did reform women's organizations. Those in Chicago, for example, included the Welfare League of Chicago, the Woman's City

Club, and the Chicago Women's Aid.[18] During the Progressive era, inner-city immigrant women, some of the most disempowered elements of society working to help others in that group, were publicly vilified as abortionists. This image replaced that promoted earlier in the nineteenth century as a "foreign-looking" man with a beard. It also signified physicians' increasing consolidation and control over this particular area of policymaking, in which they had gained the power to make midwives the scapegoat rather than their male colleagues.[19]

Very few women's organizations at the time were willing to be drawn into the public discourse on abortion, such as it was. As always, women's organizing in the nineteenth century was split by class concerns; women workers were more concerned with working conditions and labor organizing. White women of the middle and upper classes were variously concerned with abolition, women's suffrage, and birth control issues. The first organizations to call for birth control and the first woman to do it, Margaret Sanger, were tarred with a two-sided brush; while on the one hand promising "women's emancipation," they were also open to the charge of wishing to legalize contraception access to keep the new immigrant population down. Sanger herself shied away from the abortion issue as did suffragist groups. They did so to preserve their "respectability."

Various reasons have been given for why a mass women's movement failed to form in the late nineteenth century. One thought is the lack of legitimacy of a socialist movement and party during the history of state formation, based partly on the uncritical acceptance of a capitalist liberal democracy and largely laissez-faire government by the Founding Fathers in 1787. The history of social movements in the United States shows that the movements have had to pick and choose on whose behalf they are fighting; a group could be pro-capitalist and pro–civil rights (such as the National Association for the Advancement of Colored People); or it could be Marxist and pro–civil rights, in which case it would be marginalized, such as the Black Panthers. The fragmentation of the United States into 152 potential lobbying units has tended to favor the creation of interest groups or social movement organizations at the grassroots level that if not single issue in focus are heavily restricted to a few issues. The development of the U.S. women's movement mirrors this institutional reality; umbrella women's movements such as in Canada and European countries simply do not work in the U.S. setting. Instead, there have been narrowly defined groups concerned with legal change, electing women, abortion politics, mothers' rights, and so on that on some occasions work in coalition (such as for the equal rights amendment [ERA] and suffrage). Rosalind Petchesky supports her argument as to the lack of the development of a mass-based women's movement, specifically one that could champion the cause of both birth control and abortion for women, as follows:

> Sexual conservatism, professional elitism and aggrandizement, and class and race bias entwined to determine the unique role of medical professionals in formulating a state policy criminalizing abortion in the nineteenth century. . . . The absence in the U.S. of either a strong centralized church or a national "public hygiene" implementation system . . . (meant that policies of contraception to contain the poor and foreign-born) were "an emanation of 'science.'"[20]

Within this institutional setting, groups interested in furthering women's causes were subjected to the same divide-and-conquer logic as other social movement groups. Upper-class women's groups, such as suffrage groups, needed to maintain their legitimacy in the eyes of the state and wealthy society, so they would generally not champion controversial issues such as birth control. Sanger was the rare person who sprang from a comfortable background and initially identified as a socialist. As Petchesky documents, Sanger's early organizing years in her Birth Control Federation of America, founded in the 1920s, used an issue frame that partially contrasted with the prevailing state and medical discourse. Socialist feminists tended to view abortion as unhealthy and contraception as a means to the emancipation of women.[21] Petchesky notes the contradiction between Sanger's espousal of socialist-feminist themes of women's control over their own bodies and her push to gain respectability for birth control. She did this by arguing that contraception should be prescribed and dispensed only by physicians.[22] The notion of alluding to birth control only as a scientific and medical phenomenon also permitted an unfortunate association with nonfeminist supporters of eugenics. [23] Other health professionals and activists concerned with women's rights argued for an abstinence-based philosophy as a way for women to control their reproductive lives. One group opposing Sanger's attempts to work with doctors was the Voluntary Parenthood League. A representative from this group, Mary Ware Dennett, and a socialist doctor, Antoinette Konikow, both expressed views that Sanger's crusade "took the technique of birth control from a woman's own control" and simply reified the dominant understanding that birth control was primarily a medical interest."[24]

By the beginning of the twentieth century and into its early years, the Progressive coalition and its movement to clean up inner-city politics had a dominant role in the framing of governmental responsibility, especially under the presidency of Theodore Roosevelt. Sanger's organization worked most closely within the mainstream of this frame; therefore, it is probably not surprising that her organization has been viewed as the most vocal and effective one. This is both because she courted the powerful middle class, fitting in with their views and rhetoric, and "participating in the dominant ideology that surrounded them."[25] In the parlance of the "coalition of professional birth controllers" dominant within and outside the Progressive movement from the early to mid-twentieth century, the issue of birth control became "depoliticized and 'decontaminated,' reinforcing a 'hygienic' concept of monogamous sex." However, this concept applied only to the white and wealthy. Sanger and others participated in the "dominant eugenic-minded, non-feminist alliance that dominated fertility control politics in the United States from the 1920s to the 1970s."[26] In 1942, the Birth Control Federation of America became the Planned Parenthood Federation of America. Later that decade, it spun off both the International Planned Parenthood Federation (IPPF) and the Population Council. In Petchesky's view, these groups, fitting into the nonfeminist eugenicist period, shaped population and fertility policy in the United States "and its Third World dependents" until the 1970s, "persistently seeking government funding and . . . with astonishing success," receiving it.[27]

By the 1950s, the dominant understanding of abortion was still largely privatized and technical and firmly under doctors' control. It cannot be said that access to abortion and birth control even started to be discussed widely as a women's rights issue until the 1960s, at the earliest. Demonstrating their continued control over the provision of abortion services, starting in the 1950s, physicians enacted "therapeutic abortion committees" so as to put the weight of the hospital as an institution behind their decisions on limiting the number of abortions provided. Although a minority of states required the confirmation of a second doctor before an abortion could be performed, most of the committees were established at the doctors' discretion. The size of the committees was also discretionary, and it could range from two doctors upward, excluding the one who would perform the abortion. The establishment of the therapeutic committees reflected the fact that increasingly inside the medical profession as well as outside of it, questions of morality were being introduced into the discourse.[28] From the doctors' point of view, they had a legal justification for performing the abortion if the hospital committee approved, and thus they believed they could not be prosecuted individually. This, however, did not hold true, as many doctors endured horrific trials, losing their medical licenses and being imprisoned. As with making any service or commodity subject to the rules of the marketplace, those with the resources the market values the most, namely, money, are usually able to get what they want. Inevitably clients with wealth, information, and connections inside the hospital prevailed.[29] The illegal market began an upsurge, including women's travel to border cities in Mexico, such as Tijuana and Juarez, even as abortion was and remains officially illegal in Mexico.[30]

Within this largely physician-driven first period, when events began to overtake physicians' practices, doctors became convinced of the need for reforms to the laws they had helped implement. Luker has noted that by the late 1950s the discourse over abortion in the United States had become considerably more complicated. In essence, the difficulty for doctors, or the "professionals' dilemma," became that the accepted grounds for performing abortions, "'preserving the life of the woman' . . . became a medical rarity."[31] By this time, the acquiescence to abortion regulation by the states was beginning to come under fire from at least three sets of professional sources, including doctors (mainly obstetricians and gynecologists), lawyers, and psychiatrists.

The first source consisted of doctors, who realized that the TAC framework was not protecting them from prosecution. The second source was the American Law Institute (ALI), representing the legal profession, which started in 1959 to work to craft a universal model penal code. The lawyers were convinced that a uniform set of laws as to which offenses carried which penalties would be superior to the patchwork framework remaining from the statutory development of criminal law at the state levels.[32] With respect to the abortion section, the gist of the lawyers' desired changes was to remove the necessity of having the doctor teams declare the abortion therapeutic and therefore legal and to craft the basis of abortion decisions to reflect a woman's wishes. This was tricky to negotiate, for just as women's groups could not talk about women's sexual lives as reasons to reform abortion codes, the lawyers could not advocate language that sounded like abortion on demand. The result was that ALI lawyers were working to cautiously expand the "categories of lawful justification of abortion" while publicly recognizing opponents' views.[33] In 1962, the ALI passed the new model penal code, which included statutory rape in the grounds for justifiable abortion and, for adult women, when mental or physical health demanded it. The health terms were not defined, presumably so as to leave wiggle room for state legislatures to enact more precise regulations.[34]

In certain states, various actors began pressing for the types of changes envisioned in the model penal code prior to its passage in 1962. In California, a Democratic freshman, state assemblyman John Knox, proposed a bill allowing abortion in the cases of "rape, incest, fetal deformity, and threats to mental or physical health."[35] While this bill was sent to a legislative study, from which it never emerged, two sets of events happened in the middle 1960s that made some anti-reform legislators and doctors reconsider their stance. The commonality between the two sets of events was that it put physicians in the risky position of having to decide whether to perform abortions on fetuses with a high probability of deformity. In the pre-reform climate, fetal deformity was not a universally protected ground for abortion. The first case was the by-now famous 1962 case of Sherri Finkbine from Arizona, who had found out that while pregnant, she had taken massive doses of thalidomide, a tranquilizer sold over the counter in Europe but denied approval by the FDA.[36] Thalidomide had been implicated in causing severe birth defects in at least five thousand babies in Europe. The most commonly occurring defects were missing or flipperlike limbs.

One year later, the "American rubella epidemic began, and the argument rose in pitch."[37] Because an effective vaccine was not yet available and would not be for another twenty years, the medical belief was that pregnant women who contracted rubella had a 50 percent chance of bearing a baby with potentially life-threatening deformities. These included blindness, deafness, mental retardation, and various heart, blood, and bone problems.[38] By the time the epidemic of 1963–1965 had swept to the West Coast, including Hawaii, physicians realized that although potential birth defects were illegal as a grounds of abortion at that time, women claiming potential exposure to rubella could gain the approval of many therapeutic committees. The participating hospitals were most prevalent on the East and West Coasts. As shown by the statement of Alan Margolis, M.D., chief of gynecology at the University of California, San Francisco Hospital from 1965 to 1972, "anybody who had a possibility of having a deformed baby could have an abortion, it was just that simple."[39] Thus, a precedent existed for a climate of abortion on demand, on which reform-minded lawyers and legislators could base their arguments. Another piece to the rubella epidemic that brought the need for more clarity in the laws home to doctors was that in the summer of 1966, a zealous California attorney general's office had investigated forty doctors for performing abortions on women with exposure to rubella, threatening nine of them with loss of their medical license.[40] Like Finkbine, these doctors became symbols of how ordinary, law-abiding citizens could one day find themselves afoul of the current laws, which at that point were still based on nineteenth-century precedents. As noted, "these were solidly established physicians performing inpatient operations who appeared . . . to be married, earnest about their families, and generally above moral reproach."[41] In short, the political opportunity structure began to slowly swing open in the states, mostly due to division among elites and access by other elites, notably physicians and lawyers, to their legislative counterparts.

Within a two-month period in 1967, the lawyer-physician coalition had worked successfully in two states, with both Colorado and, surprisingly, conservative North Carolina, passing legislation based on the model penal code language. Other states began considering such legislation. In 1967, California legislator Anthony Beilenson, who had taken up the efforts from his freshman colleague to pass model penal code language since 1963, managed to get such legislation through the California Assembly. One person with whom Representative Beilenson had to deal was newly elected governor Ronald Reagan, six months into his term. Reagan had consistently worked to prevent the bill from coming to his desk and thus having to make a decision on it. Governor Reagan was out-maneuvered by Representative Beilenson, who had constructed a "super majority" of sponsors in the legislature, making the bill essentially veto-proof and forcing the governor to sign it. The bill's language read that abortions were to be permitted in cases of rape, incest, and danger to physical or mental health. While the provision to which Governor

Reagan objected most, fetal deformity, was dropped, it was noted that sympathetic physicians could interpret a mother's mental health as being affected if forced to bear a deformed fetus.[42] Two years later, by 1969, ten states had either adopted or were adopting some form of abortion statute reform based on the model penal code wording.[43] Early anti-abortion organizing outside the medical profession was found in a group called Fight for Life, which sprang up in practically every state where the model legislation was being debated.[44] Similarly, an early pro-choice organization was the national Clergy Consultation Service, formed from representatives of mainstream denominations.[45]

The need for further reform quickly became apparent, because even though the grounds for seeking abortion had been widened, doctors and hospitals still had the gatekeeper capacity. Examples of state failures were duly noted by the members of the professional coalition covering doctors, lawyers, and clergy. For example, in Colorado, the first state to sign the reform bill, hospitals still acted as gatekeepers, concerned that Colorado not become viewed as an "abortion mill." Similarly, North Carolina's new law completely closed off abortion access to nonresidents, and as a result some hospitals reported that abortions occurred only in single-digit numbers after that. In California, which had the most widely accessible law at the time, the California clergy service wrote in 1968 that "for every therapeutic abortion performed at the [Los Angeles] County Hospital, two are turned away." Similarly, statewide ministers in this group were "directing steady traffic to the illegal Mexican clinics a full year after the liberalization law had gone into effect."[46]

The third set of professionals wishing to reform the 1950s abortion committee system was the psychiatrists, widely viewed as the "newly-liberal and socially-activist wing of the medical profession in the post-war period."[47] The psychiatrists seemed to be almost unique among doctors in that they could see the problems for both clients and providers in the existing abortion committee system. The contradiction could be described as follows. On the one hand, psychiatrists were often part of the committee stating that a woman needed an abortion for her mental health. However, they also recognized women's emotional distress under this procedure and the absolute power the medical profession had over deciding whether the woman could have a legal abortion or not. On the other hand, psychiatrists recognized the absurdity of obstetricians' and gynecologists' position, who saw the existing problem in the law, conveniently ignoring that the bulk of the law related to the structure "created by the physicians themselves in hospitals under their control."[48] Finally, both psychiatrists and doctors performing abortions recognized that because very few abortions were actually conducted to save a woman's life, the bulk of abortions then being performed in hospitals were probably illegal.[49]

By the early 1960s, women who disliked being left out of a debate that centrally concerned them began to mobilize. One of the earliest groups was formed by a San Francisco medical technician, Patricia Maginnis. While in 1961 she began to work for reform in the existing laws, along the ALI model penal code, within a year she and associates rejected reform, believing that the new laws would also require disproportionate physician control over the provision of abortion services. This group was called the Society for Humane Abortion (SHA) and has been viewed as one of the early radical groups in that it put women's views and concerns foremost, not what was politically possible in medical associations and legislatures.[50] By taking this stance early on, the SHA found itself somewhat out of the mainstream of the public discourse at the time. Reagan notes that this work was done prior to the second wave of feminism, which was to break about five years later. Although this work could certainly be classified as women's liberation efforts, Reagan rightly notes that the term *abortion* had not yet reached the public discourse; therefore, the "second wave of feminism would follow the analysis and activism of these innovative organizations."[51]

The SHA and a similar collective in Chicago, the "Jane" collective, acted as referral organizations for women, showing that illegal abortions could be made readily available to thousands and that these women-centered organizations could coexist with the mainstream medical system to focus completely on fulfilling women's needs.[52] Like the SHA, the Jane collective occupied a unique niche in the prefeminist era, beginning by referring women for abortions to a safe doctor they knew. This started in 1967 as "the Service," providing referrals to women with no questions asked; Reagan notes that the referral group included both upper-middle-class housewives and university students.[53] The group had knowledge of which practitioners were the best and also bargained with them at times to lower their rates. What was astounding for the time was that this group "gained control over the quality and prices of illegal abortion in Chicago, and formed an alternative, feminist, health-care system."[54]

The Chicago group became dissatisfied with the quality of physician care, including the fact that some "doctors" who advertised as such had no medical credentials whatsoever. Interestingly, this mirrored the physicians' fears of the nineteenth century, forming part of the reason the regulations had been passed then. The 1960s' response was quite different; many of the women in the Chicago women's health movement trained to perform early abortions and began working within the network to provide them. Various groups active in this network included the Jane collective, "the Front," the Service, and the Chicago Women's Liberation Union. It was estimated that between 1969 and 1973, this set of providers performed up to twelve thousand abortions in Chicago.[55] Another interesting note is the shift in this group's clientele after New York legalized abortion in 1970.[56] Immediately, those with the resources began to fly to New York to have abortions done there. The Service's clientele changed to one that was 70 percent women of color, "most of whom were living on a subsistence wage or welfare with very poor health care."[57] What this trend demonstrates is the continuing saga of abortion access, where those with resources can escape the bind of illegality and obtain the procedure, while those with fewer resources clearly are in a more difficult position. Compared to the eight Chicago hospitals performing five hundred therapeutic abortions in 1970, the Jane collective performed three thousand annually. Nearly five thousand women annually presented with abortion complications at the Cook County Hospital. It was estimated by then that there were fifty thousand illegal abortions per year in Cook County and over a million in the United States.[58]

One New York organization that coexisted with the SHA in the mid-1960s was the Association for the Study of Abortion (ASA), which had been founded in 1964. Cynthia Gorney describes it as having been formed as a "genteel counterpart" to the SHA, a "resolutely scholarly organization, its letterhead heavy with M.D.'s, PhD's, and Esqs."[59] Following from its worldview, this organization used rhetoric consistent with its roots in the birth control movement of the 1950s and 1960s, including Planned Parenthood. The ASA was officially committed to the ALI's penal code model of reforming existing laws in the states. The idea behind the reforms was to expand the grounds on which women could seek abortion. Yet as many noted, such reforms would not remove the physician's or hospital's gatekeeping function. The ASA also continued Margaret Sanger's Planned Parenthood justification for making birth control methods more widely available because the "world's population was exploding and must be contained, and families in poverty must . . . keep their numbers manageable."[60]

Within the ASA, Larry Lader and a likeminded activist from Illinois, Lonny Myers, decided that substantive change of abortion laws, more sweeping than available under the reform option, was needed. In 1969, Myers and Lader put together a national conference to talk about whether abortion reform strategies were still even viable, with the sub rosa purpose of forming a new organization. At this conference, the limitations of the current strategy were boldly highlighted. From these efforts, the first national organization devoted specifically to addressing abortion laws per se, the National Association for Repeal of Abortion Laws (NARAL), was formed, with Lader as its first executive director.[61]

The first major task NARAL took for itself upon its founding was to influence the debate then going on in the New York State Assembly over change to its laws. A Republican assemblywoman, Constance Cook, one of four women in the 150-person assembly, worked with a state assemblyman from "downstate" Manhattan, a Democrat named Franz Leichter. The essence of their argument for repeal was built on two blocks: first, that there were not two people at issue, only one (the pregnant woman); and second, that abortion was a medical procedure and as such needed to be inscribed in health law and performed by doctors.[62] Since repeal of the existing law was viewed by insiders as a much harder sell than discussing reform of the present law, and there effectively was no nationwide "model repeal law" from which to work, Representatives Cook and Leichter had to work slowly and cautiously over two sessions to get their bill through. Although Cook and Leichter felt that they were working from the hard practicalities of getting the bill passed by a disparate legislature, one where many members were members of the Catholic Church, some social movement groups were convinced by 1969–1970 that even the language of the Cook-Leichter bill wasn't enough. The language of the bill, which ultimately got through the New York State Assembly in 1970, required a physician to be the one to perform the abortion and that abortions could not be performed after twenty-four weeks into the woman's pregnancy, unless (as previously the case) her life was "deemed to be at stake."[63]

The response of various groups such as NARAL, the National Organization for Women (NOW), and to the left of NOW groups that placed themselves on the radical end of the feminist spectrum, was that the New York law was ultimately not a repeal but a reform.[64] One famous response was from a young member of a radical feminist group, Lucinda Cisler, who wrote in *Ramparts,* a journal of that movement sector, that a woman must have "the full capacity to limit her own reproduction [which could not be achieved when] . . . at a certain stage, your body suddenly belongs to the state."[65] While the first part of the statement could have been written by Margaret Sanger fifty years earlier, she would have been writing from the context of approving birth control, not abortion. The second part of Cisler's sentence gets much more to the heart of what made radical feminists radical—that patriarchy was the iron-clad framework in society where men made laws and rules to control women, based on their belief that they had sexual power over all women. Thus, to radical feminists such as Cisler, an abortion law that still gave doctors the power of refusal, and routinely at a particular point in pregnancy, could not be construed as having "women have free and total control over their own bodies." The type of total control she envisioned was only provided by their movement counterparts in the Chicago-based feminist health collectives run by Jane, the Front, and the "Movement."

By contrast, NOW has always been viewed as part of the dominant liberal wing of the U.S. women's movement since the 1960s, titled the "second wave." Therefore, at the organization's founding in November 1967, "abortion" was actually the last word in the last section of the first NOW "We Demand" Manifesto. While abortion was not especially highlighted in NOW's first list of demands for which it would work, its first president, Betty Friedan, stated extremely proactive views for the time. For example, she is credited with having made the first public argument that "[a woman's] control over her own reproductive process must be established as a civil right, not to be denied or abridged by the state."[66]

Within NARAL, the ultimate shape of the New York law also "split the New York chapter into two warring camps" when the chapter voted to uphold it.[67] Thus, while radical feminists still saw physician dominance as problematical in the new law, it was for its time the most radical and open law in the United States. What made it so was the elimination of requirements for TAC decisions and psychiatrist decisions as to clients' mental health. Within the first six months of pregnancy, a woman could have an abortion simply "with her consent," and "commission of an abortional act upon herself [was] justifiable" within the same time period. The law was also a first in two other respects. It was the first of the thirteen reform states that did not require the abortion to be performed in a hospital, and it included no residency requirement. This not only eliminated the potential of prosecution, it vastly opened up the area effectively served by abortion clinics, as women could fly in and out of the city fairly easily.[68] It was signed into law by moderate Republican governor Nelson Rockefeller on April 11, 1970.[69] He publicly gave credit to women's groups for the legislation's success.[70]

The early state efforts at reform and repeal of the abortion laws all had in common that they were mainly driven by pre-existing networks of organizations, including the ALI, state chapters of the AMA, some clergy groups, and the American Civil Liberties Union (ACLU). What got the reforms passed was that they stayed within the parameters of the medical model, all except for New York stating that abortions had to be performed by physicians in hospitals. None of the reforms provided a major challenge to the authority and legitimacy of the physicians' profession, so the doctors did not mobilize against it. Similarly, medical authorities came to two important realizations by the end of the 1960s that enabled them to either be part of the move for further change to the laws, such as repeal or at least not to block those movements. The first realization was that even under the TAC system, physicians in some states were prosecuted by zealous district attorneys. Also, the rise of groups such as the SHA in California and the ASA in New York and their outspokenness on the abortion issue brought the issue of women as still underserved in the reform framework to the fore. For example, hundreds of women were obtaining illegal abortions in Mexico and the United States, ironically often of higher quality in the completely illegal Mexican system.

The Mexican argument was pointed out by groups such as SHA and ASA—that lifting restrictions on access to legal abortion did not mean increased quality, either for legal or illegal abortions. This had been among the doctors' central points for justifying the existence of legal regulations since the mid-nineteenth century. Interestingly, in Mexico where abortion was and is illegal, women were going not only to Tijuana, just over the San Diego, California, border, but into the airport of Mexico City (the capital of Mexico), wearing special ribbons to identify themselves to their contacts.[71] It would appear that the Mexican system of illegality was viewed by some in the United States as providing an important fail-safe so that U.S. legislators and doctors could go on the record against abortion or could limit the numbers they performed, even if pro-choice. Then, women who had been left behind by this system could perhaps travel to Mexico. In the United States, even under the most radically reformed or repealed state of New York in 1970, women still obtained legal, but botched, abortions and still died or suffered grievous complications.[72] Thus, from the women's point of view, which was finally being brought to the forefront, women were as much harmed by the repeal framework as doctors were.

Therefore, by the end of the 1960s, two important sets of events were occurring, indicating a new political opportunity structure. The political opportunity structure was being shifted from the ground up by a newly available alliance between medical experts and laypeople, typically women. Three new sets of groups were important in this change, including feminist groups that had formed to work for abortion rights, such as the SHA and the Jane collective; groups that were feminist but not primarily focused on abortion, such as NOW; and finally groups such as NARAL, which were formed specifically upon the idea of legalizing abortion.

Doctors became increasingly opposed to the legal framework they had agitated to put in place, as it was no longer being used to protect them.[73] In the shift between the first and the second time periods, the important parts of the political opportunity structure included the availability of allies to help move the physicians' case forward. While access to the state for physicians in the first time period (1860 to 1973) of the abortion issue in the United States was important, namely, to state legislatures to help enact rules concerning abortions and who could perform them, access to the state as gained mostly by women lawyers became the chief element of the conducive opportunity structure in the second time period (1973 to 1989) of the policy's history. Similarly, shifting alignments in the late nineteenth and early twentieth centuries had been important catalysts for the physicians to begin lobbying, particularly with the increase in urban populations and the need to define who could medically treat them. In Keck and Sikkink's terms, physicians had previously been able to use the politics of moral leverage and of accountability upon state legislators to create a framework by which there was a certain class of abortions that could be performed legally. When the state's authority no longer recognized that, the medical profession, women in activist groups, and women professionals had to begin strategizing to invoke a new type of symbolism and to try leveraging political influence around a different type of argument. This argument became the new public discourse about a woman's right to control her body. The privatization of the abortion issue between doctors and mostly male state legislators had been irrevocably blown wide open. Finally, the first period that had mostly been about physicians' claims for professional courtesy and self-regulation became, in the new understanding of the abortion issue, centrally about women's quest for abortion to have national legitimacy. Legality for women as the subjects of abortion policy rather than for physicians as the deliverers of it became the key issue in the second period.

## Period Two: Nationalization of Abortion Policy and Discourse, 1973–1989

In May 1971 the Supreme Court announced it would hear the *Roe v. Wade* case and an accompanying case, *Doe v. Bolton*. The Supreme Court's interest was based on a series of cases in 1969 involving young lawyers just out of school in certain key states who wanted to use the law as a tool of justice. In this way, they would seem to have been following Betty Friedan's 1967 statement that reproductive freedom could be ensured at the level of constitutional law. These lawyers argued that because four-fifths of the nation's laws had not yet been updated to reflect the "model penal" or "repeal" code meant there was an unconstitutional variation across the states in access to legal abortion.

Clear shifts in the political opportunity structure and conducive factors for advocacy networks brought about this second period of abortion policy. The first political opportunity structure factor was the rise of the second-wave women's movement in the 1960s and the coalition efforts of some groups (such as NOW) with those such as clinicians and nurses who had been working quietly in individual states for the previous twenty years to make abortion more accessible. In addition to the newly possible alliance between medical professionals and women's groups, the second major political opportunity structure shift involved the newly rediscovered power of the

Supreme Court. A second crucial political institutional factor ultimately helping the advancement of the *Roe* case to the Supreme Court's discretionary agenda was that over the previous decade, lawyers had worked to bring up cases in several states regarding the constitutionality of the wide variation in laws regarding the permissible grounds for abortion. Thus, as is warranted in the U.S. federal judicial system under the Supreme Court's power of discretionary review, the Supreme Court was bound to fulfill its mandate of reconciling contradictory state court rulings on the issue, particularly when affecting the U.S. Constitution.

The third political opportunity structure factor of changing political alignments was the accession of the Democrats to the presidency in 1960 after a decade of republicanism, and the legitimation of strong federal action to improve women's status, such as President John F. Kennedy's naming of the Presidential Commission on the Status of Women.[74] This third factor was likely key in reorienting the universe of actors and the definition of the issue. The main actors became the Supreme Court and the prochoice coalition (medical professionals plus newly active women's groups). The issue was defined as the constitutionality of abortion for women.

Later in the decade, under the Republican president Richard Nixon, the successful nomination by the president of Chief Justice Warren Burger in 1969 was to help women immeasurably. Although the Burger Court from 1960 to 1986 was stern on law and order issues compared to its predecessor, it holds the record for most having advanced women's Fourteenth Amendment rights and those found elsewhere in the Constitution.[75]

Many of the arguments used in the late 1960s' cases were based on questions of equal protection and rights to privacy and liberty as specified or implied in the U.S. Constitution.[76] The cases could be brought up on two grounds. The first was where a physician was potentially sacrificing his or her career either by unwittingly or deliberately being prosecuted. This would result in a court challenge. The second, most common route was that of filing a class action suit, typically on the basis of women denied abortions as forming a legal class.[77] Young attorneys all over the country were sharing arguments with each other, based on law school and feminist and professional networks, and keeping a score of which arguments won in which states.[78] With regard to advocacy network strategies, this second set of institutional arrangements and issue framings on abortion was marked mainly by a shift to moral leverage and accountability politics. Moral leverage and accountability were most overtly voiced by women's rights activists after *Roe,* with others in the coalition increasingly taking a backseat. While constitutionality was the dominant frame of the abortion issue under the second period, the idea of access was included by describing the hoped-for universality of abortion-related conditions that would follow across the states. Ultimately, this was a hollow hope, as Raymond Tatalovich has pointed out, for the states that were the most restrictive pre-*Roe* have largely remained that way.[79]

One important case paving the way for *Roe,* although based on the rights of a doctor, was the 1969 California criminal trial of *People v. Belous.* In this case, Leon Belous, M.D., was prosecuted even though he had followed the pre-reform California law and refused to perform an abortion on an unmarried woman in 1966. Bowing to pressure, he ultimately referred the woman to a newly emigrated doctor, who while licensed in Mexico was not yet licensed in California. While the woman was recovering in his office, the police raided it and found Belous's name. He was prosecuted for violating the statute of "conspiracy to commit abortion" and was fined and stripped of his medical license.[80] He was an extremely well-connected doctor, including his association with the California Committee for Therapeutic Abortion, "the first California professionals' organization to agitate for abortion law change," and filed an appeal. One amicus curiae brief filed on his behalf to the California State Supreme Court was "signed by 178 medical school deans, including department chairmen and the heads of every medical school in the state."[81] Because the "California State Supreme Court of the 1960s was regarded by many legal observers as the most influential state supreme court in the nation," with its rulings frequently looked to as a model for other states, a lot of attention was focused on the *Belous* outcome.[82]

Ultimately, the California Supreme Court overturned Belous's conviction at the lower level by a 4–3 majority, based mainly on the concept of "vagueness" of the old pre-reform statute, in that "a person of common intelligence must necessarily guess at the law's meaning and differ as to its application."[83] Justice Raymond Peters, to whom the opinion-writing had been assigned, in turn assigned it to one of his law clerks, a brilliant young woman, Abby Soven. In writing the opinion, she added in language concerning fundamental rights to privacy and liberty (as articulated in the U.S. Supreme Court's 1965 *Griswold v. Connecticut* opinion). Soven's language suggested that the lack of these words' exact articulation in either the state constitution or the U.S. Constitution was "no impediment to the existence of this right."[84] Her language, which was adopted by the California Supreme Court as its opinion in September 1969, invalidated both the pre-reform California law—and could be used for forty other states like it—allowing abortion only to save a woman's life. Her invocation of constitutional language in this instance was that "a definition requiring certainty of death would work an invalid abridgement of women's constitutional rights."[85] This was an enormously significant case, for it was the first time the Constitution was invoked to overturn a pre-reform state statute. After the successful resolution of this case, the strategy of going to court to press for change became a parallel one along with movement organizing and legislative lobbying.

The *Belous* case had at least two immediate results. It showed generally young, progressive attorneys that pre-reform (and even in some instances model penal code–based) statutes could be successfully challenged by using enumerated or implied constitutional rights. At the same time, attorneys were learning that, at the end of the 1960s, federally appointed judges were widely perceived to be more sympathetic to individual rights than most state judges. Most worked to get their cases brought to the three-judge federal panels comprising two federal district court judges and one judge from the appropriate circuit from the court of appeals. Cases that invoked national constitutional arguments against state statutes would usually have to be brought to federal court.[86] Another case that was brought on a similar issue to *Belous* at roughly the same time was that against M. Vuitch, M.D., of the District of Columbia. After the doctor was cleared at the federal district court level and the D.C. statute was thrown out, the U.S. Justice Department appealed the verdict. This action nearly guaranteed a hearing by the U.S. Supreme Court, which happened in 1971. In April 1971, the court effectively reinstated the D.C. statute by holding that its vagueness was not a fatal flaw. However, the decision opened the door to consideration of women's rights by stating that the challenged statute protected the preservation of a mother's life or health and that health could include both physical and mental well-being.[87]

Challenges in a few states deserve mention, for they laid the eventual foundations for both the *Roe* and *Doe* verdicts in 1973. One was a challenge brought to the Illinois nineteenth-century, pre-reform statute by two young women attorneys in *Doe v. Scott* in federal district court. The lawyers included Susan Grossman of the Chicago Legal Aid Bureau and Sybille Fritzsche, a German émigré working at the Chicago branch of the ACLU.[88] They worked on the *Doe v. Scott* case to challenge the Illinois statute in federal district court in Chicago. Grossman, a former federal law clerk, worked to craft a number of arguments, including both more radical and more conservative ones so that justices could select from the ones they wished.[89]

In their brief, attorneys Grossman and Fritzsche counterposed the arguments of two groups with each other, those of poor women who had virtually no access to legal abortion in Chicago, and physicians who were being prosecuted under Chicago's nineteenth-century law, allowing abortion only with respect to the life of the mother. These two "classes" of people were set up so that the attorneys could bring a class-action lawsuit on behalf of poor women who were unable to afford the fees and so often could not obtain an abortion. This violated the state and national equal protection clauses, argued the attorneys. With respect to physicians, they were said to be inno-vators in bringing the interests of physicians to the forefront of their argumentation. With regard to this group, the attorneys reiterated the vagueness argument used successfully in the California *Belous* case but also argued that the law violated the physicians' right to privacy, as well as their First Amendment freedom-of-speech rights between doctor and patient. Thus, women were a class on whose behalf the Grossman/Fritzsche team litigated, based on the class of women who wanted abortions in Illinois, could not obtain them, and could not raise the funds to travel out of state. Doctors were argued to be a class, too, that had an interest in decriminalizing abortion to eradi-cate their distress of not being able to treat patients as they saw fit and being liable to prosecution. As in the *Belous* case, there was widespread support of the medical community; for example, 120 medical school deans and faculty filed a joint motion of support for the suit.[90]

In January 1971, the federal court agreed with the attorneys, overturning the Illinois statute on the grounds of vagueness and physicians' fears of becoming felons. In terms of women's rights, the decision was written in broad terms for 1971, accepting the points that the Illinois statute intruded into women's constitutionally protected "rights to life, control over their own bodies, and to freedom and privacy in matters related to sex and procreation." This has also been noted as the first court decision to articulate a potential trimester framework for regulation, in that the state "may not prohibit, restrict or otherwise limit a woman's access to abortion." However, the argument that many feminists found most compelling at the time, that of needing to guarantee actual access to the procedure, was not dealt with by the court.[91] Thus, questions of class differentials in obtaining access to abortion is something that continues to be unresolved. Within a few days of this decision, however, it became stayed during an appeal by the Illinois attorney general. Ultimately, the final disposition of the law would have to wait until the *Roe* case.

Sarah Weddington, a young Texas lawyer, was working to craft a lawsuit following the *Belous* finding advanced by the law clerk Abby Soven that women's rights were the fundamental issue in abortion rights litigation. Weddington shared arguments with a colleague, Margie Pitts Hames, who was putting together a similar case in Georgia. In Texas, Weddington and a colleague, Linda Coffee, were introduced to Norma Jane McCorvey, "unmarried and already the mother of one child, who brought them a convincing account of the emotional and economic hardship a second child would cause."[92] While Texas's statute being challenged was the unreformed version from the nineteenth century, the one in Georgia was a post-reform model penal code statute involving a woman who had been denied an abortion by the therapeutic abortion committee.[93] Ultimately, the Texas and Georgia cases would become the companion cases (*Roe v. Wade* and *Doe v. Bolton*) that the Supreme Court bundled together in May 1971. The Texas cases came forward when an abortion referral organization asked lawyer Weddington to file a case challenging the statute. Weddington herself had had a Mexican abortion and had long espoused feminist views. The Georgia attorney, Margie Pitts Hames, was thirty-eight years old to Weddington's twenty-four years old, a veteran of private practice and the ACLU.[94] By that point, most of the young lawyers crafting challenges to the state abortion statutes were either feminists and/or members of Planned Parenthood or the ACLU. In short, they were a fairly new breed of lawyers, now working in a new system where class-action lawsuits were possible, as were abortion law challenges in federal courts.

The climate for being part of a women's rights challenge to Georgia and Texas laws was not encouraging at the time. While working to expand women's rights, the attorneys knew that they also had to construct virtually unshakeable constitutional arguments to get their state challenges to a federal court hearing. As David Garrow described, Coffee and Weddington were "intent upon filing a full-scale attack on the Texas abortion statute" [only allowing abortions where the woman's life was in danger].[95] In spring 1970, Coffee filed both *Roe v. Wade* and *Doe v. Bolton* on the same day.[96] Both cases were heard by federal courts, and both ultimately were appealed to the U.S. Supreme Court. In the *Roe* case, the Dallas-based federal district court found that a woman's right to privacy was constitutionally protected and that the Texas statute abridged that right. Curiously, however, the court refused to accomplish the accompanying order to immediately cease enforcement, as had become the norm by then.[97] The same happened in the *Doe* case; the federal district court in Atlanta found the Georgia statute to be the first model penal code (reformed) law to be unconstitutional. It found that the law unconstitutionally intruded upon the woman's right to privacy; however, because it also stated that it did not hold that the "right reposes unbounded in any one individual," the statute would not be stayed through an injunction.[98] This left the curious state of affairs whereby two federal district courts had ruled state laws unconstitutional. These were Georgia's new "reformed" statute from 1968 and that of an old Texas one dating from 1854. Strangely, these courts refused to stay the implementation of those laws. Clearly, according to attorneys Weddington, Coffee, and Hames, the next route would be the U.S. Supreme Court. In the U.S. federal system of structuring political institutions, because the federal district courts had "refused to order injunctive relief" regarding the state laws, these attorneys were within their rights to appeal directly to the U.S. Supreme Court, bypassing the usual intermediate federal level of the circuit court of appeals.[99] The U.S. Supreme Court announced in May 1971 that it would hear both cases. By the time of these decisions in January 1973, "conflicting precedents could be cited from eighteen state and federal abortion cases."[100]

The U.S. Supreme Court's decision in the 1973 *Roe v. Wade* case did not protect abortion per se. Instead, it established the constitutional right to privacy of a woman when consulting her doctor. This right was completely free from state intervention in the first trimester of pregnancy. Women most often seek abortions during this trimester, with more than 90 percent of procedures being performed then, so the *Roe* framework could be viewed as protecting the largest number of women potentially seeking an abortion. The ruling also held that in the second and third trimesters, the state would demonstrate an increasing "compelling interest" in regulating abortion procedures, based on the mother's health in the second trimester and that of the fetus in the third. Following the 1965 *Griswold* ruling on contraception for married couples, in which the majority decision stated that the right to privacy was older than the Bill of Rights itself, the seven-justice *Roe* majority ruled that the constitutional framework for women's right to privacy was also based on the Bill of Rights' First, Fourth, Fifth, and Ninth Amendments, all extended to the states through the "penumbra of rights" covered in the Fourteenth Amendment.[101]

The accompanying *Doe* decision was equally as interesting, stating the unconstitutionality of the therapeutic abortion committee system. Justice Harry Blackmun's decision in this case was that all the provisions nullified by the district court had been done so correctly, and all the exceptions under which an abortion could be sought were unacceptably narrow. Also, the Georgia law had not adequately shown why the abortion must be performed in a hospital. Thus, "just as *Roe* effectively voided the abortion laws of all thirty states whose statutes resembled the one in Texas, the *Doe* opinion invalidated the Georgia law and the generally similar reform provisions adopted by fourteen other states since 1967."[102]

As has been true in other countries, including Canada, the bulk of grassroots organizing on both sides of the abortion question came only after the federal government had acted in a highly visible manner. In the United States, the pro-choice side immediately felt that the *Roe* decision meant that the national government had listened to and understood women's concerns. The decision equally catalyzed the pro-life side, which immediately went into emergency gear to start strategizing as to how to address the ruling in the future, mainly through legislative action at the national and state levels. The mobilization successes of the pro-life movement are ultimately to be seen in the shift by the late 1980s to the third period of returning abortion policy responsibility and lobbying mainly to the state level.

Few organized pro-choice groups existed at the national level prior to 1973. Those that did included Planned Parenthood, NARAL, and NOW (which has always been a multi-issue organization). Margaret Sanger's organization had become the Planned Parenthood Federation in 1942, and the National Association to Repeal Abortion Laws became the National Abortion Rights Action League, keeping the same acronym (NARAL). Planned Parenthood became involved in abortion only after a membership vote in 1969 and lent its staff and lawyers to help prepare briefs for *Roe*.

As with many social movements, the fortunes of NARAL waxed and waned according to how well the organization articulated threats of potential crisis to its members and general supporters. For example, under a new executive director, Beatrice Blair, who brought direct-mail expertise to the organization, NARAL worked to convince members and the public that the *Roe* and *Doe* decisions had not solved all abortion questions and that further work and vigilance would be required to protect the gains won therein. The membership numbers increased in response to this work, going from about two thousand members in 1973 to about ten thousand in 1975–1976. NARAL moved to a Washington, D.C., office in 1976 and has worked continually to make the case that pro-choice Americans needed to be vigilant by continuing to join and fund organizations dedicated to the pro-choice cause. NARAL has been the largest mainly single-issue group in the pro-choice movement since the late 1970s. By 1980, its membership reached the historically unprecedented figure of ninety thousand, which increased to 140,000 with a budget of $3 million within two years.[103] Membership dropped back down to the ninety thousand level in the mid-1980s, with no immediate crisis looming, but by 1989–1990 at the time of the Supreme Court's *Webster* decision, it increased more than fourfold to four hundred thousand, with a budget of $10 million.[104] In addition to becoming a player on the Washington scene through the office and its political action committee (PAC), and increasing its individual numbers, NARAL focused on increasing the numbers of affiliate organizations in the states and, most important, training them in tactics and priorities sanctioned by the national office. This meant that by the late 1970s, NARAL had built upon and in some ways superseded its grassroots beginnings of the early 1970s. Through the late 1980s, there were NARAL affiliates in nearly every state.[105]

With respect to an active but far less visible organization, mainstream clergy in the Jewish and Protestant faiths had been working to achieve reform since 1967. Central figures in what became known as the Clergy Consultation Service included Baptist reverend Howard Moody of a Greenwich, New York, parish; clergy from New Jersey, Illinois, and California; and Reverend Ewing from St. Louis, Missouri.[106] While the Clergy Consultation Service was formed to offer counseling, it quickly got into the referral business, even though the clergy would officially deny it. For example, a co-worker of Rev. Moody's, Arlene Carmen, began keeping notes on various clinicians who were reported to be good or bad by women sent out to access their services, and she began venturing across the country to interview potential abortion providers herself. Others, as in California, maintained a referral list of trustworthy doctors in Mexico's border cities.[107]

The need for the Clergy Consultation Service, which had been at its height of activity during the 1960s, officially stopped with *Roe* in 1973. However, a new clergy group was formed right around that time. It included some of the clergy veterans of the network and expanded over time to include new, interested clergy, again usually from the mainstream Protestant denominations and the Jewish faith. The new organization became known as Religious Coalition for Abortion Rights (RCAR), and as noted by Suzanne Staggenborg, "when organized in 1973, it was legally a part of the United Methodist Board of Church and Society."[108] In 1981, RCAR severed its ties, deciding to become a separate organization not affiliated with any one particular faith. In the 1970s, RCAR focused mainly on lobbying Congress, and after *Roe* the organization tried to encourage the growth of state affiliates in states with large congressional delegations, so as to have maximum impact. Based on a lack of national resources, the organization had to abandon these plans, but affiliates did form in states where there were pre-existing connections.[109] Originally, membership in RCAR was group based (such as denomination or house of worship) with no formal requirements for level of activity. RCAR then set up a board of directors in Washington, D.C., including a representative from each national denominational or organizational member. As further noted by Staggenborg, the central working group of the board is an executive committee elected annually. The organization also includes paid staff to administer the network and sponsors such as prominent clergy who may lend their name on particular occasions. Individual memberships are also part of this framework.[110]

Staggenborg also notes that, as a federation, RCAR followed the NARAL model in gradually requiring greater accountability from affiliates to the national level. Requirements included the creation of boards of directors, or policy councils, for state affiliates and annual budget reports to the national board. Resources are provided from the national level to the affiliates, including literature, trainings for affiliate directors, and small yearly grants to assist in staff hiring. Later, one way in which RCAR loosened its structure was in allowing the creation of local "area units," which would allow for individuals located in a particular state to work with the RCAR affiliate while not being a denominational representative themselves. By the mid-1980s, RCAR could count twenty-six affiliate groups in twenty-eight states (New York and California each had two), and twenty-three area units by 1990. By that same year, the organization's national budget surpassed $1 million, from a starting point of $100,000 in 1973.[111]

Another religious pro-choice organization is the Catholics for a Free Choice, formed in 1972. They have been particularly important in working for abortion and contraceptive rights in at least two of the countries in this study (United States and Mexico) and widely in Latin America. Most recently, it has been active in campaigns to promote birth control as compatible with the majority of the world's religious teachings and also to remove the Vatican as a nonstate voting member at the UN.

The National Abortion Federation, an organization of clinics and doctors, was founded in 1977. It exists as a resource for those involved in the provision of services—(including acquiring data on the provision of different abortion techniques throughout the states, identifying which providers have dropped out of the network, and monitoring threats to providers)—and to help with legal and professional requests. It sponsors annual conferences and has a link to a Canadian network. Information sharing across national borders has become extremely important to the providers' network. Since 1973 NAF has taken on the function previously performed by the Clergy Consultation Service of putting together lists of competent and good abortion providers. Clearly this service of "vetting" providers to weed out the bad from the good has still been necessary in the post-*Roe* world. It faced a division within itself between feminists who staffed the clinics and tended to distrust the medical profession versus doctors who felt they were losing respect by being designated as generic providers.[112] NAF also conducts and provides research both to professionals and the lay public, and sometimes it lends its name to pro-choice efforts, such as the recent one against the reinstatement of the global gag rule by President George W. Bush.

The other main organization that has moved in and out of the pro-choice coalition at various times is the National Organization for Women. Throughout most of its history since 1967, NOW has been a multi-issue organization, although during certain periods, the national level has declared a primary commitment to one issue. This happened with the ERA during the state ratification period of 1972–1982. It is clear that the network of NOW affiliates and the general wider constituency put in place in key states to help with the ratification effort, starting in 1972, was an important network on which NARAL and Planned Parenthood in particular could draw after 1973. In the later 1970s, while NOW remained a valued ally to pro-choice organizations, it did sometimes strike out on broader ground than NARAL wished and used a broader repertoire of actions than NOW had suggested.[113] One example is NOW's declaration in 1978 that it would focus on reproductive choice, including with abortion the rights to child care and contraception.

Turning to the development of the U.S. pro-life movement, law professor Mary Ann Glendon has argued that *Roe v. Wade* was an abrupt break in a social consensus then developing in the United States around liberalizing abortion laws. She argues that the U.S. scenario, in which the Supreme Court played such a central role, was different from most other countries with parliamentary systems and legislative supremacy,[114] referring specifically to the genesis of the right-to-life movement (as it termed itself in the 1970s) and the strengthening of the pro-choice movement. Glendon further argues that in deciding *Roe v. Wade,* the Supreme Court ruptured any hope of social consensus around abortion politics in the United States and galvanized the hard lines of opposition that will always remain. One clear answer to Glendon's argument is that liberalization as it evolved through the late 1960s posed significant problems for women and doctors. Also, without the *Roe* ruling, states would have had the latitude, now denied to them, to keep abortion illegal.

Early pro-life groups were found in individual states in the 1960s. One of the most visible was the Citizens for Life groups, formed in every state where reform legislation was being considered. One early group with a national focus was Americans United for Life (AUL). Formed in 1971, it portrayed itself as a scholarly mainstream educational foundation. It did not support legislative lobbying nor the formation of "county by county citizens' chapter groups."[115] Its focus was to produce newsletters and in-depth studies on particular aspects of the abortion question, sent only to those who requested them. As the ASA on the pro-choice side had been heavily composed of doctors and lawyers, so too was AUL. They had been active since the late 1960s, fighting off the attempts to reform Illinois' law according to the model penal code provisions.[116] The AUL developed an LDF, or legal defense fund, "to develop a national counterpart to what appeared to be the abundant legal resources of the ACLU and Planned Parenthood."[117]

The National Right to Life Committee (NRLC) was founded as a more publicly activist organization by John Willke, M.D., and his wife, Barbara, of Ohio in 1970. They wrote anti-abortion literature and traveled the United States for years, making presentations for the pro-life side. For example, in 1972, in two states (Michigan and North Dakota) where referenda had been put on the public agenda to legalize abortion in the first twenty weeks of pregnancy, the Willkes traveled there, lectured, and helped defeat both measures.[118] As time went on, they became more sophisticated in their visuals, using pictures of near-term fetuses to imply that all abortions were done on similar fetuses. However, in that climate in the early days, they appeared to have had quite a disproportionate influence. Most of the state Right to Life Committees, some of which were formed by the Willkes (such as Ohio's), and others that were not, were viewed as being administered and financed by the Roman Catholic Church.[119] After the *Roe* decision, some states maintained active Right to Life Committees (New Jersey, New York, and Minnesota being prominent ones), and some members decided to work on taking over the NRLC. Among the key planners were a Minnesota woman who had been crucial in founding her state Right to Life Committee, a Methodist named Marjorie Mecklenberg, and an Episcopalian internist from Arizona, Dr. Carolyn Gerster. The reason their religious background is deemed relevant is that a main reason for wresting control of the organization from its priest director in D.C. was that in their opinion, the organization was viewed as being too controlled by the Church, "in lockstep with their bishop."[120] Ultimately, the organization became the "movement's heavyweight, with a big national board and regional affiliates all over the country."[121]

The NRLC tactics throughout the 1970s were mainly those of popular protest, including marches at legislatures and hospitals. While members considered themselves part of a mainstream group, those on the pro-choice side viewed them as loud and radical. This view was undoubtedly based on some of the organization's leaders, such as one president, the well-known Boston physician Mildred Jefferson, who did not shy away from publicly based tactics of demonstrations and "sidewalk counseling." As an African American, she was well aware of her minority status within a movement (and group) that was "overwhelmingly white and Catholic" in the mid-1970s.[122] In the early years of the movement, meetings of the NRLC claimed that it viewed the abortion fight as a long struggle, one that "might go on until 1980."[123] While the national committee was viewed by some as among the "radical fringe of the mainstream" movement, it took great care to have well-respected professionals on its national board. For example, women physicians functioned as president of the organization at least twice in its early years, after it had been reconvened as a secular group.[124]

Very early on, the NRLC confronted the situation endemic to social movement organizations, namely, which tactics to endorse—in short, which particular "space" of their social movement sector they would occupy. The second woman president, Carolyn Gerster, M.D., stated firmly at one NRLC conference in St. Louis in 1978 that the organization would "never condone illegal activity."[125] This was in response to some young members present at the conference who were pressing for sit-ins at clinics. The group was thus dealing with questions such as, "Where was the dividing line for nonviolent acts? Was it 'violent' to destroy property without injuring people?" One reason that this set of questions was so pressing, demanding an official stance from the NRLC, was that the previous February, a man (who was later found to be unaffiliated), "posing as a deliveryman had walked into a Cleveland clinic and flung a bag of flammable liquid into the receptionist's face before setting fire to the clinic's interior. . . . Patients had to run from the fire, and the receptionist was temporarily blinded."[126] Although every local pro-life organization denounced the attack, two things were immediately clear. One was that violence would be conducted in the name of the movement, and the mainstream organizations would have to expend much energy distancing themselves from it. The second was that this attack was only five years after the *Roe* decision, making some see the entire movement as violent from the beginning. The leaders of the NRLC were aware that they had to keep reassuring the public that they were nonviolent or else they would "alienate the broad middle class where pro-life has its basic support." One member told a newspaper that some people attending the conference did not realize that the right-to-life movement was already seen as the "radicals of our time," and that "it would be very easy for hardcore pro-lifers 'to talk themselves into a whole lot of trouble.'"[127] Mainstream tactics that had been previously used by the NRLC and evaluated at the 1978 convention included workshops on grassroots political action, working with the media, and how to effect a constitutional convention.[128]

Another right-to-life group that was part of the first wave of organized groups in the early 1970s was Human Life International (HLI), active around the world and within North America from its U.S. base. Like the NRLC, its early years were spent affiliated with the Catholic Church from which it later split. Its official formation date is not specified on its website, but it states that Father Paul Marx formed the forerunner organization, Human Life Center, in 1972 at St. John's University, Minnesota, and "out of this grew Human Life International."[129] The website also states that "Planned Parenthood has called Father Marx 'Public Enemy Number One.'" By the 1980s, HLI had developed as a separate, institutionalized entity.

Tribe has noted that the right-to-life movement implemented a two-tiered set of actions right after the momentous 1973 Supreme Court decisions. One tack was aimed at the national level, particularly in Congress. The other strategy was to emulate the pro-choice movement's history up until *Roe* and get enough conflicting state court decisions in place that the Supreme Court would eventually have to reconsider *Roe*. Although this moment did not come until 1989, the pro-life movement's patience and persistence were shown in the 1989 *Webster* decision, which began to turn back the locale of abortion regulation to the state legislative level. For at least a decade, the pro-life side operated largely in stealth mode, so that it took a while for the public to notice the internal contradictions within the pro-life strategy. The first was that of focusing on the national level; even as pro-life groups decried the national government's, especially the Supreme Court's, intrusiveness into the area of procreation, it was active at that same level and ultimately hoping for Supreme

Court action to overturn *Roe*. The second inconsistency was that the other official set of statements of the pro-life movement, and the conservative movement generally, were about shrinking the regulatory state; however, their actions from *Roe* onward had the net effect of increasing the sheer body of abortion-related regulations across the states, not decreasing them.

The congressionally based pro-life actions began within a year of the 1973 decisions. One of the earliest efforts to ban abortion outright took place just after *Roe* was handed down.[130] Senators James Buckley (R-NY) and Jesse Helms (R-NC) proposed constitutional amendments to ban abortion. However, Congressman Don Edwards (D-NY), chair of the crucial House Judiciary Subcommittee on Constitutional Amendments, refused to schedule hearings; the Senate chair, Birch Bayh (D-IN), held hearings but did not allow the proposal out of committee through 1975.[131] As will be described in Chapter 4, Senator Buckley continued his pro-life activism after his retirement. As the head of the U.S. delegation to the UN Conference on Development in Mexico City in 1984, he influenced the U.S. submission to reflect his and the Church's position.[132]

One of the most effective strategies of the pro-life movement starting in 1973 was to deny "otherwise available federal funds . . . to facilitate abortions."[133] Undoubtedly, this strategy was based on the framework of the Illinois Supreme Court ruling in *Doe v. Scott* that the Court could not address economic inequality between women and reiterated in *Roe*.[134] Congress passed legislation in 1973 denying all federal money to the Legal Services Corporation or for foreign aid used to fund abortions.[135] This predated the Mexico City doctrine, implemented at the 1984 UN Population Conference in Mexico City, where pro-life former senator James Buckley headed the U.S. delegation. The other finance-based strategy that has widely curtailed domestic access to abortion is the Hyde Amendment, named after its House sponsor, Representative Henry Hyde of Illinois, passed in Congress in 1976. This denies federal Medicaid funding to women seeking abortions, with a narrow exclusion for the "endangerment to the mother's life."[136] The funding restrictions may be viewed as a particularly callous restriction on abortion, for they clearly draw a line between those who can afford private medical care and access to abortion and those who cannot. Feminist groups argued then and since that the minority of legislators opposed to abortion should not impose their will on an entire class of people, in effect holding women below the poverty line more responsible than their middle-class counterparts. Similarly, the tactic is embedded in a belief that only women are responsible for their pregnancies, and it clearly singles out this class of women as particularly "bad."[137] The elimination of federal funding from the Medicaid program effectively cut off the ability of most Medicaid recipients to have abortions. Prior to 1976, Medicaid-funded abortions comprised one-third of all legal abortions in the United States.[138] Two important Supreme Court victories in the late 1970s confirmed the constitutionality of these policies.[139] By 2002, fewer than half of the states permitted public funding in "all or most circumstances," while nearly twice that many, thirty states, only allowed it in the cases of "life, rape and incest."[140]

Another strategy, ultimately focused on the national level, was that in the 1970s the NRLC and AUL developed a Fourteenth Amendment argument to try to counter the constitutional right to privacy that the Supreme Court articulated in *Roe*.[141] By claiming that the fetus was deserving of Fourteenth Amendment equal protection and due process clause rights, these groups were undoubtedly working toward a judicial comparison of the right to privacy with that of fetal life.

Overall, right-to-life groups after 1973 worked for legislation that "skated as close to the zone of known unconstitutionality as possible."[142] Two states in which the right-to-life movement was particularly strong and had a continuous presence after 1973 were Pennsylvania and Missouri, not coincidentally the states whose legislation ultimately provided the strongest challenges to *Roe*.[143] Right to Life Committees were organized just after *Roe* in these states, and over the years the majority of court challenges to the decision came from these two states.[144] Gorney hypothesizes that the success of the organizations' formations and passage of legislation in these two states came from shared demographic characteristics. These included the fact that they were large states, with "distant cities at either end," divided by a "wide swath of conservative farming country." They also had high membership in fundamentalist Protestant and Catholic denominations. From the point of view of legislators on the fence, the convenient fail-safe was that both states bordered on states (New York and Kansas) where abortion was fairly accessible.[145]

At the state level, the NRLC and others worked to enact restrictions upon abortion access. Lobbying efforts took place to enact twenty-four-hour waiting periods, Medicaid funding bans, parental consent laws, and a whole host of restrictions on the institutions and their personnel performing abortions. The latter included record-keeping requirements, facilities restrictions including use of zoning laws to deny their siting, and requirements of medical tests to be performed before the procedure.[146] As most of these could not be justified under the *Roe* framework as being relevant to protecting the health of the mother in the second trimester or that of the fetus in the third trimester, they were usually struck down by the Supreme Court. One restriction that notably survived was the parental-consent requirement for minors (usually with a judicial bypass provision). While some states' restrictions predated *Roe,* others have been implemented since, so that forty-three states now have such provisions. Thirty-three of those states enforce these provisions, and two of them, Oklahoma and Utah, have no bypass procedure as an alternative to a minor notifying her parents.[147] They could also be viewed as the updated residency requirements, a clever follow-up to the residency requirements made unconstitutional by *Roe* and that have outlasted that decision. Similarly, the passage of conscience clauses for hospitals and doctors had the effect of reinstating the TAC framework outlawed under *Doe*. As Tribe notes, the passage of conscience clauses covering entire hospitals had a severely limiting effect in states where there was only one hospital in a large geographic area. By 1975, he states, the conscience clauses "were at least partly responsible" for the fact that only 17 percent of public hospitals and 28 percent of private nonsectarian hospitals in the United States performed abortions.[148]

Ultimately, the second, nationalizing period of U.S. abortion policy and activism was the most high profile and productive in different senses. The women's movement and pro-choice movements came to maturation during this time, as did the pro-life movement (its designated label since the 1980s). During this period, women's right to reproductive choice was nationalized, although by its end that right was seriously under threat. Since 1992, the right to first-term abortions could be effectively said to be national, yet there is still a wide range of relevant restrictions, all upheld as constitutional. It was probably during the second, nationalizing time period in which women's rights per se were at their most dominant point in the discourse, having been interjected by a combination of feminist lawyers and members of movement organizations. Both pro-choice and then pro-life forces saw access to elites as an important political opportunity structure aid, pro-choice during the 1970s and then pro-life during the 1980s. In turn, this differential state access was due to instability of the political climate in the 1970s, switching from Democratic control to more solidified Republican control in the 1980s. Different allies accordingly made themselves available in these two decades: primarily attorneys and their organizations to women's groups during the 1970s, and conservative think tanks, attorneys, and the Republican Party during the 1980s.

## Period Three: A Return to Subnational Abortion Politics, 1989 Onward

As has been noted, one of the chief paradoxes in the pro-life movement's arguments is that while the movement decries national action as indicative of a tyrannical, intrusive state and in particular the policy role of nonelected Supreme Court justices, it successfully used them during the 1980s. The result has been to effectively disaggregate the *Roe* ruling back to the state level, where state legislatures have been given the most constitutional space on the abortion policy question during U.S. history. The effectiveness of the pro-life movement in bringing about more state regulations affecting women's access to abortion contradicts their official arguments as to not wanting a regulatory state. The official emphasis of the conservative movement is that a regulatory state is a large, intrusive state and therefore normatively bad. The irony of shifting back to the pre-*Roe* days of state abortion regulations based on a movement equally as willing to use national and international power centers as the liberals they decry should not be lost on readers.

Within the years of national political alignments making it easier for the self-described pro-family movement to mobilize and raise funds, persistence of right-to-life groups in Missouri and Pennsylvania paid dividends.[149] These were shown when the U.S. Supreme Court agreed to hear the *Webster* case coming from Missouri, based on a law passed in the Missouri Legislature at the behest of the NRLC, based on intense lobbying of more than a decade by a core of committed activists. The Missouri lawyers seeking constitutional judgment on the Missouri law restricted the Supreme Court challenge to the following pieces of the law. First, the challenge mentioned the requirement of viability testing; second, the preamble to the Missouri law stated that life began at conception. Other questions concerned the Missouri law's restrictions on public funding and use of public employees and facilities. While some questions of the challenge referred to issues of access, two of the questions referred to fundamental philosophical efforts to overturn *Roe*. The first was that of the preamble, seeking to define when life began. The second was a question in the challenge concerning whether the "trimester approach of *Roe* should be . . . discarded in favor of a rational-basis test."[150] The latter aimed to remove the right to privacy as the most protected type of fundamental constitutional right as articulated in *Roe* and move it to the lowest level of judicial scrutiny, which had never been used to strike down gender-based discrimination until 1971.

The *Webster* decision of 1989, written by Chief Justice Rehnquist, upheld the smaller pieces of the Missouri law, those requiring viability tests on the fetus in second-trimester abortions and the right of Missouri to prohibit both the use of public facilities for abortions not deemed "necessary to save the life of the mother" and public employees from performing or assisting an abortion."[151] The three blocs that had become apparent on the Court during the Reagan years divided on this decision. Because the five-member plurality contained only four members who would agree to overrule the trimester framework of "compelling state interest" in regulating abortion as established in *Roe,* the *Webster* decision stopped short of overturning it. Similarly, it agreed basically not to decide the constitutionality of the preamble to the Missouri law, arguing that it was only a philosophical statement introducing the law. Justice Antonin Scalia, never known for moderation, wrote a scathing attack on fellow Justice O'Connor because in previous cases she had hinted at the unworkability of the trimester framework but was not prepared to come to that conclusion in *Webster.* On the four-member dissenting side in *Webster* were the three remaining majority members of *Roe,* Justices Thurgood Marshall and William Joseph Brennan, Jr., and its author, Harry Blackmun, as well as moderate Justice John Paul Stevens, nominated to the bench by President Gerald Ford.[152] In the *Webster* case, the post-1980 conservative bloc (Rehnquist, Scalia, Anthony Kennedy, and O'Connor) overlapped the two dissenters in *Roe* (Rehnquist, Byron White) just enough to garner its five-member plurality. Similarly, the liberal bloc (Brennan and Marshall) overlapped enough with *Roe* author Justice Blackmun, and when joined by swing member Justice Stevens, added up to the four-member dissenting minority.[153]

The 5–4 decision in the *Webster* case held significant ramifications for future decisions. Perhaps the most important was to essentially invite states to keep legislating to find the perfect vehicle with which to impress enough Supreme Court justices to overturn *Roe*. Another was to practically reduce Justice Blackmun to tears as he took the unusual step of publicly reading his dissent when *Webster* was announced in July 1989. Part of Justice Blackmun's statement was, "I fear for the liberty and equality of the millions of women who have come of age . . . since *Roe* was decided. I fear for the integrity of, and public esteem for, this Court." On the other side, Justice Scalia invoked looking "forward to at least another Term with carts full of mail from the public, and streets full of demonstrators urging us . . . to follow the popular will."[154]

The *Webster* case has been described in the literature as a turning point for both sides of the abortion issue. On the pro-choice side, it galvanized the movement into defensive action, realizing that its work had grown exponentially overnight. It was now clear that the Supreme Court was yet another institution that could work to reduce women's rights to abortion. Combined with this scenario, NARAL and other groups would have to expand their scope of activism to watch, if not all the states, at least those that were deemed likely to pass laws restricting abortion access based on their old, pre-*Roe* records. In a 1989 head count of state legislatures, NARAL found that only nine states could report having a legislative majority in both houses in favor of protecting abortion rights, while twenty-four legislatures counted both houses in favor of prohibiting abortion. Yet many scholars view the framework of the 1990s and beyond as one at which pro-choice is still fundamentally the stronger position. One example is that of popular opinion. As recently noted by Phyllis Schlafly, "our [U.S.] population is still where it was in 1973, with 60 percent tolerating abortion, 20 percent opposing it entirely, and 20 percent firmly supporting it."[155] In light of other studies, the 60 percent should be read as including people with various degrees of reservations. Other evidence of the continuing strength of the pro-choice position in the United States is that the "strength and commitment of pro-choice voting appear to be far greater now than before *Roe*."[156] It appears that the strategy of accountability politics, holding state legislators and/or congressional members responsible for anti-choice actions, has served NARAL well as the continuing political leader of the pro-choice movement.

At the time of the *Webster* hearing, publicly active members of the women's pro-choice movement adopted the slogan "Who Decides?" based on a board meeting. This was most overtly promoted by NARAL and NOW. Basically, the slogan combined both issue stances on the evolution of the law since 1973 and fears about the future under increased pro-life lobbying. Thus, the defensive issue definition became favored within the pro-choice movement so as to emphasize the need for continued pro-choice vigilance, including lobbying, voting, financial donations, and membership. This strategy was ultimately successful into the 1990s and beyond, according to Tribe, as both the majority of Americans favor access to abortion at least during early pregnancy but also that the evolution of constitutional law beginning in the early 1970s was a significant framework for discussing women's rights. Viewing the "pro-choice political movement as part of *Roe*'s progeny," Tribe states that "prior to *Roe* a woman's most vital liberty and equality interests were all but invisible to the Constitution . . . the choice necessary for reproductive freedom and equality . . . was more a dirty secret than a constitutional right."[157]

The mobilizing success of each side of the abortion question is shown in the currently unstable constitutional position of abortion. While the feminist and pro-choice movements are sufficiently institutionalized in U.S. public policy so that probably no Supreme Court could write a decision completely overturning *Roe,* the guarantees contained in that decision after the third month of pregnancy have been severely compromised. Those contained in the first trimester, with the "unfettered right to privacy," have been no less under attack by the pro-life movement and are somewhat less compromised than procedures later in pregnancy. However, the paradox still remains for abortion of official constitutionality with less access to it in the United States than thirty years ago, due to successful pro-life lobbying at both the Supreme Court level and then in the state legislatures.[158] Part of this success may be attributed to the pro-life movement's conveying to legislators that it was extremely willing to use single-issue voting, or Keck and Sikkink's politics of accountability. Pro-choice groups, such as NARAL, later adopted this strategy in the late 1980s.

On the pro-life side, one of the movement founders, Curtis

Willke, has described the infighting between the moderate and extreme wings during the 1980s. While the pro-choice side at least had the agreement that choice had to be protected, the fundamental disagreement within the right-to-life movement was whether all abortion was murder or whether pro-life organizing could be more nuanced. The latter view, taken by the NRLC, worked on types of policies on which legislators or judges would be most willing to act. In contrast, Operation Rescue, founded in Binghamton, New York, in 1988 by the evangelical Randall Terry, used a direct-action, take-no-prisoners approach. Terry's Operation Rescue was formed on the notion that those who would "rescue" fetuses from being aborted needed to obey God's rules, the notion of natural law that rules supreme over man-made laws.[159] Terry's group became the leader of the nascent national movement of "rescuers," those who believed mainly in direct action, such as confronting people at clinics. After early successful actions in New Jersey and Pennsylvania, Terry planned and put forth a series of clinic blockades in Atlanta just before and during the 1988 Democratic National Convention. This militant part of the pro-life movement worried those such as the NRLC, who had spent at that point nearly twenty years in organizing and building up their credibility with legislators and other officials. Operation Rescue has not publicly disavowed violence, asserting instead that it is willing to take "any steps necessary to rescue children" (fetuses). Many Operation Rescue members are willing to be arrested, and in 1989 alone more than twenty thousand of the members were charged in clinic blockades.[160] Although all of the violence from the late 1980s onward cannot be ascribed to Operation Rescue alone, the organization must bear some of the responsibility as the first major group to include in the public discourse the concept of using "virtually any means to rescue unborn children."

Human Life International has evolved its focus to mainly include the transnational and international levels of government. It is the central pro-life group within Mexico, called Vida Humana. Both Vida Humana, coming from HLI in the United States, and Matercare, based in Canada, are identified by the pro-life movement as the chief sources of "pregnancy crisis centers" in Mexico and Canada.[161] In the United States, the "women's help centers," as pro-life groups call them, date back to the early 1970s, begun actually in Toronto as an organization called Birthright. Currently, "many of these centers employ medical professionals, use sophisticated medical equipment, including ultrasound machines, and [are] staffed almost entirely by females."[162] HLI is said to have a de facto head in Columbus, Ohio, Margaret Hartshorn, M.D., president of Heartbeat International.[163]

Pro-choice activists counter that these centers, which often buy buildings next to abortion and contraception clinics, confuse women by claiming to offer information on all options, but once there, women are bombarded with information on only the pro-life side. They point out correctly that abortion clinics, as government-regulated entities, must obey the laws and can only counsel on both sides of the question (and not on abortion in cases where prohibited). However, pregnancy crisis centers neither identify who they are nor operate within boundaries of the law as required of pro-choice clinics. There is likely a division between professional clinics, run by doctors with medical equipment and which must be government licensed (but do not necessarily identify themselves as part of the pro-life movement) and those that are simply counseling centers, which are neither licensed nor clear about their affiliation. Many on the pro-choice side view the establishment of the pregnancy crisis clinics as the lower-decibel version of Operation Rescue tactics adopted in the 1990s; while Operation Rescue and others picketed and confronted women going to clinics offering contraception and abortion, HLI and Matercare set up the crisis or help centers.

Interestingly, each side of the abortion question publicly claims that the other has been better funded and organized from the 1980s onward. What is undeniable is a shift in strategy within each side. Jack Willke notes that in the 1980s, the National Right to Life Committee became the dominant pro-life organization, "growing from five to fifty employees between 1980 and 1991, went from a cash flow of $400,000 annually to fifteen million, and has affiliates in all fifty states."[164] Willke contrasts this situation with the best-funded and oldest pro-choice organization, Planned Parenthood, "with an annual income of over $700 million in 2001."[165] It should also be noted that while the NRLC is a single-issue organization, Planned Parenthood is not, working around the world on matters of contraceptive information, research, and allocation, as well as research on abortion procedures and alternatives. Similarly, Planned Parenthood is the organization that has lost millions of dollars through its refusal to abide by the international gag rule in place under the presidencies of Reagan, George Bush the elder, and George W. Bush. The other interesting comparison made by pro-life organizations is that they claim to be grassroots, that is, expressing the will of the people, as opposed to the so-called hierarchical structure of pro-choice organizations. The subtle link to feminism as a military-style hierarchy and the pro-choice movement as not supporting women is clear. Both sides have state affiliates, both sides have Washington offices and PACs, and the NRLC noted its success in Washington under the Reagan administration from 1980 to 1988, "where pro-life leaders worked both with and within the administration."[166]

## Conclusion

The shift to the third major period in U.S. abortion organizing and policy exemplifies the contrary positions of abortion policy in the United States. While there is a constitutional guarantee of women's ability to access the procedure unfettered at least during the first trimester of pregnancy, states are not required to offer abortion procedures. One study has noted that in fact the best predictor of post-*Roe* laws is the state's status in the pre-*Roe* framework, showing that in fact state legislative change does not occur by leaps and bounds. The thirty-two states that had anti-abortion statutes in 1973 currently retain legal restrictions to access.[167] The legal framework is as similar to the pre-*Roe* framework as opponents of reproductive choice have been able to make it. Although states are not allowed to outlaw abortion, nor to enact residency requirements as they could before 1973, the only time at which a woman is guaranteed to be able to have an abortion is in the first trimester; after that, other restrictions may be imposed. However, given the power of insurance companies and state legislators in certain states, women may not even be allowed to access abortion unless they can pay for it.

Different studies show the vast inequality of abortion access across the United States, which is in itself superimposed upon the unequal nature of the U.S. health-care system. For example, the vast majority of states (forty-five) have conscience clause enactments, meaning that medical personnel who are opposed to abortion can opt out of the procedure. While 70 percent of adults receiving Medicaid are women, more than half of states limit public funding for abortions to cases of life endangerment, rape, or incest, and Medicaid funding for all Native American reservations is limited. Other regulations in forty-three states require parental notification or consent for minors; forty states and the District of Columbia ban postviability abortions, and twenty-two states have mandatory waiting periods. In addition to these figures, about 61 percent of women within the eighteen to sixty-four age group have employer-provided health insurance. Although these plans may or may not cover women's needs for abortion-related procedures or contraceptive access, it is clear that women without health insurance have even higher barriers to care. A NARAL study showed that in 1997, the average fee for abortion was $316 for procedures going to just past twelve weeks, $618 at sixteen weeks, and $1,109 at twenty weeks.[168] Related to the framework of citizens' dependency on employer-provided health care in the United States is the fact that in 1999, a mere 37 percent of Americans were covered by an employer-provided health plan that covered abortion services. One study conducted the same year showed that in North Carolina, 37 percent of women who would have accessed abortion had public funding been available instead carried the pregnancy to term.[169]

The irony is that abortion is currently less constitutional in terms of having fewer protections than it was in the 1970s, and it is certainly less accessible. The nationalized period, where women felt they had unqualified access to abortion services across the United States, lasted only about fifteen years. Following from the election of a socially conservative president in 2000, the rhetoric of states' rights remains supreme, as does the ability of states to regulate whether women can have certain types of medical care, a procedure not true for men. The Alan Guttmacher Institute states that 87 percent of counties in the United States have no abortion provider. This fact is also relevant to the demographics of abortion, where abortion rates have slowed in thirty-five states (those with restrictions) and risen in fifteen other states with relatively wider access from the years 1973 to 2000.[170] Another paradox in which U.S. women live in the post-2000 years is that while restrictions have been reinstated on the provision of U.S. funds for global abortion programs (including women in the U.S. military or dependents of men in the military) through USAID, the U.S. Agency for International Development, those funds have at other times (under President George W. Bush, for example), been used to provide Depo-Provera to women in Asia, Africa, and Latin America, in effect "free testing" for U.S.-based pharmaceutical companies (such as Upjohn) that manufacture the drug. The internal contradictions in U.S. abortion policy are highly problematic. Those with money, such as pharmaceutical companies, in effect get free support from the government, and women with money can afford any type of reproductive care. Yet those who either have to depend on governmental assistance through Medicaid or military insurance or even private insurance are truly on their own. This contradiction has been exacerbated by the new federalist policy period of turning abortion regulations back to the states.

In the evolution from a pre-nationalized period of abortion regulation and activism (starting in the nineteenth century) to a nationalized one (beginning in the early 1970s) and back to a subnationalized, new federalist period (since 1989), some similarities can be found across relevant aspects of Tarrow's political opportunity structure framework and across Keck and Sikkink's strategic repertoire for advocacy networks. These include the fact that in all three time periods, access to the state was probably the most important structural aid to the group that ultimately won: physicians in the first period, women's pro-choice groups in the second, and pro-life organizations in the third. The notion of instability of political alignments was especially helpful to physicians in the first period, where they could take advantage of the dramatically changing demographics of the U.S. population, from rural to urban, and to use moral leverage and symbolic politics to convince state legislators that licensed doctors should be the only ones to perform abortions. Changing political alignments were also important to the ushering in of the new period, particularly in the rise of the second-wave women's movement and the increased legitimacy of the Supreme Court. In the third, devolutionist period since the late 1980s, both pro-choice and pro-life sides have used moral leverage, the former to appeal to legislators and justices to keep abortion safe and legal and the pro-life side to try to instill protections for fetal life. As both movements have matured, they have been willing to use accountability politics, such as electoral targeting, and have been successful in doing so. As with the other two time periods, access to the state has been important in this third period, particularly in helping the pro-life movement to access state legislatures to instill restrictions since the 1989 *Webster* decision. Access to the state has also been occasioned for the pro-life movement with nearly constant Republican presidential administrations willing to continue Reagan's Mexico City policy via executive order and, since 1994, solid Republican majorities in both houses of

Congress and across the nation's governorships. Many have seen this changed set of political alignments as a Republican political realignment since the 1980s.

## Notes

1. Kristen Luker, *Abortion and the Politics of Motherhood* (Berkeley: University of California Press, 1984), 14–15.
2. Ibid., 15, 18–35.
3. Ibid., 15.
4. Luker, *Abortion and the Politics of Motherhood,* 27. Luker also cites James Mohr, *Abortion in America: The Origins and Evolution of National Policy* (New York: Oxford University Press, 1978) on this point.
5. Luker, *Abortion and the Politics of Motherhood,* 14–20; also Rosalind Pollack Petchesky, *Abortion and Women's Choice: The State, Sexuality, and Reproductive Freedom* (Boston: Northeastern University Press, 1985), 78–82.
6. Luker, *Abortion and the Politics of Motherhood,* 20.
7. Leslie J. Reagan, *When Abortion Was a Crime: Women, Medicine, and the Law in the United States, 1867–1973* (Berkeley: University of California Press, 1997), 82.
8. Ibid., 82.
9. Ibid., 89.
10. Ibid., 109.
11. Cynthia Gorney, *Articles of Faith: A Frontline History of the Abortion Wars* (New York: Simon and Schuster, 1998), Ch. 3.
12. Luker, *Abortion and the Politics of Motherhood,* 40.
13. The earlier penalties against poisoning were typically used to push midwives out of the practice; the later addition of instruments was specifically aimed at physicians. With regard to harassment and prosecution of physicians, Gorney (*Articles of Faith,* 27, 42–43, 52–53) offers various examples of well-regarded doctors being sent off to do prison terms in the 1950s and of criminal investigations into forty physicians by the California attorney general in 1966. See Luker (*Abortion and the Politics of Motherhood,* 53) on this point as well for a documentation of state-by-state prosecutions; she comes to the opposite conclusion from Gorney, however, arguing that convictions were disproportionately few among physicians prosecuted for performing abortions in the late nineteenth and early twentieth centuries.
14. Laurence Tribe, *Abortion: The Clash of Absolutes,* 2nd ed. (New York: W.W. Norton & Company: 1992), 34.
15. Reagan, *When Abortion Was a Crime,* 91.
16. Ibid.
17. Ibid.
18. Ibid., 105–109.

19. Ibid., 86–87. Two plates shown here from the *Chicago Times,* December 23, 1888, fulfill the adage as to how important pictures are in constructing public viewpoints.

20. Petchesky, *Abortion and Women's Choice,* 83.

21. Ibid., 90.

22. Ibid.

23. Ibid., 92.

24. Ibid., 91.

25. Ibid., 93.

26. Ibid.

27. Ibid., 117.

28. Luker, *Abortion and the Politics of Motherhood,* 46; while she notes here that from 1926 to 1960 abortion did not appear to become either easier or harder to obtain, nor were there particular geographic patterns in place as to its provision, the one striking finding as to the arbitrariness of availability and physicians' discretion is found in that "abortion in the most liberal settings was fifty-five times more frequent than in conservative settings."

29. Ibid., 56–57.

30. Gorney, *Articles of Faith,* 32–35.

31. Luker, *Abortion and the Politics of Motherhood,* 67.

32. Gorney, *Articles of Faith,* 45.

33. Ibid., 46. As Gorney notes, the ALI approach was turning on its head the "cherished if imperfectly applied American principle that was more than one hundred years old," stating, in part, that "abortion, at least in early pregnancy . . . involves considerations so different from the killing of a living human being as to warrant consideration not only of the health of the mother but also of certain extremely adverse social consequences to her or the child."

34. Ibid., 47–48.

35. Ibid., 49.

36. Ibid. As Gorney notes, the Arizona law at the time permitted abortion only in the case of danger to a woman's life. While Finkbine had procured the necessary doctors' approval on "therapeutic" grounds, she was unsophisticated enough to grant a newspaper interview the night before her scheduled abortion. The hospital immediately withdrew its consent, and ultimately Finkbine flew with her husband to Sweden, where even under that liberalized climate they had to wait thirteen days for the Royal Swedish Medical Board to approve a therapeutic hospital-based abortion. Ultimately the abortion permission was granted, but Finkbine became a galvanizing symbol for pro- and anti-abortion forces, as she was covered in many magazines, including *Life,* as either pregnant or sitting with her four other children.

37. Ibid., 51.

38. Ibid., 51–52.

39. Ibid., 52.

40. Ibid.

41. Ibid., 52–53.
42. Ibid., 57–58.
43. Ibid., 60.
44. Ibid.
45. Ibid. Gorney discusses the roots of this coalition in Missouri, Chs. 1–5.
46. Ibid., 71.
47. Reagan, *When Abortion Was a Crime*, 218.
48. Ibid.
49. Ibid. Reagan notes the physicians' fear of prosecution in the 1950s for even discussing abortion publicly. For example, a small, unpublicized Planned Parenthood–sponsored conference was held in 1955, where physician participants were assured that they could have the notation of their participation deleted from the published conference proceedings. This was partially based on the occurrence from a previously held Planned Parenthood conference in 1953 in which one physician had been called to the grand jury simply as a result of making remarks about abortion at that meeting (p. 219). Thus, it would be appropriate to state that within the medical profession in the 1950s, as in the legal profession, there was knowledge that the therapeutic abortion committee structure would in the long run prove to be a house of cards built on too many contradictions to survive. Yet physicians in particular were made aware of the dangers of speaking out publicly about this until the mid-1960s.
50. Ibid., 223.
51. Ibid.
52. Ibid., 223–225.
53. Ibid., 224.
54. Ibid., 225.
55. Ibid. Reagan gives a detailed history of these groups.
56. Gorney, *Articles of Faith*, 83–93, gives a detailed account of the repeal effort in New York.
57. As discussed in Reagan, *When Abortion Was a Crime*, 225.
58. Ibid., 240.
59. Gorney, *Articles of Faith*, 83.
60. Ibid., 84.
61. Ibid., 84, 90.
62. Ibid., 84–86.
63. Ibid., 89.
64. Ibid., 86–92.
65. Ibid., 88–89.
66. Ibid., 88.
67. Ibid., 90.
68. Ibid., 91.
69. Ibid., 93–94.
70. Bill Kovach, "Rockefeller, Signing Bill, Credits Women's Groups," *New York Times*, April 12, 1970, cited in Tribe, *Abortion*, 141, n. 9.
71. Gorney, *Articles of Faith*, 124.

72. Ibid., 125, 131.

73. Reagan, *When Abortion Was a Crime*, 234.

74. Cynthia Harrison, *On Account of Sex: The Politics of Women's Issues, 1945–1968* (Berkeley: University of California Press, 1989).

75. Judith Baer, *Our Lives Under the Law* (Princeton, N.J.: Princeton University Press, 1999).

76. The various state efforts at repeal conducted through the courts are addressed in Reagan, *When Abortion Was a Crime,* 234–245; Gorney, *Articles of Faith,* 140–160; and David Garrow, *Liberty and Sexuality: The Right to Privacy and the Making of* Roe v. Wade (New York: Macmillan, 1994), 389–600.

77. Gorney, *Articles of Faith,* 142.

78. Ibid., 155.

79. Raymond Tatalovich, *The Politics of Abortion in the United States and Canada: A Comparative Study* (Armonk, N.Y.: M.E. Sharpe, 1997), 27–29.

80. Gorney, *Articles of Faith,* 131; Reagan, *When Abortion Was a Crime,* 235.

81. Gorney, *Articles of Faith,* 131.

82. Ibid., 131–132.

83. Ibid., 133.

84. Ibid., 133–134.

85. Ibid., 134.

86. Ibid., 143–144.

87. Ibid., 141, 151; Garrow, *Liberty and Sexuality,* 407–408, 424.

88. Reagan, *When Abortion Was a Crime,* 235.

89. Ibid., 235–240. *Doe v. Scott* is comprehensively described here.

90. Ibid., 236–239.

91. Ibid., 239–240.

92. Gorney, *Articles of Faith,* 143.

93. Ibid. As Gorney details, the Texas, Georgia, New York, Ohio, and Kentucky cases used pregnant women as their lead plaintiffs, those who were denied their rights by the law; Illinois used both doctors and pregnant women as respective classes, and the New Jersey case combined doctors and women "affiliated with women's organizations" (pp. 142–143). Similarly, the old law being challenged in Texas was that only allowing "life of the mother abortions"; that in Georgia, reformed in 1968 under the model penal code, provided also for abortions as a consequence of rape, to prevent "serious and permanent damage to a woman's health," and to prevent the birth of a baby who would "likely have some grave, permanent, and irremediable mental or physical defect" (pp. 150–152).

94. Ibid., 153–154.

95. Garrow, *Liberty and Sexuality,* 404.

96. In confusing fashion, Garrow (*Liberty and Sexuality*) identifies April 16 as the filing of the *Doe* case on p. 428; however, on p. 433, the date of both *Roe* and *Doe* filings are listed as March 3, 1970.

97. Susan G. Mezey, *In Pursuit of Equality: Women, Public Policy, and the Federal Courts* (New York: St. Martin's Press, 1992), 216.

98. Garrow, *Liberty and Sexuality,* 458.

99. Ibid., 460–462.

100. Tatalovich (*The Politics of Abortion in the United States and Canada,* 56–57) writes that "during those years the statutes of Connecticut, Georgia, Texas, North Dakota, Kansas, New Jersey, Wisconsin, California and Florida had been nullified, while existing laws in Kentucky, Louisiana, North Carolina, Ohio, Utah, Indiana, Mississippi, and South Dakota had been upheld."

101. Tribe, *Abortion,* 82–83.

102. Garrow, *Liberty and Sexuality,* 595.

103. Ibid., 158–159.

104. Ibid., 160.

105. Ibid., 64, 160.

106. Gorney, *Articles of Faith,* 32–36.

107. Ibid., 35.

108. Suzanne Staggenborg, *The Pro-Choice Movement: Organization and Activism in the Abortion Conflict* (New York: Oxford University Press, 1994), 60.

109. Ibid., 60–61.

110. Ibid., 160.

111. Ibid., 160–161.

112. Gorney, *Articles of Faith,* 290–291.

113. Staggenborg, *The Pro-Choice Movement,* 107.

114. Mary Ann Glendon, *Abortion and Divorce in Western Law* (Cambridge, Mass.: Harvard University Press, 1987); cited and discussed in Tribe, *Abortion,* 71–76, and Tatalovich, *The Politics of Abortion in the United States and Canada,* 78–81.

115. Gorney, *Articles of Faith,* 435.

116. Ibid., 436.

117. Ibid., 435.

118. Tribe, *Abortion,* 50.

119. Gorney, *Articles of Faith,* 107; Tribe, *Abortion,* 145–146.

120. Gorney, *Articles of Faith,* 178–179, 439.

121. Ibid., 247–248.

122. Ibid., 246.

123. Ibid., 245.

124. Ibid., 245–247.

125. Ibid., 261.

126. Ibid.

127. Ibid., 262.

128. Ibid., 260.

129. HLI website, www.hli.org, accessed 3/18/03.

130. Tribe, *Abortion,* 143.

131. Ibid., 144.

132. As described in Marilen J. Danguilan, *Women in Brackets: a Chronicle of Vatican Power and Control* (Manila: The Philippine Center for Investigative Journalism, 1997), 13.

133. Tribe, *Abortion,* 145.

134. Ibid.; Reagan, *When Abortion Was a Crime*, 235–245.

135. Tribe, *Abortion*, 145.

136. Ibid., 153–154.

137. Ibid., 152.

138. Ibid., 151.

139. *Maher v. Roe* (1977) upheld the denial of state portions of Medicaid funding, whereas *Harris v. McRae* (1980) did the same for federal funds. See Susan Mezey, *In Pursuit of Equality*, 244–252.

140. NARAL, *Who Decides? A State-by-State Review of Abortion and Reproductive Rights*, 11th ed. (Washington, D.C.: NARAL Foundation, 2002), 20–21.

141. Staggenborg (*The Politics of Abortion in the United States and Canada*, 188, n. 2) has written that the usually accepted terminology by those who were active in abortion politics before 1973 was "abortion rights" on the side of abortion access and "right to life" on the anti-abortion side. After 1973, the more common definition preferred by each side was "pro-choice" and "pro-life." Staggenborg notes the normative issue of writing from a pro-choice perspective. This author does as well, and uses the terminology preferred by each side.

142. Tribe, *Abortion*, 144.

143. Gorney, *Articles of Faith*, 155–164; Garrow, *Liberty and Sexuality*, 681.

144. Gorney, *Articles of Faith*, 439.

145. Ibid., 439.

146. Ibid., 144.

147. NARAL, *Who Decides?* 11–12.

148. Lucy Komisar, "Sellout on Abortion," *Newsweek*, June 9, 1975, cited in Tribe, *Abortion*, 145, n. 26.

149. Gorney, *Articles of Faith*, 439–440.

150. Ibid., 465–466.

151. Ibid., 487–488.

152. Ibid., 490–492.

153. James Q. Wilson, *American Government*, 5th ed. (Lexington, Mass.: DC Heath & Co., 1992), 412.

154. Both statements are from the *Missouri v. Webster* opinion, 1989, cited in Gorney, *Articles of Faith*, 490–491.

155. Phyllis Schlafly, "Principle or Pragmatism? Abortion Politics in the Twenty-First Century," in Teresa Wagner, ed., *Back to the Drawing Board: The Future of the Pro-Life Movement* (South Bend, Ind.: St. Augustine's Press, 2003), 169.

156. Tribe, *Abortion*, 193.

157. Ibid.

158. NARAL report, cited by E. J. Dionne, "On Both Sides, Advocates Predict a 50-State Battle," *New York Times*, July 4, 1989, cited in Tribe, *Abortion*, 178, n. 29.

159. Gorney, Articles of Faith, 461–462.

160. Tribe, *Abortion*, 172.

161. HLI website, accessed 2/20/03; Austin Ruse, "The International Scene," in Wagner, *Back to the Drawing Board,* 317–318.

162. Jack Willke, "A History of Pro-Life Leadership: *For Better or Worse,*" in Wagner, *Back to the Drawing Board,* 128–129.

163. Ibid.

164. Ibid., 127.

165. Ibid., 136, n. 7, cites "Stopp International, the Ryan Report," April 2001.

166. Ibid., 125.

167. Tatalovich, *The Politics of Abortion in the United States and Canada,* 202.

168. Figures are drawn from the following: NARAL website, www.naral.org, accessed 5/2003; NARAL Foundation, "The Reproductive Rights & Health of Women of Color," Washington, D.C., 2000, 21–22; and Women's E-News, Jodi Enda, "Geography Rules U.S. Women's Access to Health Care," www.womensenews.org, accessed 7/17/03.

169. Kaiser Family Foundation, "Employer Health Benefits: 1999 Annual Survey, 2; Philip J. Cook et al., "The Effects of Short-Term Variation in Abortion Funding on Pregnancy Outcomes," *Journal of Health Economics* 18 (1999), cited in NARAL Foundation, "The Reproductive Rights & Health of Women of Color," 21–22.

170. IPPF (International Planned Parenthood Federation), *News,* 1/14/3003, citing *The Alan Guttmacher Institute Report on Public Policy,* www.ippf.org.

# 3

# Canada: Limited Access Despite Public Health Care

Canadian abortion policy has hardly been clear-cut. From the early era of abortion rights to the current environment, Canadian policy has fluctuated and suffered the same ambiguities found in policies employed by the United States and Mexico. For example, the first Canadian abortion policy period from 1869 until 1967 resembled both the early U.S. policy and the current Mexican one in that abortion was either tolerated and largely unregulated (as in the United States) or nationally illegal while unofficially available. The second Canadian policy period on abortion, from federal reform in 1969 through the Canadian Supreme Court's 1988 *Morgentaler v. The Queen* decision striking down those reforms, was said to establish but not mandate a nationalizing climate for abortion constitutionality and potential access. Finally, since 1988, the Canadian situation has remained closer to that of the United States than Mexico in that abortion is legal nationally while access to it is declining. This chapter describes these three policy periods in terms of the interaction of Canadian federal structures and the elite tolerance of ambiguity between constitutionality and availability and between federal versus provincial policies. It also describes pro-choice and pro-life strategies during these three periods to either narrow the zone of ambiguity or enlarge it.

In assigning relevance to the role of political opportunity structure components and advocacy networks' strategies, it is clear that in Canada as in the United States, "access to the state" has been a main defining factor across all three policy time periods. More specifically, the nature of the Canadian state as a typically closed access structure and some of its fundamental institutional transitions since the 1980s, which are discussed in this study, have shaped the policy environment for network actors. These changes, such as the establishment of national insurance (Medicare) in 1966 for the provision of health services that are privately provided but government funded, had a great effect on the Criminal Code of Canada omnibus revision bill (Bill C-43) in 1969. Although the Canadian medical system is privately delivered, it is also publicly funded, where physicians are most often paid by the provincial government. Canadian medicine therefore has kept its interests in influencing the state at the forefront, much more than in trying to influence decisions of private finance.[1]

Similarly, the passage of a nationally supreme, entrenched Charter of Rights and Freedoms in 1982 elevated the power of the federal judiciary, especially the Supreme Court of Canada, to being level with Parliament, a totally new occurrence in the Canadian political system. This national event ultimately enabled the 1988 *Morgentaler* ruling. Sidney Tarrow's second political opportunity structure criterion of access to allies, such as between physicians and women's groups, was extremely important particularly at the beginning of the third period in their joint lobbying to keep abortion from being recriminalized. The third opportunity structure aspect of instability of political alignments was also seen in the third period starting in 1988, where the federal Conservatives governed from 1984 to 1993 under a cost-cutting mantra, including health care, repeated by Liberal governments since then. The shift to a Conservative government, particularly in 1984, is termed an example of "instability of alignments," for it was the largest federal electoral majority ever won in Canada's history and a highly unusual event for the Conservative Party, because it had governed nationally only rarely during the twentieth century.

In terms of Margaret Keck and Kathryn Sikkink's framework, physicians used both morality and accountability politics in the second and third time periods. They defined the abortion issue as a more general one of Canadian values for providing equal health benefits for all (only enshrined as national law in 1966, nearly one hundred years after Canada's founding). Established women's and pro-choice groups, including the transnational Planned Parenthood Federation and the Canadian Abortion Rights Action League (CARAL), were in the same position. It can be safely said that material leverage politics were not used, as the Canadian political system does not use the same type of private election finance system as found in the United States.

## Period One: Abortion Hovering Between Federal Criminality and Sub Rosa Access, 1869–1967

In 1869, the first federal criminal laws on abortion in Canada, laid out in Sections 209, 237, and 245 of the criminal code, made it illegal to "procure and perform an abortion" and "to kill the fetus," but they also contained the exceptions of being "performed with reasonable care and skill" or "to preserve the life of the mother." In the 1940s, Canada followed the 1939 British *R. v. Bourne* precedent, establishing the defense of "medical necessity" for women and physicians if continuing the pregnancy would harm the "life or health" of the woman.[2] Similar to the United States, the first era in Canadian abortion policy regulation was primarily centered upon the organizing of national physicians' organizations. Later, the introduction of national health insurance began to make it possible for the federal government to talk about which medical services the federal government would and could provide through funding and those it would not. For abortion, this would involve revisions to the federal criminal code.

One study of the Canadian health-care framework describes the establishment of hospital jurisdictions and areas of medical expertise as "allopathic," based on viewing the patient's body as "sick" and needing treatment by surgery and/or drugs.[3] This model was not atypical of industrialized societies by the early twentieth century, which placed physicians at the top of the health-care pyramid to describe and prescribe the problem and its treatment.[4] The early acceptance of the allopathic model can be traced to the founding date of the Canadian College of Physicians and Surgeons, the regulatory body, and its incorporation into many jurisdictions by the mid-nineteenth century.[5] The mainstream physicians thus "were successful in using their political connections to win state support and exclude competition." This led not only to giving doctors in the provinces great autonomy to decide what services should be offered where but also the graduates of which university programs—and therefore what classes and races—could be represented in the medical profession.[6] By the 1940s, the Canadian Medical Association had "established itself as the representative body for Canadian medicine at the federal level" and could speak for the entire membership, unlike other countries where the association's representation has been split between generalists and specialists.[7] Physicians had themselves sorted out by specialty and into regulatory and lobbying mechanisms by the 1940s.

The next major structuring event in Canadian medical history was the introduction of publicly funded health insurance. The insurance framework may be seen as the most public part of the Canadian health-care system, for the vast majority of Canadian hospitals, 95 percent, are private and nonprofit.[8] The health-care framework is described by its overseeing department, Health Canada, as a "predominantly publicly-financed, privately-delivered health-care system," or as described by another author, "public payment for private practice."[9] In addition, the federal department of Health Canada describes the concurrent administration by federal and provincial governments of the Canadian health-care system as belonging mostly to the provinces.

Before the introduction of provincially administered and provincially and federally funded public health insurance, gaps were present in health insurance coverage. Until the 1950s, only a minority of Canadians purchased private insurance.[10] By 1961, though, about 53 percent of Canadian citizens had some type of commercial medical insurance.[11] The first public insurance plan, covering inpatient services, was introduced by the progressive Cooperative Commonwealth Foundation government of Saskatchewan in 1947. By 1950, three other provinces had joined the system.[12] Based on an agreement reached in 1961, the federal government contributed 50 percent of the costs, covering hospital and diagnostic services for inpatient hospital treatment. In 1966, the federal Liberal government passed the *Medical Care Act* but delayed its implementation until 1968. This action extended the federal government's 50 percent cost-sharing role to physician services performed outside of hospitals.[13] By 1972, this extension of coverage was complete across all provinces and territories and was deemed to have reached the goal of universality. All Canadians, but not all services, were covered by the publicly funded insurance plans.

The four principles "understood" as included in the *Medical Care Act* were that (1) the scope of covered services would include all types of physicians, both general practitioners and specialists; (2) coverage needed to be universal (cover all residents of a province on uniform terms and conditions); (3) the plan had to be publicly administered by either the provincial government or a nonprofit agency; and (4) Canadian citizens' mobility had to be recognized, and "full transferability of benefits" needed to be provided when people moved across provinces.[14] Another criterion was added by the time of the act's passage, which allowed for "extra billing" of physician services to clients, restricted only in that it should not "impede reasonable access to the procedure."[15]

The recognition of both the publicly funded and provincially administered concepts of the Medicare (public universal insurance) system from the beginning of the national Medicare system in 1966–1968 are important to this study. The reason is that the funding and administration issues are the main ones available to pro-choice and pro-life organizing from the 1990s onward, as will be shown. In Canada, the most public intertwining of the rights questions over abortion and its funding has been public at both federal and provincial levels since abortion was decriminalized in 1969 and publicly funded health insurance was introduced one year prior to that. The Canadian universal principle that health insurance is publicly funded has meant that funding has nearly always been raised in the public discourse over abortion-law rights reform by pro-choice and pro-life groups. In the United States, the inclusion of funding in the abortion reform discourse has gradually become more public since the 1980 *Harris v. McRae* decision by the Supreme Court stating that both federal and state governments could deny public (Medicaid) funding for abortions. In Mexico, the funding discourse has been the least publicly broached because abortion remains nationally illegal. However, among feminist abortion-law reform groups such as the Group for Information on Reproductive Choice and among medical providers, the notion of equitable funding and access to safe abortion has gradually become more public since the 1980s. Clearly the universal nature of public health insurance, applying to all Canadians, has shaped the Canadian discourse about abortion law reform more strongly than in the United States and Canada. It has also given pro-choice and pro-life groups material leverage and accountability levers with which to lobby their federal and provincial legislators.

Organized medicine was not initially in agreement with this legislation, fearing an income loss. First, the CMA and commercial insurance companies previously in the field supported public funding only in the limited cases of social assistance recipients and/or low-income earners: to cover only inpatient hospital services, and these would continue to be payable to commercial insurance companies or voluntary plans.[16] One example of physician opposition was seen in a twenty-three-day strike in Saskatchewan just before the extended insurance program (covering inpatient and outpatient services) was implemented in 1962. What ended the strike was the agreement that physicians could continue the practice of extra billing, where doctors could opt out of the government program and thereby bill the patient directly for fees above and beyond those allowed and remunerated by the province.[17] Despite the understanding about the principle against unreasonable extra billing enshrined in the 1966 *Medical Care Act,* physicians in at least seven provinces had virtually unlimited freedom to set their own rates in this regard until the 1980s, ultimately leading to a cost imbalance. It is important to remember that despite the system's self-described universality, doctors lobbied to remain free of payment ceilings and were largely successful at this until the 1980s.

Ultimately, however, physicians came around to supporting the universal, publicly paid framework. In return for "ceding professional discretion over price," they were allowed to maintain their autonomy in clinical decisionmaking and keep a "private fee for service practice."[18] There was also a noted decrease in "doctors' hours of work, housecalls and telephone conversations," with a corresponding increase in their incomes after the introduction of Medicare.[19] Thus, by the late 1960s or early 1970s in most provinces, doctors had come on board to support the federal government's proposal, with part of the added sweetener being the ability to conduct "reasonable" extra billing. There is still a (smaller) role for private insurance companies in covering out-of-plan providers such as dentists, optometrists, and chiropractors.

Another potential source of opposition to the Medicare system was that provinces felt themselves unduly burdened by its administration requirements. The framework has been described as extraordinary "in its degree of federal control," in that "every essential requirement for the operation of the program was prescribed." Provinces were required by the federal government to establish hospital planning boards; license and supervise hospitals, their budgets, and equipment purchases; collect "prescribed statistics" and submit them in final reports; and submit all hospital expenses to federal audit. Finally, services had to be available "on equal terms and conditions."[20]

Fairly early on, the bubble started to burst with regard to the health insurance system, because a fiscal imbalance appeared in universal health-care insurance within a decade of its implementation. For example, the Economic Council of Canada stated in its 1970 report that if the then-current trends in health and education spending continued, these items alone would absorb the entire gross national product within thirty years.[21]

At the close of the first period of abortion-law crafting and health-care insurance administration in Canada, there was lobbying to open abortion service provision. At the same time, there was a recognition by the provinces that the administration of national publicly available health-care administration was making an ever-increasing dent in their discretionary social spending revenues. The ultimate need to reconcile nationally enshrined rights to access with the on-the-ground reduction in funding was starting to be felt.

## Period Two: Nationalization of Abortion Law and Medical Insurance Funding, 1969–1988

The reformed Criminal Code of Canada provisions of 1969 have been described as a statutory "catching up" to the practices already employed by a number of doctors.[22] By the early 1960s, even though abortion was still in the criminal code, about 120,000 were performed each year, many by unqualified people and not in medical settings.[23]

Although some movements had been made within the House of Commons in the mid-1960s toward pushing reform of the criminal code, they were conducted either by non-Cabinet (i.e., backbench) members of the governing Liberal Party or by the opposition social-democratic New Democratic Party (NDP). Thus, they did not form part of the government's legislative program.[24] In 1967, the Liberal government, at that time a minority government, introduced legislation to reform the criminal code, but it died when the election was called. Returned as the head of a majority government in 1968, Liberal prime minister Pierre Trudeau proceeded with the plan to conduct the omnibus revisions to the criminal code, which became law by the end of that summer. With respect to the provisions on abortion, the new law stipulated that abortions were required to be performed only in qualified hospitals, where the request was approved by a therapeutic abortion committee. Comprising three doctors from the hospital, the TAC would certify that the abortion was medically necessary because the pregnancy threatened the mother's life or (undefined) health. The result was that women still had to go to hospitals, not clinics, to have abortions performed, and they had to be performed by doctors only (not physician assistants, for example). Hospitals were not required to set up TACs, so there was no guarantee of equal access across Canada. A woman procuring an abortion, or someone providing one, outside this framework would still be liable to prosecution. What is also important to note and undoubtedly influenced the acceptance of the government's legislation was that by 1968 Medicare (public) insurance coverage was in place. This insurance would be applicable to most hospital-based abortions.

The absolute numbers of Canadian abortion procedures as officially reported showed some peaks after the 1969 legislation went into effect. There was a large upswing in procedures performed in the immediately proximate years, from a report of 11,152 such procedures in 1970 to 37,232 in the next year; the corresponding rates per 1,000 females were 6.6 and 9.9, respectively. Overall numbers and rates of abortion procedures increased steadily, not drastically over the next ten years, with the next major increase happening between 1981 and 1982, with the absolute numbers going from 71,911 in 1981 increasing to 75, 071, with the figures then declining. The next large increase in numbers and rates to date happened between 1989 and 1990, from 79,315 procedures, a rate of 12.6 per 1,000 women, to 92,901, a rate of 14.6.[25] Clearly, access to abortion procedures was something Canadian women felt was a reasonable legal guarantee after 1969, despite the fact that hospitals performing abortions tended to cluster around a few large urban areas.

The second-wave Canadian women's movement was institutionalized during this second phase of Canadian abortion policy. This event provided physicians with important allies in watching the implementation of abortion policy after 1969 and provided Canadian women (to a certain extent) with access to the state at various junctures to enable their policy input. Most scholars have described the Canadian women's movement as dominated by the liberal, mainstream strand (concerned with improving women's rights through legislative and other policy means) with a "state-centered" focus.[26] This latter focus includes having received funding from national and provincial governments. As noted by one Canadian women's movement scholar, the fact that the Canadian women's movement has been found most often at the liberal mainstream end of the spectrum does not mean that its tactics are limited to that arena. Various groups, including on abortion policy, have used a combination of insider and outsider strategies. Examples include demonstrating outside Parliament at one point, then becoming lobbyists inside its walls at other points, whenever the relevant forum shifted.

A state-based infrastructure to represent women's policy issues before government and the opposition parties, and to convey governmental positions to nongovernmental organizations (NGOs) and vice versa, was established through the recommendations of the Royal Commission on the Status of Women. The commission was begun under the national Liberal government of Prime Minister Lester Pearson in 1967 but reported under Prime Minister Trudeau's leadership in 1970. While constrained by the liberal democratic language of its day as the only official representative of women's concerns, the commission's report issued some far-reaching conclusions among its 167 recommendations, including those related to reproductive control. Various women's policy agencies emanating from this commission included the minister responsible for the Status of Women in 1971, a "junior" post created as a partner position to a more senior portfolio assigned to the same minister, and the Department of Status of Women Canada as a quasi-Cabinet department. The other two elements of this infrastructure included the (officially nonpartisan) Advisory Council on the Status of Women—having a more public function of acting as liaison between the public generally, NGOs, the House of Commons, bureaucracy, and the Minister Responsible for the Status of Women—as well as the Women's Program in the Department of the Secretary of State. The presence of this official infrastructure to represent women's concerns between the public and government and back again gave women a strong toehold into state representation that has not been seen in the United States. Examples have included regular conferences, held several times per year, sponsored by the Advisory Council on various issues and often held in parliamentary conference rooms. Similarly, the Advisory Council on the Status of Women, which was divided into separate offices until

1995, regularly published reports on various issues related to the high-profile priorities of the Minister Responsible for the Status of Women and the government of the day.

With respect to specifically abortion-related groups, CARAL has been one of the two most high-profile pro-choice groups active since the institutionalization of the second-wave women's movement. It was founded in 1974 to both work for women's reproductive rights and to help with the various defenses of Henry Morgentaler, M.D., who had been trying to challenge the TAC system since its formalization in 1969. CARAL, independent of the similarly named U.S. pro-choice group, is most properly placed within the liberal mainstream part of the women's movement spectrum. Throughout its history, it has mainly been interested in changing abortion laws to benefit women as well as working with the relevant actors, such as Parliament and the judiciary, to achieve this. By 1990, it had a membership of eighteen thousand individuals and thirty chapters.[27]

The other pro-choice group that has been involved in efforts to change national policy to about the same extent as CARAL is the Ontario Coalition for Abortion Clinics (OCAC), formed in 1982. In terms of its feminist analyses of power relations, OCAC is to the left of CARAL. It tends to use radical feminist analysis in explaining the patriarchal (and often capitalist) domination of women's reproductive and life choices. OCAC was founded specifically on the issue of helping to bring freestanding clinics to Ontario, particularly its largest city, Toronto. To that extent, it was also involved with Dr. Morgentaler's campaigns to establish a clinic there, prior to the legalization of such venues by the Supreme Court's action in 1988. Planned Parenthood has been active in various lobbying campaigns when necessary, such as those around changes to national legislation and in trying to establish freestanding clinics; otherwise, it is known mainly as a provider organization for birth-control resources and general reproductive rights information.

Other groups that have been active in the pro-choice coalition at strategic points include the largest national women's organization in Canada, the National Action Committee on the Status of Women (NAC), formed in 1972. By 1990, it was said to have a membership of three million Canadian women and more than five hundred groups. Its counterpart in Quebec has been the Fédération des femmes du Quebec (Federation of the Women of Quebec, FFQ), formed in 1966. Like NAC, the FFQ has functioned as an umbrella organization consisting mainly of liberal feminist organizations. Other groups that joined the pro-choice coalition, especially on issues of legal strategy, include the Women's Legal Education and Action Fund (LEAF) of Toronto, a feminist legal defense fund founded in 1985, and the National Association of Women and the Law (NAWL) of Ottawa, formed mainly of legal scholars and practitioners.

The main right-to-life groups have included the seemingly marginal Campaign Life as well as REAL Women of Canada, formed by the same woman, lawyer Gwendolyn Landolt of Toronto. Campaign Life has been most successful outside of Canada, working with other groups, notably Human Life International Canada (HLIC), to work the rules and representational structure at the UN in New York and to send as many participants as possible to UN conferences.

In addition to the availability of allies by the formation of women's groups that strengthened the coalition between Dr. Morgentaler, CARAL, and OCAC and between physicians and other women's rights groups, access to the state was an important part of the second period on abortion policy, involving a visible role of the national government in setting national standards. Access to the state was seen for the reception of doctors' and lawyers' concerns by the relatively quick action taken by the Trudeau government in 1968, as well as the tweaking of the national health insurance framework to allow physicians to extra bill the government for years after the system was put into effect. It should be added that the publicly funded insurance system also was an important element of access for women, as women tend to be disproportionately numerous clients of health-care systems. Also helping women was the embedding of women's policy agencies into the federal structure. This would help women's NGOs gain access to state structures at strategic points over the course of the development of abortion policy.

Another important element of state access that happened during the general "national state expansion" project of the Trudeau Liberal government from 1968 until 1984 was the passage of one of the prime minister's pet projects, a supreme Bill of Rights (Charter of Rights) in 1982. This shaped access to the state mainly for NGOs that had previously felt shut out of the Canadian lobbying system of highly limited access. One important way was in the entrenchment of freedom of speech and association guarantees in Section 2, very similar to the U.S. Bill of Rights' First Amendment.

Another important opening for women's influence was in the government's invitation to groups to make public presentations to the Special Joint Parliamentary Committee in 1981, prior to the Charter's consideration in the full House of Commons. It was clear from the outset of the Liberal government's introduction of the Charter that at least one equality clause for women was to be included, a guarantee of "equality before the law," which had been in the statutory Bill of Rights enacted in 1960 but never used to strike down gender-based legislation. In addition to this guarantee that would be strengthened by being in a Bill of Rights, which was supreme over legislation—not at its same level—other changes were finally wrought by women's groups after a great deal of lobbying. They included strengthening Section 15 to add "equality under the law" (to enable results-based jurisprudence) and adding an ERA-type clause, known as Section 28, stating that "the rights and freedoms in this Charter are guaranteed equally to male and female persons." Another clause, ultimately Section 7, promises "life, liberty and security to the person." This was the subject of lobbying by both pro-choice and pro-life groups, the latter wanting to get fetal life acknowledged in the Charter. They were unsuccessful in that task. The relative degree of influence that feminists had at the expense of nonfeminist counterparts was to make a great deal of difference in cases litigated before the Supreme Court less than ten years later.

The abortion policy regime enacted in 1969 governed the provision of abortion services until the Supreme Court heard the *Morgentaler* case in 1988. The case came because of Dr. Morgentaler's challenge of the federal laws, by setting up and operating freestanding (nonhospital) clinics in Montreal and Toronto. Prosecuted, jailed, and then acquitted by successive Quebec governments, he became a visible national figurehead of the pro-choice movement, even though Dr. Morgentaler identified himself as aligned with the Humanist Association of Canada rather than feminist groups. Dr. Morgentaler wished to show that the then-current federal regime was still too restrictive. However, courts in other provinces, such as Ontario and Manitoba, rejected his "necessity" defense, based on the 1939 British *Bourne* case.[28]

The main advocacy network tactics used by the women's movement in this second abortion policy period in Canadian history included symbolic politics, particularly from the 1970s onward, as the movement institutionalized itself. It claimed that most of the abortion debate until that time had been about the rights of doctors and not women, and that because women voted too, their rights should be respected in national policies. This became an even stronger argument after the Charter's implementation in 1982, where the rights of women were constitutionally specified. Abortion opponents, seeming highly outnumbered and fairly weak in the 1970s and early 1980s, such as Campaign Life, used moral leverage arguments like their U.S. counterparts that fetal life deserved protection as well. This included argumentation both about the Charter framing and in post-1988 legislative debates over the fate of the 1969 omnibus legislation.

## Period Three: Returning Abortion and Funding Administration Primarily to Provinces, 1988 Onward

One important event shifted the political opportunity structure toward a new framework for discussion of and advocacy on Canadian abortion politics in the 1980s, culminating in the start of the third period on abortion policy from 1988 onward. This was the 1984 Conservative Party victory by the largest federal electoral mandate in the history of Canada. Related to this, there was increasing evidence that the federal capacity and will to fund the health-care system was declining and became part of the overall Conservative drive to reform federal budgets. The sharpest division yet within the division of publicly provided health care took place under the Conservative mandate, that of differentiating between the fact that all Canadians are covered but not all services are. In budget-cutting times such as the 1980s, the federal transfers for service coverage in provinces began to decrease.

Within this third period, pro-choice forces and physicians and others from the medical establishment have successfully been able to use the politics of accountability, as well as moral leverage and symbolic politics. These groups have used the intertwining arguments about rights and universal insurance coverage for all as historically protected concepts in Canada. They have been helped in this by one of the key opportunity structure shifts from the second period, that of the national entrenchment of the Bill of Rights: the Charter of Rights and Freedoms. Feminists for example have been able to rely on the gender-equality rights provisions found in Sections 15 (including affirmative action) and 28. Pro-life groups in Canada and the United States have to use the symbolic and moral leverage politics of working to raise the fetus to the same constitutional level of scrutiny as those considered "persons" in the law. The attempts so far have failed. One possible reason is that a decision to move the definition of personhood forward would result in considerably increased costs to the health-care system.

It would be no mistake to state that the Canadian Supreme Court's *Morgentaler* decision of 1988 was made possible by the 1982 entrenchment of the Charter of Rights and Freedoms. The relevant part of the Charter to the *Morgentaler* decision was Section 7, promising "life, liberty and security" of the person. Dr. Morgentaler had centered his argument against the TAC system as denying women's security across Canada, as not everyone could secure a TAC-approved abortion and thus a criminal defense.[29] It also discriminated economically between those who could access the insurance-covered system and those who could not, as OCAC pointed out. In all but two provinces, the number of hospitals with TACs in place had declined from 1975 to 1986.[30]

The first woman justice of the Canadian Supreme Court, Madame Justice Bertha Wilson, agreed with Dr. Morgentaler's argument, as did five other justices. Hence, the requirement for TAC approval and that abortions be hospital based was struck down. Justice Wilson's decision closely followed the reasoning in *Roe v. Wade,* but unlike Justice Harry Blackmun's decision, which suggested the trimester framework to determine the progression of compelling state interest in regulating the procedure, the *Morgentaler* case did not. In the sense of the traditional Canadian polity, following the Westminster parliamentary model, the Supreme Court did not flex its newly found muscles too much. Instead, it suggested that Parliament was the proper actor to legislate the time frame, alluding to a potential "gestational limit." The criminal code provision that survived the case and the test of time is the requirement that only physicians are allowed to perform abortions in Canada. In effect, the Canadian situation since 1988 is that there is no national law governing abortion policy.

Although it may not have been realized then, at the same stroke the *Morgentaler* decision did what twenty years of U.S. constitutional abortion jurisprudence had done, from *Roe* in 1973 to *Harris* in 1980 and through to *Planned Parenthood v. Casey* in 1992. At the same time it nationalized the constitutional right to abortion, it effectively delivered the policymaking weight back toward the provinces, which had always been the major health-care administrators in Canada. In the context of federal cuts to provincial health-care funding, the Court decision ensured that the discourse and strategies around access to abortion rights would become increasingly fiscalized in Canada. The Canadian commitment to universal health insurance since the 1960s and that this system has included abortion coverage in at least some facilities is helpful to Canadian pro-choice groups in arguing that collective commitments to Canadians' health care exist. While health-care funding has been cut back from certain abortion facilities, Canadian women at least can claim to be part of the collective Canadian-ness, due to constitutional equality provisions, constitutional abortion rights interpretation, and universal health-care coverage.

In the United States, by contrast, pro-choice groups have neither a constitutional ERA nor a historic commitment to equal public insurance coverage. They are limited in the reach of their discourse to the constitutional abortion rights status as interpreted in *Roe,* considerably narrowed by *Casey* in 1992. The right to abortion access in the United States has thus been as individualized and privatized as many other social rights, due to the private nature of health insurance coverage. The U.S. abortion-rights discourse is thus linked more to a vague "fairness and equity" sense based on a now somewhat-outdated judicial commitment to constitutionally based access. Unlike its Canadian counterparts, it lacks the historic funding arrangements to argue that abortion should be as equally funded as other primary health commitments and trigger punitive federal sanctions if not. On another facet of abortion access, that of the gestational limit, U.S. women would seemingly be in a somewhat better position than their Canadian counterparts because at least the constitutional basis for guaranteeing abortion during the first trimester—when more than 90 percent of abortions occur—was validated in *Casey.* While constitutional gestational limits for abortion services were not provided in *Morgentaler,* it is also true that the lack of a regulatory framework concerning gestational limits, leaving it up to hospital procedure, can be helpful. For example, abortion services can be arranged in Canada significantly into the second trimester, into the fifth month. The problem is to be able to pay for it if, for example, one goes to a hospital where one's Medicare coverage is inadequate. Finally, future protection for first-trimester abortion in the United States is not guaranteed, as four justices went on record in *Casey* as opposing it.

After Canadians believed the abortion issue to be mostly settled by the 1988 *Morgentaler* interpretation, two cases came to the fore that made the issue politically toxic again. These two cases had to do with pro-life efforts to get constitutional rights of protection for fetal life. The first case was brought by former provincial legislator Joe Borowski, a "life-long pro-life crusader."[31] He had begun his challenge of the Criminal Code of Canada in Saskatchewan courts, losing at both levels, before the Charter had been entrenched in 1982. When *Borowski v. Canada* came to the Supreme Court of Canada for review in 1989, Borowski tried to use the same Section 7 argument for life, liberty, and security of the person as used by the Supreme Court in its *Morgentaler* decision, only on behalf of the fetus. On narrow, technical grounds, the Supreme Court ruled his case moot, referring back to the original criminal code provisions then superseded by the Charter. The second case was *Tremblay v. Daigle* of 1989, heard by the Supreme Court after the Quebec Court of Appeals granted an injunction to Chantal Daigle's former boyfriend against her having an abortion, since it interpreted the Quebec Charter (Bill of Rights) as protecting fetal life. Although Daigle went to the United States to have the abortion procedure denied to her in Quebec, the Supreme Court of Canada overturned the Quebec ruling in its November 1989 decision, stating that the fetus was not a juridical person in either civil or common law systems in use in Canada.[32] This case has been described as the most troubling to the Conservative government, for it realized it would have to take the abortion issue up in the House of Commons, an issue the government had hoped to avoid during its second mandate from fall 1988 onward.

Although Parliament did try to legislate in two separate attempts in 1988 and 1989 that split the governing Conservative Party in half, it was not successful.[33] Heavy lobbying by both medical associations and women's groups, particularly CARAL, OCAC, NAC, LEAF, and Planned Parenthood, is given a large part of the credit for the bill's defeat. CARAL has reported that after the attempts of the Conservative federal government to reintroduce criminal sanctions on abortion after the 1988 *Morgentaler* decision, many physicians quit the field and did not return even after the bill's defeat. Nearly a hundred doctors out of 275 who threatened to quit medicine in the face of the proposed legislation did so.

Without the overarching criminal code provisions, the principal means by which the federal government can still regulate provincial delivery of health-care services is through the federal spending power and the standards within the national health insurance system. This constitutional division of powers has been of help to the pro-choice movement in Canada and the doctors regulated by this power sharing and has not provided the opportunities for state access that have been provided nationwide in the United States since Supreme Court rulings of 1989 and 1992. Unlike the U.S. *Webster* and *Casey* decisions, the 1988 *Morgentaler* decision did not contain language about which provincial restrictions upon abortion might be acceptable.

Thus, the chief means used by provincial governments that might be opposed to broadening abortion access has been to defund clinics, whether hospital based or freestanding. Although pro-life groups have worked with and learned strategies from the U.S. network—such as picketing clinics and constructing "false" clinics next door to pro-choice ones—they simply have not had the same means to affect provincial legislation in the manner as their U.S. counterparts. It has not been shown that provincial assemblies, which are unicameral and rather limited in their powers, are in any way desirous of getting into the abortion policy field to pass restrictions such as waiting periods, gestational counseling, or what other types of issues may be addressed in publicly funded clinics. Instead, the overall procedure has been one to either deny licenses for new clinics to open or to shrink funding for existing clinics. From the pro-life side, the rhetoric has changed a bit as well to emphasizing that abortion funding should not be considered a core priority of federal and provincial governments because pro-lifers believe abortion equals murder.

Further changes have been made in the federal-provincial mix, such as through the Canadian Health and Social Transfer Program in 1995 that consolidated federal payments to an even greater degree through social services block grants to the provinces. This has meant that social services, traditionally comprising the highest percentages of provincial budgets, now have to contend with each other for funding within the same grant. Given the increasingly expressed provincial discontent with being shortchanged, a series of federal-provincial meetings resulted in the late 1990s that left the federal government promising to restore transfer payments to their 1995 levels.[34] Since the 2000–2002 federally appointed Romanow Commission on the Future of Health Care in Canada, there have been two sets of federal-provincial agreements to restore much of the funding for provincial services that was cut. The priority areas include pharmacare (pharmaceuticals coverage), home care, and primary health coverage (although not abortion).[35]

The demographics of abortion in Canada since the momentous Supreme Court decision of 1988 include the following. The number of abortions performed rose in Canada between 1988 and 1998 and have declined thereafter. In 1988, there were 72,693 abortions performed in Canada overall. By 1992, the figure had reached 100,497. By 1997, the overall figure was 114,666 but dropped to 110,331 in 1998.[36] Another result of the *Morgentaler* decision is that it seems less necessary for Canadian women to go to the United States for these procedures. In 1987, it was reported that 2,757 Canadian women went to the United States for abortions, whereas by 1998 the figure was 300 women.[37]

Another important shift in abortion services has been their locale. Initially few were clinic based, but by the mid-1990s one-third of abortions in Canada were performed in clinics; currently, about 40 percent of them are.[38] This figure acknowledges the complete lack of clinics in the provinces of Saskatchewan and Prince Edward Island (PEI). The shift between hospital- and clinic-based abortions began right at the time of the *Morgentaler* decision; the rate of Canadian abortions that took place in hospitals, which was 100 percent through 1977, dropped to 95 percent and stayed there through 1987. Nineteen ninety-eight saw the first drop in hospital-based abortions (where 93.6 percent of abortions were performed). It appears that immediately after the court decision, and the establishment of a legal choice of venue, women began to use the clinics to avoid the hospital waiting time and the often daunting bureaucracy. By 1992, the shift between hospital-based and clinic-based providers was quite pronounced: from 94 percent of abortions performed in hospitals in 1988 down to 71 percent of them being performed in hospital-based settings that year. Clinics, correspondingly, were busier; from accounting for 6 percent of Canadian abortions in 1988, they accounted for almost 30 percent by 1992, four years later.[39] The increased importance of clinic providers is quite apparent.

Other demographics of note are that the most common group to access abortion services are women in their twenties, who accounted for half of abortion procedures performed in Canada in 1998.[40] The use of abortion services from 1996 to 1997 increased among three age groups: those twenty to twenty-four (the largest increase, at about one-half of 1 percent), those thirty-five to thirty-nine, and those in their forties. About twenty-seven women of every one thousand in their twenties obtained an abortion.[41]

With regard to hospitals, there were 191 Canadian hospitals performing abortion services in 1990 but only 163 performing them as of 2000.[42] A geographic illustration of these services reveals even more. Among three of the prairie provinces—some of the physically larger provinces with high percentages of rural populations— Saskatchewan and Manitoba each have two hospitals that perform abortions, and Alberta has three. The highest numbers of clinics are found in the central provinces of Ontario and Quebec, and those two provinces and British Columbia (BC) have the three highest numbers of hospitals performing abortions (seventy-six in Ontario, thirty-seven in BC, and thirty in Quebec). Each of the three territories, Yukon, Northwest, and the newest one, Nunavut, have zero clinics each, again with large land masses to travel. When added to the zero-clinic provinces of PEI and Saskatchewan, this means that five Canadian jurisdictions out of a total of thirteen (ten provinces and three territories) have no clinic services.[43] In Canada, the second-largest country in the world in terms of land mass, geographic barriers are quite real. The geographic barriers are emphasized by the clustering of most abortion services in larger cities, necessitating travel by rural residents. For example, residents on the outport side of Newfoundland must travel completely across the province to access the only clinic there.

To complete the hospital picture, there have been many mergers in the 1990s and hospital closures in the face of the government's restructuring of national budget priorities and interest in decreasing the national budget deficit. In the 1990s, 257 hospitals in Canada were either closed or merged with another hospital. There are an estimated 781 such facilities left across the country, which means that roughly 20 percent of Canada's hospitals were closed in one decade.[44] Many of these were rural hospitals, which did not offer abortion services, but there have also been very noticeable mergers that resulted in the loss of abortion services. Both the Toronto Women's Hospital and Wellesley Hospital, two large providers of abortion and contraceptive services, were merged with Catholic

Church–run hospitals, and the result in the first case was outsourcing to a women's clinic open one day per week and the complete loss of abortion and contraceptive services in the latter. The five clinics located in the metro Toronto area perform a quarter of all abortions in the province of Ontario.[45] Given that the most likely hospitals to keep performing abortions are the first-tier research hospitals, generally in urban areas, or the second-tier general hospitals in surrounding areas, their closure is particularly significant for the question of abortion access. Many hospitals are also feeling shortages in operating room time due to the closures; for example, one BC provider's office reported that they are lucky to get one day per week in the operating room, in which perhaps ten abortions can be performed. This then entails a waiting list of at least a month between confirmation of pregnancy and abortion date for women choosing to access hospital facilities. Because hospitals are usually more fully covered than clinics by Canadian health insurance, many women choose the wait, which causes anxiety for them and possible complications. In direct violation of the 1988 *Morgentaler* ruling, New Brunswick and Newfoundland/Labrador continue to adhere to a TAC system, where the requirement of approval by two doctors must precede a hospital-based abortion in the former and one doctor in the latter.[46]

The BC Women's Equality minister reported a 20 percent decline in the numbers of physicians performing abortions in that province since 1994, and another particularly hard-hit area has been the southern Ontario area surrounding Toronto and south of it.[47] Given that physicians are the only ones allowed to perform abortions in Canada, the fact that they are vacating the field is troubling. If we accept the numbers of surgeons trained in ob-gyn as the most likely to perform abortions, their current figures across the provinces are highs of 645 in Ontario, 407 in Quebec, but only 3 across the three territories (indeed, some Ontario-based providers fly to the territories once every two weeks or even once a month). In 2001, there were 1,577 ob-gyns registered to practice across the country, with a population of thirty million, or about fifteen million women.[48]

Another point about the clinic issue is that freestanding (nonhospital) clinics are usually easier to access in that they have shorter time constraints but, again, may require out-of-pocket fees from clients as these clinics are less prone to being covered by Medicare. Because each province except Ontario and Quebec has fewer than five clinics, provincial government actions and those taken by the regulatory bodies (the provincial and national College of Physicians and Surgeons) on the issues of clinic licensing and protection are significant. The provinces of Manitoba and New Brunswick have actively worked to prevent Dr. Morgentaler's plans to establish the first clinic in each of those provinces. New Brunswick, for example, passed the *Medical Services Act* to require that abortions could be performed only in hospitals, flying in the face of the 1988 *Morgentaler* decision. The New Brunswick College of Physicians and Surgeons complied, and Dr. Morgentaler's license to practice outside hospitals was revoked. He did win the license back at trial, and when this judgment was appealed by the New Brunswick government, Dr. Morgentaler won again. However, New Brunswick, like a handful of other provinces, refuses to contribute the provincial component to health insurance coverage for abortions performed in the only clinic there, so women have to pay the $450 up front themselves. Abortions are performed every two weeks at the Morgentaler clinic in Fredericton by two doctors who fly in from outside the province, providing about five hundred abortions per year on that basis.[49]

In Manitoba in 1993, the provincial government similarly took action in the face of Dr. Morgentaler's already established clinic by passing the *Health Services Amendment Act,* excluding (publicly paid) insurance funding for clinics. Again, the only clinic in the province was (and is) Dr. Morgentaler's, so the target seems clear. Even more overt was the provincial government's suspension of the previous agreement to operate Dr. Morgentaler's clinic as a nonprofit medical service as of April 1, 2001. If this proposal had passed, the clinic would have been fully funded under national health-care insurance rules. The Manitoba government's actions make little sense in party terms. Manitoba is currently governed by the social-democratic NDP, the party that in its federal program has consistently been the most open to abortion provision and against any restrictions.[50]

Quebec and Nova Scotia do not fully fund their clinics. There is little the federal government can do about Quebec, as it operates on a somewhat different basis within the national framework, but Nova Scotia has been fined by the federal government for refusal to fully fund the clinics, which is within the scope of the federal government's action. However, by 2000, only $200,000 in penalties have been collected since 1995, whereas the fines levied were $130,000 per year.[51] With respect to reciprocal billing, that of provinces allowing health insurance funds to be used for abortions obtained outside of the province, the Atlantic provinces are at the forefront of refusing to cooperate in this system. Ontario will only pay limited fees.[52] In response to the decision of the Manitoba government to renege on its prior agreement with Dr. Morgentaler, a class-action suit was brought against the Manitoba government at the end of July 2001. The plaintiffs' contention was that fully funding abortions performed in hospitals, while requiring a $400 up-front fee for clinic-based abortions, constitutes a two-tier system, violating Canadian health insurance standards.[53] In December 2004, the plaintiffs won in Manitoba, but funding is currently pending before the Supreme Court of Canada.

It is important to note the different actions by the provincial Colleges of Physicians and Surgeons in two neighboring provinces. While the College in Saskatchewan voted to uphold the clinic ban in 1996, that of Alberta refused to redefine abortion as an excluded (i.e., nonmedically necessary) procedure when the provincial government moved to delist the procedure from Medicare insurance coverage in 1995.[54] The degree of provincial government and organized medical group variation is clearly a reality with which the pro-choice movement has had to contend.

Nova Scotia has flouted the *Canada Health Act* requirements against extra billing since 1995, although it has not been fined anywhere near the possible $130,000 annual level. Given that all services deemed to be medically necessary are now required to be funded on an equal basis to provide universality and accessibility, and abortion was included in this list by the federal government in 1995, there is no longer any policy reason for PEI to provide no abortion services whatsoever, for Saskatchewan not to have clinics, for most of the Atlantic provinces to refuse to participate in reciprocal billing, and for Manitoba and New Brunswick to charge user fees for clinic-based abortions.

Transnational institutional linkages have been formed on both sides of the abortion question since the 1980s. On the pro-life side, tactics of the violent wing of the pro-life movement have increasingly begun to resemble those of the U.S. movement. Harassment of clinics and their personnel was widespread in the 1990s, as service access has shifted there. The Morgentaler clinic in Toronto was burned, twice partially and once completely. That in Edmonton, Alberta, has had gasoline and butyric acid attacks. Picketing has been a consistent problem in Vancouver, BC, and a "bubble zone" was enacted there to keep protesters fifty meters away. Two doctors, Garson Romalis of BC and Hugh Short of Ontario, were shot by James Kopp, currently on trial for the murder of Barnett Slepian, M.D., in the United States.[55] Operation Rescue and the "Army of God" routinely boast about their actions across the border and how many followers they have picked up in Canada. A more mainstream tactic of the pro-life movement, following U.S. strategy, has been to establish "clinics," which unlike their federally funded pro-choice counterparts, do not have to offer information on both sides of the question.

The pro-choice movement, particularly CARAL, Planned Parenthood, and the Childbirth by Choice Trust, has become increasingly active in the National Abortion Federation, headquartered in Washington, D.C. In this network, organizations have worked together to share information on violent offenders such as James Kopp and Joseph Scheidler of Chicago. This cooperation resulted in Kopp's arrest. NAF also holds annual conferences at which providers from the United States and Canada meet to discuss the situation of abortion provisions nationally and subnationally, as well as the new positive and negative developments. This network has clearly been facilitated by the widespread use of the Internet since the mid-1990s. In essence, as the opposition has heated up its attacks and been shown to be increasingly willing to cross borders for annual protests on both Parliament Hill and Capitol Hill, attempts at blockades and unrest outside of clinics, and to attend recent papal visits in Toronto and Mexico City, the pro-choice network has realized that it has a transnationally focused movement with which to contend. Its strategies have been both defensive, in terms of keeping more legislatures and the U.S. Congress from whittling away existing abortion rights but also a highly sophisticated strategy of information sharing across borders on a consistent basis to describe common tactics of pro-life groups and especially to alert other countries when violent offenders seem to be headed there.

## Conclusion

The Canadian and U.S. trajectories on abortion policy since the 1860s are the two most similar in this study. Both tended to parallel the process of professional organization of the medical profession and to follow the relative weight of that profession when it lobbied at different levels of government. In the United States, the relevant lobby site in the first period was the state legislatures, for states have the bulk of criminal law responsibilities, the exact opposite of Canada, where the criminal code is mainly federal. In both countries, where physicians saw that increased federal attention would decrease their chances of prosecution, they lobbied for increased federal policy attention to the issue. While the enactment of the 1969 Canadian legislative reforms and the 1973 *Roe v. Wade* decision did impose a greater degree of national standards and some sort of parameters within which women would know where they could obtain a legal abortion (which was largely absent in the two countries' first policy periods), neither was so strictly formulated as to impose absolute consistency. It is within these spaces that the pro-life network began to work to particular success in the United States, turning the abortion policy period since 1989 (the *Webster* decision) back to one of state regulation on an order not seen since before 1973. The main exception is that states since 1973 cannot declare abortion illegal and neither can provinces.

Thus, there have been three period shifts in abortion policy in Canada and the United States, from subnational regulation in the United States (and some language in the Criminal Code of Canada), to the most visible national regulations constructed through alliances of medical professionals and women's movement activists, and then to a state of devolution under different legal frameworks. However, they have had different outcomes. The relevant parts of the political opportunity structure have been, first, access to the state (physicians in the first period, physicians and women's movement in the second period, and the U.S. pro-life movement in the third). And second, access to allies between the women's movement and physicians was most pronounced in the second and third time periods in Canada, in first bringing about *Morgentaler,* then successfully lobbying to prevent abortion from being returned to the criminal code after that court decision. This alliance was most pronounced and helpful in the United States during the second period, leading up to *Roe* and the decade following it.

Instability of political alignments, or a great sea change in electoral fortunes of parties, was important in bringing about the third devolutionary period in both Canadian and U.S. politics. In the United

States, the rise of the Republican Party nationally from 1980 onward has given institutional linkages and ideological cover for the pro-life movement, which has operated across state legislatures given the shifted policy pressure point since the *Webster* and *Casey* decisions have allowed greater latitude to states in formulating restrictions. In Canada, the rise of the Conservative Party in its largest electoral success in the twentieth century, a party internally conflicted between social and economic conservatism, helped bring in the third period. However, the third period of abortion policy in Canada was most directly brought in by, first, entrenchment of the Charter during the second period in 1982, then the use of the Charter to overturn the disparities contained in the 1969 abortion legislation in the 1988 *Morgentaler* case. Where the accession of the Conservative Party to government from 1984 to 1993 became significant was in its attempts along the federal continuum of party governments to rein in health-care costs by shifting more costs to the provinces, as well as its inability to override the 1988 framework of having no national law on abortion. As in the United States, this has shifted the locus of attention to provincial legislatures and health ministries, but with a far different message. While the Canadian pro-life movement borrows some tactics from its U.S. counterpart, buys land next to them, and demonstrates outside clinics (and the pro-choice movement must respond, namely, by instigating actions to force the pro-choice movement to respond), the major focus for the Canadian pro-choice movement has been to ensure that funding for abortion access in hospitals and free-standing clinics (as well as the development of other methods like RU-486)—and the discourse surrounding these issues—is largely based on the terms of "funding" and "medically necessary services" as set forth in the revised criminal code.

The messages or framing strategies of advocacy networks, as described by Keck and Sikkink, also varied across the time periods. In the first period beginning in each country in the nineteenth century, doctors used "moral leverage" to proclaim that their expert opinions were to make sure that legislatures (state in the United States, national in Canada) regulated the conditions of abortion performance. As some accounts have demonstrated, this was probably equally about establishing professional turf and keeping women from self-administering contraception or abortion or excluding a role for midwives. Seemingly, there was also a hidden material component, which was not made public: only the moral type of leverage was used. In the second time periods in the United States and Canada, where medical professionals and women's movement activism were dominant in ensuring more federal action to protect women's right to choose and doctors' freedom from prosecution, the dominant discourse among women's movement actors was a liberal, rights-based type of moral leverage, demanding accountability from legislators.

In both countries, due to *Roe* in the United States and the Charter implementation in Canada, the pro-life movement got into full swing by the 1980s. While it has had more impact in the U.S. policy system, which is now devolved throughout fifty states, the rhetoric used by this advocacy network has been similar in both countries. First, it has used the moral and symbolic leverage to try to gain equal protection for fetal rights, a strategy that has failed in both countries. Where the network has been more successful is in portraying itself as the materially poorer side of the movement, not receiving government funding like the pro-choice movement. Again, this has been a particularly successful strategy in the United States, convincing the majority of presidents since 1980 to retain the Mexico City strategy of denying pro-abortion funds through the U.S. Agency for International Development. On both sides of the abortion question, the movement became a much more transnational one from the 1980s onward. There are at least two reasons for this. One was the publicity surrounding UN conferences on population and development and on women, which in essence facilitated strategic options and rhetorical consultation among members of the same network in different countries, both before and during the conferences. The second is that actors on both sides of the question recognized the similarities between the processes in Canada and the United States, particularly when *Morgentaler* directly incorporated language from *Roe,* and first U.S. pro-life actors began to work with their Canadian counterparts. Pro-choice actors soon followed suit.

What has also been seen as a key similarity between the United States and Canada in the evolution of abortion policy is that both moved from a period of largely subnational control and sub rosa access to abortion until sometime in the twentieth century. For each country, there was a correspondingly brief time when the national government was willing to be the primary guarantor of abortion access. This period stretched from 1973 under the *Roe* framework in the United States to either 1980, 1989, or 1992, depending on which set of allowable subnational restrictions one chooses to highlight. The *Harris* case of 1980 allowed the federal and state governments to deny Medicaid funding for abortions, which is now the case in thirty-five states and the District of Columbia. The 1989 *Webster* case enlarged the allowable scope of prohibition to include mandatory counseling and the exemption of public hospitals; the restriction of mandatory counseling is now present in twenty-eight states, with twenty-six of them imposing a waiting period, allowable since the 1992 *Casey* decision. Finally, forty-five states allow refusals by hospitals or doctors to participate in abortions, at both public and private hospitals.[56] Since the *Morgentaler* decision in 1988, which broadened the constitutional guarantee of abortion access, the time frame since the 1990s has seen a set of mainly financial decisions that have hurt women in this position. Clinics have been defunded; hospitals have been shut down or merged; the first generation of doctors to perform abortion in Canada since its decriminalization in 1969 are increasingly retiring; and certain provinces, such as Nova Scotia, Manitoba, and New Brunswick have openly defied attempts to establish clinics there. Thus, the period of national supervision of the abortion policy framework lasted a mere nineteen years in Canada, from 1969 until 1988. In both countries since the 1980s and 1990s, the federal governments have increasingly turned back the administrative requirements for abortion procedures to the subnational governments, and the picture for women's access has worsened. In Canada, due to the historic Medicare commitments, women have sometimes been able to practice material leverage against provincial governments (such as in Alberta) in pressuring them not to delist abortion services from the list of insured medically necessary services. As discussed, this type of option is not really available in the United States because all Americans are not guaranteed access to health insurance. Following a relatively short nationalized period of policy control in Canada and the United States, policymakers appear to have been extremely willing to tolerate the ambiguity present in having no national standards and allowing larger degrees of subnational variation. While policy ambiguity may serve women in other domains, there are no ways to frame it as a positive choice for women regarding abortion access.

## Notes

1. Carolyn Tuohy, *Accidental Logics: The Dynamics of Change in the Health Care Arena in the United States, Britain, and Canada* (New York: Oxford University Press, 1999), ix.

2. Raymond Tatalovich, *The Politics of Abortion in the United States and Canada: A Comparative Study* (Armonk, NY: M.E. Sharpe, 1997), 30; Jane Jenson, "Getting to *Morgentaler:* From One Representation to Another," in Janine Brodie, Shelley Gavigan, and Jane Jenson, eds., *The Politics of Abortion* (Toronto: Oxford University Press, 1992), 24.

3. Pat Armstrong and Hugh Armstrong, *Wasting Away: The Undermining of Canadian Health Care* (Toronto: Oxford University Press, 1996), 19.

4. Ibid., 20–21.

5. Ibid., 23–24.

6. Ibid., 24.

7. Tuohy, *Accidental Logics,* 42.

8. Health Canada website, "Canada's Health Care System," www.hc-sc.gc.ca, accessed 7/2004.

9. Ibid.; David Naylor, *Private Practice, Public Payment* (Montreal: McGill-Queen's University Press, 1986), cited in Armstrong and Armstrong, *Wasting Away,* 60.

10. Malcolm Taylor, "Health Insurance: The Roller Coaster in Federal-Provincial Relations," in David P. Shugarman and Reg Whitaker, eds., *Federalism and Political Community* (Peterborough, Ontario: Broadview Press, 1989), 73–75; Armstrong and Armstrong, *Wasting Away,* 58–60.

11. Tuohy, *Accidental Logics,* 49.

12. Taylor, "Health Insurance," 77. The three provinces that had joined the system were Alberta, British Columbia, and Newfoundland.

13. Health Canada website, www.hc-sc.gc.ca, accessed 7/2004; Taylor, "Health Insurance," 79–81.

14. Cited in Taylor, "Health Insurance," 80–81.

15. Ibid., 81–82.

16. Ibid., 80.

17. Tuohy, *Accidental Logics,* 53.

18. Ibid., 207.

19. Armstrong and Armstrong, *Wasting Away,* 60.

20. Ibid., 79.

21. Ibid., 83.

22. Gail Kellough, *Aborting Law: An Exploration of the Politics of Motherhood and Medicine* (Toronto: University of Toronto Press, 1996).

23. Alphonse de Valk, *Morality and Law in Canadian Politics: The Abortion Controversy* (Dorval, Quebec: Palm, 1974), cited in Jenson, "Getting to *Morgentaler,"* 25.

24. Tatalovich, *The Politics of Abortion in the United States and Canada,* 32.

25. Ibid., 203.

26. Pauline Rankin and Jill Vickers, "Locating Women's Politics," in Manon Tremblay and Caroline Andrew, eds., *Women and Political Representation in Canada* (Ottawa: University of Ottawa Press, 1998), 342–343; Alexandra Dobrowolsky, *The Politics of Pragmatism: Women, Representation, and Constitutionalism in Canada* (Toronto: Oxford University Press, 2000).

27. "CARAL Executive Summary of Brief to Legislative Committee on Bill C-43," 1969, 1.

28. As described in Tatalovich, *The Politics of Abortion in the United States and Canada,* 30–31.

29. Mollie Dunsmuir, *Abortion: Constitutional and Legal Developments* (Ottawa: Library of Parliament, Parliamentary Research Branch), Paper Number 89-10E, August 1998.

30. Donley Studlar and Raymond Tatalovich, "Abortion Policy in the United States and Canada: Do Institutions Matter?" in Marianne Githens and Dorothy Stetson, eds., *Abortion Politics: Public Policy in a Cross-Cultural Perspective* (New York: Routledge, 1996), 86.

31. Quoted from Tatalovich, *The Politics of Abortion in the United States and Canada,* 79.

32. Janine Brodie, "Choice and No Choice in the House," in Brodie, Gavigan, and Jenson, *The Politics of Abortion,* 91–96.

33. Melissa Haussman has described these events in "Of Rights and Power: Canada's Federal Abortion Policy, 1969–1991," in Dorothy McBride Stetson, ed., *Abortion Politics, Women's Movements, and the Democratic State* (Oxford, UK: Oxford University Press, 2001).

34. Tuohy, *Accidental Logics,* 105.

35. Health Canada website, www.hc.gc.ca, accessed 6/2004.

36. References from Tatalovich, *The Politics of Abortion in the United States and Canada,* 203, Table 7.1; data compiled for CARAL in March 2000 by the Canadian Institute for Health Information (CIHI) and Statistics Canada, and a report by Judy Lee in Statistics Canada's *The Daily,* www.statscan.ca, accessed 12/18/00.

37. Interview with Marilyn Wilson, executive director, CARAL, Ottawa, July 24, 2001.

38. CARAL information sheet, "Abortion in Canada Today: Province-by-Province Status," Spring 2001.

39. All figures from Tatalovich, *The Politics of Abortion in the United States and Canada,* 203, Table 7.1. The clinic-based figures as of 1992 reflect only seven provinces; this is explained by the fact that PEI has no facilities performing abortions, Saskatchewan continues to refuse to allow freestanding clinics to operate in this area, and the first clinic was established in New Brunswick by Dr. Morgentaler in 1994.

40. Lee, report in *The Daily.*

41. Data computed for CARAL by CIHI and Statistics Canada and Lee, report in *The Daily.*

42. Computed from Tatalovich, *The Politics of Abortion in the United States and Canada,* 208, Table 7.4 (1990 figure); for 2000 data, CARAL fact sheet, "Access to Abortion Services Across Canada," 2001.

43. Computed from CARAL fact sheet, "Abortion Services."

44. Computed from CIHI and Statistics Canada data, Summer 2001, and from CARAL fact sheet, "Abortion Services."

45. CARAL information sheet, "Abortion in Canada Today," 8.

46. Ibid.

47. Ibid., 1–8.

48. Canadian Medical Association, Masterfile, January 2001.

49. CARAL information sheet, "Abortion in Canada Today," 10.

50. Canadians for Choice press release, "Women's Health Endangered by Provinces Refusing Funding for Abortion Care," May 4, 2001.

51. CARAL website and Pro-Choice Action Network, "Abortion History—Chronology of Events," www.caral.ca, accessed 2001, 2002, and 2003.

52. CARAL, "Reciprocal Billing Agreements for Abortion Services under the *Canada Health Act*," 1999.

53. Tom Brodbeck, "Hope Government Pays: Morgentaler Applauds Class Action," *Winnipeg Sun*, July 28, 2001, A5.

54. CARAL website and Pro-Choice Action Network, "Abortion History."

55. Ibid.

56. Data from NARAL website, "State Legislation," www.naral.org, accessed 9/29/04.

# 4

## Mexico: Contradictions Between Written Laws and Women's Lives

This chapter describes the paradoxical nature of the Mexican political system apparent at many levels and its historic effects upon women's organizing. Abortion is generally illegal in Mexico with only the exemption of rape shared by the thirty-one states and the Federal District of Mexico City, the location of the federal government. Despite the official prohibition that has been in place from 1931, the government provides annual statistics as to the number of abortions estimated to have taken place, stated for the 1980s as perhaps up to 850,000 annually. Other non-Mexican sources, such as international NGOs and agencies, estimate the figure as being likely twice that number, up to about 1.5 million.[1] In terms of women's overall participation to increase abortion access, some of the major parties have included decriminalization in their platforms, yet the issue has not been brought up in the federal Congress since 1979.[2]

To discuss reproductive rights and women's organizing on this topic, it is necessary to embed these points in a larger discussion of the beginnings of the "modern" era in Mexico during the 1910–1920 revolution, resulting in the 1917 Constitution.[3] We will then examine how the Mexican political system functioned and changed during the late twentieth century. Since the 1980s, shifts in political allegiances—in response to international and domestic economic crises as well as civil society changes in the views of the Catholic Church and opening of the media—have opened the public space in which social movements have contested for rights in Mexico. Thus, the first policy period covers Mexican social and political arrangements from the early 1920s until the 1980s and the extraordinary degree of control afforded to the ruling PRI during that time. Period two, operative since the mid-1980s, illustrates the effects of intracoalitional fractures across the parties, including a large shift in member and voter support from the PRI to the more rightist PAN, which strangely opened the political opportunity structure to more progressive actions. These included international influence through the UN Conference on Population and Development (ICPD) and the UN World Conference on Women, the development of a critical social movement structure, and more high-profile women's activism across a number of issues.

In certain ways, the second period of Mexican politics is most similar to the first Canadian and U.S. counterparts. This is because there has not yet been in Mexico a consistent and concerted federal program to help women obtain access to their reproductive rights. Nor is there likely to be as long as the Church retains strong influence in politics and Mexico is governed by a Christian Democratic party. As in the first periods of abortion policy in the United States and Canada, the current period in Mexico is one where subnational legislatures largely have the space in which to make policy and where at least pro-life lobbyists concentrate their efforts. Feminist lobbyists tend to concentrate their efforts mainly at the national level, recognizing that the federal Congress and president are the most powerful legislators in the country. Unlike the current Canadian and U.S. situations, there is no backbone of a federal judicial interpretation to which pro-choice organizers in Mexico may point as underlining a national set of rights or access to abortion choice.

## Period One: Construction of an Autocratic "Democracy," with No Official Role for Women

This first aspect of Mexican history is largely background material, for women's rights as such were not officially implemented to any measurable degree, yet it did form an important structural basis for Mexican politics and understanding how the system worked up until the late 1980s. For this first period, it is largely irrelevant to discuss political opportunity structure and advocacy network concepts as pertaining to strategies to affect the state. While it is true that Mexican women have been active off the radar screen since "colonial times," the institutionalized movement has been present largely since the 1970s.[4]

## Political Institutional History

The 1917 Mexican Constitution and government laid the groundwork for regimes that had to pay at least official attention to the various groups in society.⁵ After a series of coups and murders of government elites, "regular" elections began in 1934. In 1929, the Party of the National Revolution (PNR) was formed by Plutarco Calles, to extend his personal influence. This began a Mexican tradition of a single ruling party, "functioning as an extension of political power."⁶ By 1934, the first election was held, where Lazaro Cardenas, who was brought forth as the only "candidate" to succeed Calles through the traditional *dedazo* (fingering) method, was elected for what would become the traditional *sexenio* (six-year presidential term), not subject to re-election. Cardenas has been described as Mexico's "first and last revolutionary president." On one hand, the 1917 constitutional order did not touch the traditional aspects of Mexican society, such as the army and Catholic Church dominating rural society, and "foreign investors and Mexico's oligarchy keeping exploitative economic structures firmly in place."⁷

Paradoxically, the 1917 Constitution also enshrined seemingly revolutionary principles, such as "the most progressive social rights of the time," including an eight-hour work day, minimum wage, rights to organization by unions, and requirements that employers fund health, education, and housing. Other stated rights were the *ejido* system of land tenure, distributing land to the native population and the nationalistic declaration "establishing the government's control over natural resources."⁸ Indeed, Cardenas was said to be the first and last president who accomplished major land reforms and redistribution.⁹ What the PNR and its renamed successors, the Party of the Mexican Revolution (PMR) in 1938 and finally the Institutional Revolutionary Party in 1946, accomplished was the establishment of one-party rule for almost one hundred years, convincing many people for a long time that they were the true heirs of the Mexican Revolution, "committed to greater social justice, economic equality, popular participation, and economic nationalism" as enshrined in the 1917 Constitution.¹⁰ Cardenas was known for building basic infrastructure (such as roads, irrigation projects, and electricity) and "strengthening the country's financial system," all to promote the Mexican domestic market. He also nationalized the oil industry in 1938 after British and U.S. firms "declined to meet worker demands." Cardenas is given credit for three decades of economic growth after he left office.[11]

Although the Constitution promised many rights and freedoms never before articulated in Mexican history, many have never been implemented. It also contained anti-clerical provisions and stated that Mexico was formed on a secular basis, yet the Church remains a powerful political player today, especially in the areas of family law and women's lives. Similarly, while land reforms and natural resource nationalizations took place in the name of the people under President Cardenas in the 1930s, they have often been gutted by PRI presidents since the 1980s.

The reason for assessing the Mexican political system as a paradox is that while many freedoms for the people were written into the Constitution, many ways have been found to circumvent them. A highly developed system for continuation of the PRI as the government of Mexico was begun in 1917 and furthered over time. One notable way of controlling popular sentiment and channeling it only into the PRI was through the system of "corporatism," begun under Cardenas and continuing to a lesser degree today. Through this framework, the national government (PRI controlled from the 1920s until 2000) would selectively bargain with formal organizations comprising peasants, unions, and the "popular" sector (mainly civil servants), recognized as the pillars of society. Established under Cardenas, this system gave the state the role as the rector of society to "enact popular support for a stable state where capitalism could flourish." Although there was some degree of popular sovereignty in the early years, by the mid-1940s, under President Miguel Aleman, the "corporatist sectors degenerated into instruments of state control." Thus, these parts of society were virtually completely managed in their internal governance by the PRI and expected to show their support through votes in return.[12] The trade-off has been one where officially sanctioned unions, such as the trade sector (Confederation of Mexican Workers, or CTM), public sector, educators' unions, and National Peasant Confederation (CNC), were given official status to bargain for their communities at the price of autonomy.[13] Overall, the framework has been one where the executive-centered system, known as *presidencialismo,* "has masked dictatorial rule through populist posturing and corporatist structures. The government seeks to co-opt and incorporate dissidents" through the corporatist system and, according to most accounts, did so successfully until about the late 1960s, when the first cracks in the foundation began to appear.[14]

The overarching mechanism of presidential oversight of Mexican political life is that the president historically has had control of most institutions that would be deemed representative ones. These include the national Congress, which until 1997 contained a huge majority of the governing PRI. Moreover, "Congress has never failed to pass a bill proposed by the President and has never overridden a presidential veto."[15] Also, subnational "legislatures" (usually containing fewer than fifty members) have virtually no independent power. Even if controlled by an opposition party, the history has been one where the results of state-level voting had to be ratified by the national PRI to see if the results would be allowed to stand. As Tom Barry notes, "the President appoints and removes [the thirty-one] state governors at will, completely disregarding the voters who put the state leaders in place." Thus, opposition party control in some of the state legislatures has by no means brought about their independence; it simply means that the process of policy coordination between the national ruling PRI (until 2000) and the state legislatures was a tiny bit more difficult, having to putatively involve members of the Christian Democratic PAN in negotiations. It is also true that the president "installs and dismisses leaders of Congress, the Supreme Court, PRI, public-sector labor unions and midlevel administrators through staged elections, rubber-stamped ratifications, and letters of 'resignation.'"[16] The Mexican system may be viewed as an executive-centered one, where the executive was controlled by the same party from the 1920s until 2000.

Similarly, membership on the country's highest courts is determined by the president, although appointments to the Supreme Court require a two-thirds' Senate approval.[17] This has historically been forthcoming because there were no opposition Senate members before 1988.[18] Although the Supreme Court has the power of judicial review comparable to its counterparts elsewhere, it is not yet autonomous of national party and executive control. Unlike the United States and Canada, which are generally common-law countries whose constitutional law builds upon precedent, Mexico is a civil law country. It shares this status with Louisiana in the United States and Quebec in Canada. The most important difference between a common-law and civil-law system is that the latter denies the autonomous weight given to courts to discover a law's constitutionality based on previous rulings. In Mexico, the best way to view policy change traditionally is that it has emanated from the president's office and has been implemented by the massive bureaucracy controlled by the president's party in the DF.

The Congress, divided into a Chamber of Deputies (House) and Senate and meeting usually for two legislative sessions per year, has a staggered election schedule. Neither House nor Senate members can stand for consecutive re-election, similar to the president. Based on reforms in the 1970s and 1980s, the Chamber of Deputies has five hundred members, three hundred of whom are directly elected in legislative districts, favoring the PRI, and two hundred of whom are "distributed among the parties according to proportional representation [PR]." The reforms of enlarging the chamber and adding seats elected through PR were brilliant, according to many observers, as they had the effect of conveying legitimacy by allowing opposition parties to be elected, while keeping the opposition fragmented.[19] The Chamber of Deputies is elected both during presidential years (at the beginning of the *sexenio*) and at the midterm, because their terms are three years long. The Senate's size was also doubled in the reform of the 1980s, from two senators per state (and two for the DF, a total of sixty-four) up to 128. The other sixty-four senators are divided into two halves, where one-half of these seats go to the second-place party in each state (further fragmenting opposition parties), and the rest are "national senators" who are distributed according to the proportion of each party's national vote, on a PR basis.[20] Senate terms are for six years each, with half of the Senate being voted on in each set of elections conducted for the House.

The PRI was historically said to have no coherent ideology other than "gaining and keeping state power."[21] According to many scholars and journalists, the PRI's ability to retain the presidency until 2000 was based as much on outright coercion and fraud as anything else. At a few notable times, it has been possible to see shifts based on something like ideological disagreements within the PRI. The shifts have been defined mainly by economic views. Roughly, the left has been generally more willing to use nationalist rhetoric to try to "return control of Mexico's resources to the people" and to attempt to expand social policy provision. This wing was in power most notably in the party under the *sexenios* of Cardenas, 1934–1940, and under President Luis Echeverría, 1970–1976. Otherwise, the rightist faction has controlled the party, being less willing to negotiate with labor and more willing to rely on a techno-cratic elite to run the economy. The rightist faction has generally taken a more pro-continentalist stance and since the late 1980s has favored continental free trade, a vision later expanded by joining the World Trade Organization.

The most recently publicized split within the PRI occurred in 1987. At that time, Cuauhtemoc Cardenas, son of "revolutionary" PRI president Lazaro Cardenas, left with other nationalists ostensibly opposed to the neoliberal and free-trade-friendly economic model then dominant in the PRI. This faction, calling itself the Democratic Current, had at first contested the presidential selection process within the PRI. After that, Cardenas formed a new leftist party, the Party of the Democratic Revolution. Many believed that Cardenas milked the "revolutionary" symbolism of his father's party, which had been called both the party of the national and Mexican revolutions.[22] However, its main legacy to date, a party termed by Barry a "one-man organization," was to capture the mayoral election in Mexico City (DF) in 1997, which it has retained.

The left historically had trouble practicing legitimate politics in Mexico, for leftist parties were not allowed to officially register until the 1970s. The main actors in the leftist coalition have included the Communist and Socialist Parties, as well as the PRD, officially formed in 1989. There was a leftist front, Grupo Parlamentario de Izquierda (Parliamentary Group of the Left) operative in Congress in the 1970s when these parties became legal. The importance of the left has shrunk due to strategic voting for the PAN, as well as the PRI's concessions in the 1988 election of control of fifty-two munic-ipalities to the PRD, where "many Mexican observers attributed this to U.S. criticism during the sensitive negotiations on NAFTA [North American Free Trade Agreement]."[23]

The internal PRI split over economic policy helped the right end of the party spectrum even more than the left. At the national level, the Christian Democratic PAN has been the most viable contender against the PRI. It was founded in opposition to the revolutionary reforms of 1917, including labor rights and land reform.[24] It has real-ly only come into its own since the 1980s, finding ways to overcome the PRI-governmental control of the electoral structure. The PAN won the mayorships of five cities in 1983 and its first gubernatorial election in Baja California state in 1989. Vicente Fox, running under its banner, won the governorship of Guanajuato state in 1991 and the presidency in 2000.[25] In Congress, the PAN similarly won a majority of House seats in 1997, and increased its share in 2000, having been helped by the PR seat arrangement in the House that year.[26]

Similarly, the important role of business shifts away from the PRI to the PAN in 1985–1986 must be recognized as a historically crucial factor as to why political competition began to open up to the extent it did at that time. The worldwide drop by half in oil prices at precisely that time caused business to shift its alliances; another catalyst was the 1985 Mexico City earthquakes and the government's insufficient response.[27] The PRI was being squeezed from both left and right, which opened up the gubernatorial elections in 1985–1986 to a polarized set of elections between the PRI and the PAN. Ultimately, both the PAN and the PRD were the main beneficiaries.[28]

With respect to women's issues, including abortion, the parties obviously have varied platforms. These platforms coexist with the creation of a "woman's bureau" or such within each national party.[29] The official discourse of the PRI is that it supports the national Constitution's Article 40, promoting the fact that "women and men are equal before the law." Following from this emphasis, the PRI emphasizes the need for women's equal participation in the formal structure of government, although the interpretation by both Priista women and men is that this is usually and should be accomplished on an individualistic basis, that if women try harder, they will win more. As the longest-running party that still competes today, the PRI then has the oldest "*sector femenil*," founded in 1934. It has been stated that the PRI has always included women as a pillar equivalent to its three main ones within the party structure, the others being the Confederation of Mexican Workers, the National Peasant Confederation, and the National Confederation of Popular Organizations (CNOP).[30] However, the internal women's bureau within the PRI has not been afforded the same "corporate" status when negotiating with the national government; while the bureau may be equivalent within the party, it has not been treated as equal outside of it. Other PRI issues concerning women have included health and education, such as programs about HIV/AIDS, birth control (legal since 1973), and the need for all women to be educated about sex and similarly about domestic violence.[31] The platform has also emphasized giving women the power to decide the size of their families, which has been enshrined in the national Constitution since the early twentieth century and has repeatedly been emphasized as a major theme both at the UN World Conference on Women, where Mexico has been represented, and in the Mexican feminist movement. The PRI's stance on education has been to encourage girls to stay in school and to improve literacy levels to fuller enhance their participation in society.

Victoria Rodriguez's excellent study of the changing roles of women in Mexican electoral politics points out the changes within the PAN after the 1970s structurally and 1990s rhetorically. From 1957 until 1970, the PAN had a separate women's section like that retained by the PRI. After that time, however, much like its Republican and Tory counterparts in the United States and Canada, it changed women's representation to incorporate it in all party committees through a secretariat entitled "Promocion Politica de la Mujer [Women's Policy Bureau, PPM]"[32] The emphasis on women as the "giver of life" and their responsibility to promote their "dignity and femininity," as well as their emotional differences from men and their "spiritual and moral leadership abilities," has been the consistent view of women in the PAN platform. However, in the 1990s the women's secretariat, PPM, began to be more vocal on women's inferior roles within the party, especially the obstacles placed in candidates' paths. Rodriguez notes that certain leaders of the PPM have made it "without question the best-organized group of women in any of the three major political parties," working to increase women's roles in the party leadership, candidacies, and also in holding women's candidate training schools throughout the country.[33] The PAN is clearly a party whose platform and presence of women are highly inconsistent with each other.

Finally, even the PRD, along with the Greens, one of the two most socially progressive of the congressional parties, does not mention abortion in its platform. Instead, it alludes to "full access for women to health" (in addition to other goals such as education), "responsible paternity and maternity," and the reiteration of the "safer" constitutional language appearing in the PRI platform, "the right to determine the number and spacing of one's children."[34] Where Rodriguez highlights the PRD's progressive agenda is in its platform commitment to specific reforms, such as equal pay in the workplace and constitutional reform to violence against women laws. In this way, the PRD sets itself apart from the PRI and the PAN, accusing them of "listing only generalities related to family-oriented issues" by claiming to represent women as workers and public actors as well.[35]

Despite the fact that, for the most part, these party platforms need to incorporate a fuller view of women in society, Mexico has placed women in national politics in ways yet to be seen in the United States. For example, in 1993, women led both houses of the Mexican Congress; there has yet to be a woman majority leader in either the U.S. House or the Senate. Canada has bypassed both countries in terms of having women lead not only both houses of Parliament but having an interim woman prime minister for four months in 1993.[36] Also, the PRI appointed its first woman party president in 1994, following that lead again in 1999.[37] In the United States, only the Republican Party has had a national woman chair, Mary Louise Smith, in the early 1980s. Other notable events concerning the representation of women in Mexican electoral politics include the PRD's early 1990s requirement of 30 percent quotas for women on its candidate lists and the surprising follow-up by the PRI in 2001 to "outdo" the PRD and propose a 50 percent quota for women on its candidate lists.[38] Although these quotas have not yet been achieved, they are worthwhile goals. The PAN, the party of individual enterprise, business, and faith, opposes quotas for women, similar to its Republican Party counterpart in the United States.

## Economic History

Many see a paradox in the structure of the Mexican economy as well, for it has never become as vibrant as the possession of great natural resources would indicate. Mexico's historic role in the international market as a resource producer and seller, including oil and agricultural products, has made it greatly subject to the fortunes of international markets. Under the import-substitution period of the 1940s to 1970s when Mexico turned inward to meet its production needs, the country was termed an "economic miracle." Yet that same period is noted for creating inefficient Mexican industries.[39] Others blame the PRI for creating "crony capitalism" in which friends and allies were rewarded by state largesse.[40]

The global recession of the mid-1970s hurt the developing countries' export markets, including that for Mexican oil. By 1976, economic growth was one-half of what it was four years earlier; 8.5 percent in 1972 versus 4.2 percent. Because the Mexican population was growing at 3 percent per year, the economy was barely keeping up.[41] Within that same period, President Luis Echeverría had to devalue the peso for the first time in fifteen years due to the "persistent account deficit, inflation, capital flight, deficit spending, and growing debt," especially to the International Monetary Fund (IMF).[42] The discovery of new oil fields in Mexico shortly thereafter seemed to promise relief from financial problems. However, this scenario crashed with the global price drop of 1981–1982 even worse than in the 1970s, for the Mexican government had vastly overborrowed capital based on the promise of its oil revenues. By 1982, "Mexico devoted two of every three dollars received from exports to debt service" and therefore declared itself "unable to continue debt service payments."[43] While the Mexican economy seemed to struggle back to its feet, the closely following chaos of the Mexico City earthquakes in 1985, causing $4 billion in damage, sent the economy reeling again. The Mexican government immediately had to increase its debt to the IMF, then it was "bailed out" in 1989 by the United States assuming a greater role in renegotiating Mexico's debt with creditor banks.[44] Thus, while the macroeconomic situation seemed to be temporarily relieved, the social impacts of austerity, both internationally and domestically imposed, were huge. State employment was slashed by 20 percent by President Miguel De la Madrid in the first half of his *sexenio;* between 1982 and 1988, the number of publicly owned companies in Mexico, one of the largest sectors of employees, had fallen by nine-tenths, from 1,155 to fewer than 150.[45] The rate of public sector employment cuts had a huge impact on the 85 percent of the population who depended on employer-financed health insurance and salaries.

## Social Policy Framework

In terms of income disparity, Mexico is one of the worst cases in Latin America.[46] Also, by 1990 due to cutbacks, only about half (53 percent) of Mexicans were covered by a health-care program. As with the income disparity measurements, the lack of widespread health-care coverage put Mexico near the bottom of the Latin American scale.[47] Scholar and current Federal District minister of health for the PRD, Asa Cristina Laurell indicts the neoliberal project of shrinking social-welfare spending on various grounds. She characterizes the six-year presidency of De la Madrid (1982–1988) as the preparatory phase for neoliberal reforms accelerated since 1988 under Presidents Carlos Salinas de Gortari (1988–1994) and Ernesto Zedillo Ponce de León (1994–2000).[48]

Given that Latin American countries, including Mexico, have large pockets of extreme poverty and a historic dependence on the state as the economic engine for capital growth as well as the provision of social policies, it is not surprising that the imposition of cutbacks on developing countries around the world caused these nations such great pain. Developing countries outside of the United States, Canada, and Western Europe simply did not have the same social safety net in place so that under conditions of austerity the poor became relatively more harmed in developing countries than in developed ones.

Prior to 1988, "Mexico [had a] long history of social programs directed to the poorest of the poor," which had concrete bases in certain ministries and were thus "incorporated into the established national welfare structure."[49] The long-term shifts over the 1980s and 1990s involved at least three distinct sets of changes: (1) a commodification of the health-care system, where fee-for-service requirements were introduced; (2) overall cuts in the health-care budget totaling 50 percent; and (3) a shrinking of the services that were offered under insurance packages.[50] During that time period, the "IMSS [Mexican Social Security Institute] lost about five times its total budget because of falling wages, and government subsidies were simultaneously reduced."[51] The IMSS administers the public insurance program provided by employers, which covers about 85 percent of the insured. The other insured population typically purchases private insurance.

When it can access health, the nearly 50 percent of the population that is uninsured has been included in programs run by the Ministry of Health. The government sharply cut the types of services offered free to the poor; "the federal government [since 1996] only has a long-term commitment to finance a 'basic package' of public health interventions . . . containing substantially fewer services than the Ministry of Health previously provided to the poor."[52]

The differences in health-care provisions between rich and poor women come into play with respect to the country's abortion laws. The Criminal Code for the Federal District (encompassing Mexico City, the seat of Mexican national government), as established by the presidential decree of January 2, 1931, included abortion as a criminal offense. The exceptions to that for the DF only included rape, risk to the woman's life, and spontaneous abortion.[53] In the other thirty-one states, the exemptions developed mainly during the 1980s included abortions performed as a result of "negligence by the pregnant woman," if the pregnancy resulted from rape, or if continuing the pregnancy would "endanger the woman's life."[54] Typically, they had to be performed within the first twelve weeks of the pregnancy. A therapeutic abortion committee system is also included in this framework, where doctors must "obtain the opinion of another physician" that any delay in performing the abortion would endanger the woman's life. This is similar to the requirement of two other physicians' consent present in the United States from the 1950s through the early 1970s and in Canada from 1969 until 1988. In Articles 320–334 of the Mexican Criminal Code for the Federal District, penalties are provided for those performing abortions with or without the woman's consent (apparently those that could not come under the TAC loophole), and women themselves may be prosecuted.[55]

Other examples of the most permissive laws concerning abortion in Mexico include that in the Yucatan, one of the southernmost and poorest states in Mexico, where the social welfare code specifies that a woman with at least three children who can demonstrate serious economic reasons may have an abortion; whether she can access a trained doctor is another question entirely. The state of Coahuila allows abortion in the case of potential "severe physical or mental genetic or congenital defects."[56]

In the 1980s, political opportunity structure elements were shifting to usher Mexico's political alignments into a more modern period. Changing party alignments and access to allies by social movement groups were important factors in moving social movement protest and lobbying into a more prominent place in the Mexican political scene. In turn, we locate the climate on abortion policymaking since the 1980s in a new, second period in which the federal government, including opposition parties, is at times responsive to pressure by organized women's groups on the abortion issue. The case should not be overstated, however, because nobody sees the federal criminal sanctions on abortion changing while the PAN holds the presidency. It appears that this newer, second period of abortion policymaking in Mexico resembles the first period of the two other countries under study, being nationally illegal with inconsistent subnational exceptions. The catch-22 in the Mexican situation is that the country needs a period of federal willingness, impossible under the

PAN, to shepherd reforms through in order to make it to the next, third stage of abortion policy. At the third stage, some essence of a federal framework guaranteeing either rights (as in the United States) or access (as in Canada) would exist in Mexico.

## Period Two: The Opening to Civil Society Participation, 1988 Onward

The relevant accounts of state-society changes in Mexico use different starting points, but they all acknowledge that by the late 1980s, the traditional corporatist form of bargaining with and control of social groups was finished. The persistence of corporatism for much of Mexico's twentieth-century history as a way of accommodating difference through the "pyramidal structure of the ruling party state" had made any other type of collective action "risky."[57] While Chappell Lawson's account of the freeing of the Mexican media from governmental control begins in the 1980s and Heather Williams's analysis of economic protests in Zacatecas heavily emphasizes economic shocks around the time of NAFTA's implementation in 1994, both studies convey the importance of viewing the interlocking authority between party, state, and economy for most of Mexico's history as the primary factor in continuing social repression.

These studies help to understand why, unlike in the United States and Canada where the second-wave movement of feminist groups in the 1960s and 1970s produced an almost immediate expectation that women would be included at the table in government policy choices and public debate, women's groups in Mexico were operating mainly outside of the officially sanctioned area of public space until at least the 1980s. An important reason, but by no means the only one, is that women as such were not part of the corporatist pillars with whom the PRI government negotiated, and the construction of an enlarged liberal mainstream public discourse and institutions did not occur in Mexico until at least ten years after those in Canada and the United States.

Both accounts share an understanding of the acute irony of long-term changes occurring in society—along class and electoral lines since at least the 1970s—combined with the fact that they were too entrenched by the time the PRI noticed them to turn back the tide.

Thus, events that in nearly any other country would seemingly solidi-
fy governmental control over society, such as the adoption of free
trade in 1994 and privatization of the media, had the opposite effect
in Mexico; they simply widened the gaps in which popular movements could mobilize. At least two factors that were specific to the
Mexican situation helped this turn of events. The first factor was that
Mexico was a pseudo-democracy throughout the bulk of the twentieth century; although elections were held, they were generally rigged
or interpreted after the fact to support the PRI. As part of this pseu-
do-democratic framework, the dominant media cartel, Televisia and
print journals such as *El Heraldo, Excelsior,* and the government-
owned *El Nacional,* knew that their existence depended on being
friendly to the PRI and publishing virtually no opposition-driven
events.[58] The second relevant factor is that the powerful Catholic
Church began to critique the government in the face of international
media attention focused on Mexico after the famous electoral fraud
of the 1988 presidential election and protests under economic scarcity from 1982 onward. Where much of the Church hierarchy had been
previously willing to quietly tolerate PRI corruption so as to receive
the benefits of state protection, the landscape was changing to favor
Church rupture from basking in PRI approval after the 1980s.
However, President Salinas tried to keep the Church within the PRI-
supporting fold by overturning the 1916 constitutional prohibition
about recognizing the Church as a legal political entity.

## Women's Organizing

In a comprehensive account of Mexican women's strategies to gain
entry into the public sector dialogue, Rodriguez divides women's
formal activism into what could be called the analogue to first-wave
feminism in other countries, from 1916 through the early 1950s, and
a second wave, from the 1960s onward. The first wave as in most
other countries was concerned largely with suffrage and citizenship
questions, and women were granted suffrage between 1947 (municipal) and 1953 (federal), after having organized over the issue since
the time of the revolution in 1916–1917.[59] The second wave is
described by one of its founders as having begun in the early 1970s,
organized into a collection of small groups discussing gender issues
and concerned mainly with three interrelated issues that women
viewed as most oppressive in a state dominated by the PRI and the

Catholic Church: voluntary maternity (including reproductive rights
and abortion), freedom of sexual choice, and violence against
women.[60] As in many countries, usually industrialized ones, the
"foremothers" of the second-wave women's movement have been
described as largely middle class, as they are typically the ones with
both financial resources and time to contribute.

Many view the catalyst of women's organizing in the 1970s as
the preparation for the 1975 UN World Conference of the
International Women's Year in Mexico City. The feminist movement
is described by Rodriguez as having reached a turning point at about
that time, shown by its decision to boycott the official 1975 proceedings and to hold a counter-congress to highlight the fact that Mexican
women did not feel their government was very responsive to their
concerns. Various types of organizations were formed after the conference, including the national Coalition of Feminist Women.[61] The
coalition lobbied Congress for a voluntary maternity law, which did
not make it out of committee. Other groups were formed, some on a
feminist basis, others on a more broadly gendered basis. Similarly,
groups began to be formed outside of Mexico City, both in northern
and southern states. Given the historic barriers posed to organizing of
any activity in the regions more distant from Mexico City, this was
an important step. A national umbrella organization, Frente Nacional
por la Libertad y los Derechos de las Mujeres (the National Front for
Women's Rights and Liberty, FNALDM), which not only contained
groups representing the plurality of women's experience but was also
explicitly linked to parties of the left (Communist and workers), was
formed in 1979. While the FNALDM undertook a second lobby ini-
tiative on the voluntary maternity law, it too went nowhere, likely
because the new PRI president, Lopez Portillo, came from the right
wing of the PRI and was not receptive to this type of reform.[62]

What has been noticed by many is that the 1970s marked a turning point where cross-class organizing took place in civil society, and
this became true in the women's movement as well.[63] An important
example of this was the Coordinadora Nacional del Movimiento
Urbano Popular (National Coordinating Committee of Urban Popular
Movements, CONAMUP), founded in 1979 to organize the inhabi-
tants of the *campamentos* (urban squatter "camps") begun outside
Mexico City earlier that decade. It has been noted that most of the
participants were women, usually recent migrants to the *campamentos*.[64] By 1983, women had organized a Consejo Regional de

Mujeres (Woman's Regional Council, CRM) within CONAMUP. In addition to their previous issue focuses on property rights and basic services such as water, sewage, schools, and health centers, the CRM specifically worked "as a forum to voice women's demands and obtain basic services for the community" by offering collective kitchens, self-help workshops for women, and government-funded children's meals.[65] The presence of CRM within CONAMUP was sufficiently institutionalized by the mid-1980s that the Woman's Council was able to push CONAMUP to seemingly more radical statements, such as in a 1985 Monterrey meeting that "the family, school and Church were perpetuating patterns of women's submission and passivity."[66] To mitigate these problems, CRM members present at the conference proposed sex education workshops for the entire family, help for rape victims, harsher punishment for rapists, and self-defense courses. CRM members also addressed the other major issue of the 1980s, economic scarcity and how it disproportionately impacted women both as consumers and in terms of needing to fight price increases, as they saw a "rapid decline of their purchasing power."[67] Other examples of cross-sector organizing included the Network Against Violence Toward Women and the Feminist Peasant Network.[68] Finally, women's organizing across classes and across parts of the popular movement sectors was so well entrenched by the middle 1980s, partly in response to the economic crisis, that "in 1986 the International Women's Day march was convened by low-income women and industrial workers for the first time, rather than feminist organizations."[69]

One unfortunate outcome of the period of economic austerity and general social conservatism dominant in party politics in the late 1970s and early 1980s was the disaggregation of the women's movement. Rodriguez notes that "after 1984, the Mexican feminist movement was, for all intents and purposes, no longer a movement."[70] What happened instead was increasing "niche specialization," as would be described by social movement theorists. New types of organizations were also being formed, which was important. In addition to the multiclass basis of organizing, another was the creation of many new NGOs outside the parties. Rodriguez notes that fifty-one NGOs were created in the 1980s alone. Most of these viewed themselves as gender based rather than explicitly feminist; another study showed that the most prevalent type of NGOs included those related to women's health in some fashion. This study, conducted by Maria

Luisa Tarres, also noted that, despite their overall issue emphasis, one-quarter of the organizations surveyed also worked on the "discussion and dissemination of feminism or activities oriented to the construction of a new identity."[71] Two important new NGOs formed during this period included Grupo de Educacion Popular con Mujeres (the Group for Women's Popular Education, GEM) and Grupo de Informacion en Reproduccion Elegida (the Group for Information on Reproductive Choice, GIRE).[72] The importance of the NGOs founded in the 1980s has been through linking to popular women's groups. For example, after the 1985 Mexico City earthquakes, women's groups helped the female garment workers' unions to take care of survivors and clear the rubble in the face of government inaction. As Carmen Ramos Escandon has described, the rage of the forty thousand women left unemployed by the earthquake and the indifference of the government and factory owners toward the fate of women trapped in the rubble fostered another new type of organization in Mexico, a women's union. This union was led by Evangelina Corona, elected by the seamstresses' organization, to run independently of the traditional union structure, the CTM, which was controlled both by male bosses and the PRI.[73] This courageous move in fighting both the PRI and male-dominated union sector to form the "19th of September Garment Workers' Union" showed that women could organize to fight corporate and PRI Mexico, raising money for the women unemployed and hurt by the earthquake and being a powerful presence in labor politics. One study has noted the cross-class nature of the alliance, such that "middle-class, feminist advisors" helped the union with legal advice and in staging demonstrations.[74] The 19th of September Union is still independent, having been able to stay outside the corporatist structure. Another such independent women-run union is the flight attendants' union. Although it is 80 percent female, it was run by men until 1995. The woman elected to its presidency, Alejandra Barrales, worked to improve the image of flight attendants and to clean up the union generally. She was elected a PRD member of the House in 2000.[75]

By the late 1980s, recognizing the need to have a more institutionalized presence in representative politics, women also organized liberal electoralist organizations concerned with electing more women and making government policy more women friendly. One group, Women Struggling for Democracy, was formed to organize "female PRI and PRD members in elected offices."[76] Another was the Benita Galeana Coordinating Committee, to integrate low-income women into electoral politics.

## Social Movements and Abortion

For work that is specifically abortion related, the second period of policymaking and lobbying holds some legal contradictions. Women's movement organizations and others are increasingly able to enter these contradictory spaces to make them public and to attach accountability to legislators and the president, basically using the leverage strategies (material and moral).

One such source of contradiction to traditional state and Church opposition to contraceptive information, for example, is that there have been international, U.S.-based groups working for reproductive rights (later including abortion access) in Mexico since at least the 1950s. The International Planned Parenthood Federation was the first to become involved, mainly through UN development funding. The IPPF asserts its right to discuss abortion within clinics, leading it to reject the global gag rule of funding by the U.S. Agency for International Development. Its director is Alexander Sanger, grandson of Planned Parenthood founder Margaret Sanger. A similar NGO, the Population Council, states on its official website that it has worked in Latin America since the 1960s, with an office in Mexico City since 1979.[77] The Population Council was founded in the early 1950s by David Rockefeller and continues to receive a high proportion of its funding from the Rockefeller Foundation. It holds the U.S. rights to mifepristone (a key ingredient of RU-486) for early pregnancy termination. The council tested mifepristone in the United States and in China, Cuba, and India while awaiting FDA approval, which ultimately came in September 2000.[78] It defines its mission as "managing programs on a broad range of reproductive health issues, including ecp [emergency contraception], HIV/AIDS/STI prevention and care, abortion and postabortion care, and safe motherhood." Moreover, it states that it has been working with the Health Ministry in Mexico to "shift [abortion] treatment from dilation and curettage to manual vacuum aspiration."[79] An important provider of such manual aspiration equipment and training to use it is IPAS (a nonprofit organization that protects women's reproductive health and rights in the United States and abroad), headquartered in North Carolina. In certain respects, it appears that international organizations are allowed to maintain a toehold in Mexico as long as there is no scandal involved, and if their activity involves promoting abortions, this seems to be officially overlooked.

The Mexican affiliate of the IPPF is Mexfam, founded in 1965, describing itself as a "pioneer of contraception in Mexico." However, contraception was not legalized there until 1973.[80] Mexfam is probably best viewed as the Mexican participant in the long-term internationally funded "orthodoxy" that works both in the officially sanctioned contraceptive areas and in the mainly ignored abortion areas. Its website states that Mexfam's "community health programs operated in almost all states of the Republic," where twenty-three programs work in "slum areas" and thirty-two are located in rural communities. It also states that Mexfam has twenty-five medical clinics and 250 medical offices in twenty-eight states. Many of these centers offer emergency contraception for preventing pregnancy after intercourse. Mexfam lists its goals as "responding to the unmet need for family planning and sexual and reproductive health among the marginalized [urban and rural] populations; empowering women . . . in relationships," and "[increasing] the number of quality and avant-garde sexual and reproductive services offered."[81] While the latter is not specified, it may be assumed that "avant garde" would translate into not-yet universal services, perhaps such as in vitro fertilization and abortion. It is also referred to as "implementing the recommendations of the Cairo and Beijing Conferences," invoking progressive international norms and the UN authority for availability of wide-scale reproductive services.

Among Mexfam's funders are Abbott Labs, maker of pregnancy test kits, and Similac, maker of baby formula and hospital equipment, including IVs and diagnostics. (It should also be noted that in direct violation of the Constitution, many employers require on-site pregnancy testing, presumably with the use of the kits.) Many U.S.-based foundations are also Mexfam funders, including the IPPF and the Population Council (both funded by the UN). Other funders include Washington- and Mexican-based Rotary Clubs; the Packard, MacArthur, Rockefeller, Hewlett, Gates, and Turner Foundations; and the Canadian and Japanese Embassies.

Another U.S.-based maker of medical equipment, IPAS, has worked with the Federal District Ministry of Health and hospitals located in Mexico City to study the readiness of public hospitals to provide legal abortions, after the Criminal Code for the Federal

District was liberalized in 2000.[82] Certain turning points between the 1980s and 2000 seem to have widened the space for liberalization of certain abortion laws in Mexico; one of the key ones was the capture by opposition parties of municipal offices, usually the PRD, but also increased opposition strength in state legislatures. A second key turning point was the "ICPD +5" review undertaken just before the "Beijing +5" conference taking place in New York City in the summer of 2000. The effect of the international framework upon Mexico was that at this review in 1999, "Mexico along with other countries reaffirmed its commitment to [take steps to] ensure that unsafe abortion would be addressed as an important public health problem." Given the immediate question of how far Mexico would go in this matter in that the criminal circumstances surrounding abortion far outnumber the legal exemptions, it is seen that "few resources have been designated for training and equipping health care providers in public health systems to offer legal abortion services."[83] Finally, a third trend that seems to have been apparent is that reproductive rights groups, such as GIRE, saw the successful resonance of their framing the reproductive issue only in the late 1990s when the PRD became more powerful along with other leftist parties. Their issue framing and that of much of the feminist movement since the early 1980s, as noted by both Marta Lamas and Victoria Rodriguez, was for the overarching goal of "voluntary motherhood," premised on comprehensive sexuality education, inexpensive and reliable birth control, sterilization only at a woman's request, and "legal abortion as a last resort."[84]

In retrospect, the feminist groups and particularly the pro-choice ones such as GIRE, the oldest and most well known along with a group called Epikeia, an NGO offering legal defense and advocacy in reproductive and sexual rights, and the national umbrella group, the FNALDM, framed women's reproductive rights in a gradualist strategy where each of the four points previously mentioned could be checked off one by one as time permitted. The ways in which time permitted this were in the twenty-year disaggregation of PRI control over politics and of civil society, as well as the rising strength of opposition parties, where at least some of those on the left were willing to press for women's reproductive rights. Thus, the first battle won in the four-part set of goals was clearly that of contraceptive legality and access, stemming from 1973 onward. The sexuality education part seems to have followed closely, given Mexfam's intense programming around it, with an entire subset of its efforts devoted to the "young people's" education program. The anti-sterilization and pro-abortion access campaigns have taken longer and have involved more strategic twists and turns. GIRE was also a leader in the transnational "Campaign for Decriminalization and Legalization of Abortion in Latin America and the Caribbean" along with Catolicas por el Derecho a Decidir (Catholics for a Free Choice, CCFC), a pro-choice group in Brazil called CIDEM, and the Women's Health Network of Latin America and the Caribbean based in Brazil.[85]

Another interesting link between some Mexican national agencies, international population programs, and their national links such as Mexfam is in making the case that increased availability of reproductive health services in clinics is good for the business climate. For example, a role is apparent for the Mexican National Population Council, established in 1974 to be responsible for the demographic planning of the country and where the National Women's Office was housed until 1994.[86] When the Mexican National Population Council website is accessed, it directly connects one to the website of the International Labour Organization. Many corporations whose relationship to Mexfam is not immediately discernible fund it, including a large hotel chain, a car and motor company, and Cuervo Tequila. The Inter-American Development Bank, which frequently works with the World Bank, is a pro-investment organization, founded in 1959 as a development assistance program.[87] National agencies in Mexico also providing funding include the Institute for Social Development and the IMSS, which administers the employer-funded insurance system. Mexfam describes on its website how it has begun an "enterprise program" to "bring family planning services and education to factories whose owners are interested."[88] In addition to the DF and Puebla, adjacent to the DF, the other two cities are Tijuana and Monterrey, large border cities that are sites of trade and manufacturing. Relatedly, Mexfam states that it works in joint ventures with Planned Parenthood affiliates along the Tijuana–San Diego, Monterrey-Dallas and Phoenix-Hermosillo corridors (the latter the site of a large Ford factory in Mexico).

There are numerous ways in which one could speculate about the overt links between the international development community, corporations and NGOs, and government agencies in Mexico. The traditional way in which the international development community (most overtly seen in UN bodies and conferences) worked was to promote international development and family planning as necessary counter-weights to the thesis that the developing world would overuse the bulk of the world's resources. Many studies have shown how badly this theme was received, both by those receiving the development assistance and by the Catholic Church and ultimately the New Right, who decry that justification as "the false Malthusian hypothesis." It is true that the UN's international assistance programs and women's and children's conferences after the 1970s made a sharp centrist turn away from what was seen as racist first-world imperialism and, as newer studies have documented, began to use a language of "women and children's empowerment."[89] Although it may be assumed that the set of interests at work is complicated and varied, it is clear that UN groups and international foundations and their affiliates have invested since the 1950s in a development agenda for the less-developed world, including Mexico. Another truism is that companies making obstetric and gynecological equipment have historically found a ready testing ground in Mexico. This is based on the tradition of a disempowered population and the unilateral ability of the minister of health to make decisions as to what types of contraceptives will be allowed in clinics. Groups such as the Population Council, Mexfam, and IPAS conduct studies in hospitals and clinics as to the efficacy of the provision of contraceptive, childbirth, and post-abortion services. Finally, it appears that while the development agenda was that fueling UN and foundation interest in Latin American, Asian, and African states through the 1970s, the more recent examples from Mexico show that employers can be persuaded to make training sites and funding available for reproductive health programs.

In terms of pro-choice discourse, both the internationally based institutions and the Mexican NGOs such as GIRE may be viewed as operating somewhat in a bind that has loosened but not disappeared over time. As has been noted, GIRE and other feminist groups historically advocated for voluntary motherhood because that principle was enshrined in the 1917 Constitution (and the PRI platform) and then they worked in a sub rosa fashion for access to abortion training and provision. Another related tactic both of GIRE and Mexfam has been to point out that unsafe abortion, which is much more likely to happen to the poor and rural, is the fourth largest cause of maternal mortality in Mexico, a country that virtually enshrines motherhood in its political and religious dogma. Pro-choice groups in Mexico were also strengthened by the 1995 UN World Conference on Women Plan of Action, which stated that where legal, the abortion provision should be safe and that "forced motherhood was condemned as a violation of women's human rights."[90] Armed with both UN declarations and the 1917 Mexican Constitution, Mexican pro-choice groups had stronger ground than ever on which to argue for safe abortion services, both in the cases where it was legal and in the more numerous (often illegal) cases where women would go for "follow-up" treatment to a hospital, having begun the procedure themselves. UN-collected data indicates that at least 24 percent of Mexican women of childbearing age have had an abortion.[91]

The National Population Program and the Reproductive Health and Family Planning Program (RHFP) for 1995–2000 announced by President Zedillo incorporated many recommendations of the Plan of Action from the 1994 Cairo ICPD. The general sets of recommendations for Mexican policymakers included "comprehensiveness of care (integrality), the evaluation of preconceptional risk, and a gender perspective," as well as the provision for "sexual and reproductive health services to adolescents."[92] These recommendations were framed within the overall agreement with the Plan of Action's call for "the delivery of a wider range of reproductive health services" to countries' populations. Specifically, the report put out by the RHFP had among its goals the reduction by at least one-third of the population growth rate and fertility rate within that time frame.[93] Another goal was to get contraceptive use to 70 percent (a nearly 10 percent increase). These rather stringent targets seem to show that the earlier "development" language used by UN-affiliated international organizations was still alive and well after the 1994 Cairo conference recommendations had been accepted by Mexican policymakers and would provide a round-about justification for surveying the available abortion facilities in Mexico. In fact, the Cairo and then the Mexican RHFP reports provided a technical opening in which the expertise of groups such as the Population Council, International Planned Parenthood, and IPAS could be solicited to officially quantify the existence of different types of facilities and training programs, where previously this seemed to have been impossible at the national level.

Official studies showed that if Mexico were to reduce its fertility and population growth rates, it would have to do more than increase contraception use. A study of twenty-five health centers in eight Mexican states (disproportionately centered in urban areas) conducted by the General Direction for Reproductive Health for the federal Health Ministry stated the following: While most of the health centers could provide most of the typically needed reproductive health services, the least-available, found in only 16 percent of the health centers, was the capacity to treat incomplete abortions (as opposed to prenatal provision in all of the health centers, 36 percent providing birth services and 92 percent providing postnatal care). Similarly, "when consultations were observed, it was found that service providers screened for the need and gave reproductive health services to less than 40% of the women." With respect to contraception, "providers showed a bias towards providing the IUD, monthly injectable (Depo-Provera) and combined pills. . . . An additional bias is the belief that . . . it is better that the physician and not the user chooses the method." On another point, the importance of the media, particularly broadcast, in reaching the population is shown in that the vast majority of women (88 percent) received information on health topics through the media rather than through a first contact at the center. At the other end of the equation, when doctors and nurses were asked which trainings they needed the most, both included "treatment of incomplete abortion" as among their top priorities.[94] This information is somewhat stronger than would typically be expected from a government survey.

Similarly, another study undertaken by IPAS concerning a related 1995 reform, creating clinics for "comprehensive care for victims of sexual violence in three public hospitals in different zones of Mexico City," showed the inconsistent nature of access to abortion in public hospitals. The main factor affecting whether the hospitals offered legal abortion services was the "medical director's personal attitudes."[95] Unfortunately, "direct care for providing comprehensive care was not instituted," and another hospital illegally reinstated the therapeutic abortion committee requirement, even though the 1995 law directly overrode that practice. Thus, as IPAS noted, "access to safe, legal abortion services continues to be extremely limited."[96]

With regard to pro-choice advocacy since the Cairo conference and the Zedillo reproductive health plan, there are examples of the increased availability of public spaces within which pro-choice advocates could organize, helped by some international groups and these advocates' awareness of what strategic options to pursue. In short, this particular case study of the so-called Robles law, passed in 2000 in Mexico's Federal District, demonstrates the social movement learning curve about which options are available and most promising. As has been noted, none of the Mexican parties include the increased right to abortion in their platform, despite the increasingly sharp pronouncements of the UN conferences on this issue. Even lacking concrete platform commitments, male party leaders have felt free to promise to liberalize abortion laws during elections, probably assuming they will not be held accountable to this promise.[97] Feminist groups in Mexico, however, have started to do exactly that.

In 1997, pro-choice and generally feminist groups worked together in a coalition of forty groups, known as the Campaign for Access to Justice for Women, on issues including domestic and sexual violence, the rights of children and young people to be free of violence, freedom from discrimination, and "the right to abortion as part of the right to health."[98] GIRE was a central player in this coalition and in fact had been working on these issues since 1991 in response to the granting of legal rights to the Catholic Church in Mexico at that time. Another major coalition partner was the Mexico City Women's Health Network, "representing one of the most active currents of the Mexican feminist movement."[99] They met with Cuauhtemoc Cardenas in May 1997, at that time the ultimately successful PRD candidate for Mexico City mayor. At that meeting, Cardenas signed a letter "containing a number of commitments that he would fulfill were he to be elected mayor, including a public consultation on abortion law reform."[100] With his PRD majority of 42 percent, an absolute majority in the Legislative Assembly of the Federal District, it was hoped that Cardenas would press for the reforms he had publicly supported two weeks earlier. This did not happen, and feminist groups in the Access to Justice Campaign found themselves gearing up in earnest to work with the PRD in the assembly toward the latter half of the three-year (1997–2000) legislative term, in 1999.

The major political shifts that had to happen to get this proposal onto the agenda of "viable political opportunities" include the following, as described by Marta Lamas, a long-term feminist political activist in Mexico.[101] For the first time ever, the PRI was seen to be in grave danger of losing the presidential election in 2000, as ultimately happened. However, both the PRD and the PAN thought they had credible hopes of winning this, so ultimately the PRD leader, Cardenas, disavowed his earlier commitment to abortion law reform.

As we know, the PRD picked up seats in the House based on split voting, as did Vicente Fox and the PAN, but ultimately the PAN won the presidency. The second major shift that had to happen was that action would only take place after the federal election was decided, in favor of the PAN at the presidential level. At that time, "it became politically useful for the PRD and PRI to demonstrate their sensitivity about abortion."[102] What was also needed was a feminist leader in the assembly, who became available when Cardenas resigned from the mayorship in spring 2000 due to his interest in running for president that year. Rosario Robles, a young feminist PRD member who had been appointed interim mayor of Mexico City after Cardenas's resignation, put forward the decriminalization bill at the continued urging of the Access to Justice Campaign.[103] It may or may not be significant that she was a lame duck mayor who had already been elected to the national House seat for which she ran in July 2000 and therefore had absolutely nothing to lose on this issue, a rarity in Mexican politics. Other key factors in this particular window of opportunity were the PRD's feminist party leader Amalia Garcia, who ensured that the upper echelons of the party supported it. This measure, expanding the exemptions to criminal prosecution in the DF from the prior ones of rape, risk to the woman's life, and spontaneous abortion to include those of fetal impairment and risk to the woman's health, was passed in August 2000, one month before the DF elections.[104] Interestingly, the PRD retained control of the DF afterward.

With these amendments, the Federal District law, which had been one of the most conservative, joined the ranks of the more liberalized states. What had probably delayed this change for so long was Mexico City's prominence in national politics and the unwillingness of PRI-controlled legislative sessions from dealing with the issue. Interestingly, a month after these reforms had passed, the odd coalition of the Green Party and PAN challenged the law on the fetal malformation ground.

The Mexican Supreme Court upheld the law in a "groundbreaking judgment" in January 2002 and interpreted the law more broadly than it was written, stating that the District Public Prosecutor's Office could "authorize abortions in cases of rape and forced insemination."[105] The Robles law and its support by the Supreme Court are viewed as positive steps toward reorienting abortion law away from the traditional interpretation of, "perhaps women's rights may prevail if fetal rights are presumed not to trump them" to [the fact that] "the ruling recognized that the fundamental rights of women may in some circumstances prevail over those of the fetus" and that "religious values can and should be put aside."[106] In other words, the Robles law may be termed "positive law" and indeed a positive step in more concretely defining the circumstances under which abortion is legal in public hospitals in Mexico City, rather than the hypothetical definition of when abortion services may be legal (but were not necessarily followed up in that manner). To further broaden the nature of abortion rights and access in Mexico, feminist NGOs have held national and international conferences since August 2000. These conferences, "aimed at physicians [particularly obstetricians and gynecologists] . . . focus on violence against women and [preventive measures], including safe, legal abortion services."[107]

Although the trends toward progressive interpretation of the laws within Mexico and the DF Health Ministry's increased willingness to work with UN agencies and UN-funded agencies show an opening of some aspects of abortion policy, the single most important block constitutes the "Foxista" government, as it is termed in the Mexican press. In addition to his public statements about being pro-life in all circumstances, and his appointment of Pro-Vida–affiliated women to the executive branch, another example of this mindset was the bill passed by the state of which Fox had previously been governor, Guanajuato, one month after his election to the presidency. This legislation made abortion for rape survivors illegal and included penalties of one to three year prison sentences for both the woman and the doctor.[108] Many viewed the legislation as a direct order from Fox to test the potential for future restrictions in other states. As Lamas and Bissell note, this was probably the most public set of demonstrations against abortion policy used by the women's movement. Some public action was taken on behalf of the Robles law, such as taking to the airwaves, but the Guanajuato law set into motion a coalitional effort to embarrass the PAN and the Guanajuato legislature. For example, GIRE, CCFC, and "the feminist political association DIVERSA" held a press conference in front of the national party headquarters of the PAN.[109] Similarly, various sectors of civil society demonstrated at the Guanajuato Legislative Assembly while the governor reviewed the bill as well as in the DF in front of national party headquarters and Fox's presidential office. Related to the learning curve of social movement organizations, Lamas and Bissell state that "activists traveled back and forth from Guanajuato to Mexico City, strategizing on how to impede the process and meeting with representatives" from the parties represented in the Guanajuato legislature, including the governing PAN.[110] Experts were brought into the coalition opposing the bill, including doctors, public servants from all parties, civic leaders, and NGOs, stating that the bill violated religious freedom, separation of church and state, democracy, and the right to choose.[111] Ultimately, in the face of strong public opposition, the governor vetoed the bill at the end of August 2000.[112]

## Mexican Pro-life Organizing

Attempts to discern the breadth and depth of opposition groups in Mexico are highly difficult, for a few reasons. The first is the relatively recent nature of civil society organizing. The second is that Pro-Vida as with its parent organization, Human Life International, is linked to the Catholic Church and is extremely secretive about its chapters and members. Also contributing to the difficulty is that Pro-Vida is a linked group to HLI's Miami office, Vida Humana, representing Latin American outreach. As one source described in July 2002, "the [Mexican] movement is based in the US."[113] Scholarly accounts of Pro-Vida as a group do not exist, only scattered accountings of their actions. One action, for example, took place through lobbying against the Robles law of 2000, when "[Pro-Vida] called in experienced anti-choice activists from the U.S. and Canada," who rallied in front of a newly opened legal public abortion clinic in the Yucatan as well as one in Mexico City and in the main plaza in Mexico City. However, they were soon deported under Mexico's strong laws against foreign participation in Mexican politics.[114]

The specifics that have been gathered about Pro-Vida is that the group was formed in the late 1970s by Jorge Serrano Limon of the Mexico City Archdiocese. Its regular activities include acting as a "mass pressure organization that holds weekly vigils and pray-ins outside of health secretariat offices for family planning and AIDS-prevention programs." In Mexico, Pro-Vida has undertaken campaigns against the "mass sterilization of poor Indian women" as well as filed suit against the World Health Organization and health secretariats for distributing condoms in the anti-AIDS effort.[115] Interestingly, the group claims that the latter is a conspiracy of the World Bank and the IMF. Its principal funder is said to be Jorge Barroso Chavez, "an immensely wealthy Catholic businessman whose ties to conservative members of the Mexican Episcopal

Conference [of the Catholic church] have given him the status of a lay bishop."[116] He is also a ranking member of the Knights of Columbus and the Legionnaires of Christ. Pro-Vida has enjoyed the backing of the PAN (and current President Fox) as well as "the two highest-ranking and wealthiest cardinals in Mexico," one of whom, Cardinal Rivera "tends the largest diocese in Christendom" (twenty million followers).[117]

Another example of Pro-Vida's work is seen in the following case. In 1999, a thirteen-year-old girl, Paulina, was raped and impregnated, and in her home state of Baja California, the law covered abortion for up to nine days in this circumstance. However, when she went with her mother to the public hospital in Mexicali, despite having obtained the necessary form from the state prosecutor's office, the staff gave the family the runaround, keeping her there for a week. While waiting in the hospital with her, Paulina's family slept on floors and had six thousand pesos (about $600) extorted from them by various medical staff who promised "treatments" for Paulina that were never delivered. Ultimately, no doctor at the hospital was willing to perform the abortion, despite the fact that Paulina had the state's "permission" and that it was legal.[118] While in the hospital, staying in the maternity ward, two women from Pro-Vida illegally obtained access to her and showed her various inflammatory materials. Similarly, Paulina's mother was told by medical staff that her daughter could die, although she was well within the first trimester of pregnancy. After Paulina's baby was born, she attempted to have it baptized. The Catholic Church in Mexicali refused, ostensibly because the godmother was prochoice.[119] Another piece of the explanation for this outcome is that by this time, the governor of Baja California was a PANista, and likely the chain of command in Baja state bowed to the general Christian Democratic and specific Foxista anti-abortion views. Thus, changing party politics and their representation within the federal structure denied this young rape victim access to an abortion under the legal circumstances that she had met.

## Conclusion

This discussion demonstrates how tenuous the right to choose still is in Mexico. It also shows that where a woman lives (just as in Canada and the United States) determines whether she has the same rights as someone elsewhere in the country. Of course, the right to choose is still more developmental in Mexico, both because of the power of hospital administrators and the Catholic Church to get involved in these decisions and that the health-care system is so uneven. Needless to say, it shows the degree to which health-care systems and political decisions about them have influence, specifically, over the lives of women.

Access to the state was increased in the Mexican polity since the late 1980s, given cracks appearing in the political system from both below, from grassroots peasants, native, and women's movements, and from above, in terms of the PRI's inability to contain either its left or right wings. Thus, in Mexico, access to the state as found in the second policy period actually was caused by the other two elements of Sidney Tarrow's political opportunity structure framework: changing of political alignments and availability of allies in coalitions for change. This is an interesting difference from what was shown in Chapters 2 and 3, where one political opportunity structure concept was not found to have a causal relationship with another, simply an associative one.

Also particularly important in the second period operative on Mexican abortion policy and politics in general since the late 1980s have been elements of the advocacy network strategies. The Mexican political system still has a ways to go in terms of holding politicians directly accountable for their actions, as few have that kind of responsibility. However, the strategies of moral leverage on the part of civil society in general and a reverse "material leverage" as well were shown to be useful in the 1980s and 1990s in that the coalitions for change claimed that bad economic policies, including free trade, had caused much of Mexico's poverty. As has consistently been the case across Mexico, Canada, and the United States, the pro-life movement has invoked the symbolism of fetal life as sacred and has had additional reference points in this example. Some of the overtly pro-life PANistas, especially the current president's wife, have also claimed that a return to women's traditional roles of supporting their husbands at home would help Mexican society. Mexican women's movements generally have sometimes used moral leverage, such as "women's particular sensitivities," to show that it was largely women's groups who helped Mexico City after its devastating earthquakes. The largest pro-choice organization, GIRE, as well as some of the newer, more electoralist organizations, tend to frame their discourse in the liberal, equal-rights-oriented terminology of their Canadian and U.S. counterparts.

In terms of women's potential to increase their control over their health lives in general and reproductive lives more specifically in Mexico, the prognostications are varied. The PAN party is Christian Democratic and affiliated with Pro-Vida and powerful Mexican Catholic bishops. The Catholic Church has the most overt power to organize politically it has ever held in Mexico. However, transnational linkages have appeared between the IPPF and its Mexican, Canadian, and U.S. offices—IPAS and the DF Ministry of Health—to provide aspiration equipment. Links have also been established between GIRE and the Center for Reproductive Law and Policy in New York to research and publicize the uneven nature of access to abortion in Mexico. Most recently, the widening civil society spectrum of participation and women's activity in NGOs (both within Mexico and in UN conferences), as well as slowly increasing their representation in electoral politics, bode well for pushing the boundaries of public discourse to include women and reproductive rights, however potentially easier without the PAN controlling the presidency and Congress. The fact that there are still hundreds of thousands of abortions performed every year in Mexico, most of them illegally, indicates that the gap between rhetoric and reality persists. It will likely take years more of pressure from inside electoral politics and NGOs working with the UN and internationally based NGOs such as the International Women's Health Coalition to bring more leverage to bear on this problem of unequal access and rhetoric versus reality.

## Notes

1. Figures are provided by GIRE, the largest and oldest reproductive rights group in Mexico, founded in Mexico City (officially known as the DF, or Distrito Federal) in the early 1970s. The figures are drawn from the article "Issues of Abortion in Mexico" in GIRE's "Trimestral Bulletin on Free Choice," September 1996, cited in Center for Reproductive Law and Policy (CRLP) and GIRE, *Women of the World: Issues and Policies Affecting Their Reproductive Lives, Latin America, and the Caribbean,* 1st ed. (New York: CRLP, November 1997), 152, nn. 194, 195.

2. An excellent chapter on the changing role of women in autonomous movements and party politics is that of Carmen Ramos Escandon,

"Women's Movements, Feminism, and Mexican Politics," 207, in Jane Jaquette, ed., *The Women's Movement in Latin America: Participation and Democracy,* 2nd ed. (Boulder, Colo.: Westview, 1994), 199–221.

3. As Tom Barry notes in *Mexico: A Country Guide* (Albuquerque, N.M.: Inter-Hemispheric Education Resource Center, 1992), 3–4, most observers inside and outside of Mexico acknowledge the revolution's starting year as 1910, when the autocratic president Porfirio Diaz (in place since 1876) was overthrown, yet some acknowledge the ending by the 1917 Constitution, and others view the revolution as continuing at least until 1920.

4. Escandon, "Women's Movements, Feminism, and Mexican Politics," 199.

5. They were, respectively, those of 1824, upon independence from Spain, and that of 1857, a product of a Liberal reform, "both of which challenged the society's colonial and feudal structures" (Barry, *Mexico,* 5).

6. Ibid.

7. Ibid., 4.

8. Ibid., 5–7.

9. Ibid., 6.

10. Ibid.

11. Ibid., 7.

12. Ibid., 6–8.

13. Daniel C. Levy and Kathleen Bruhn, *Mexico: The Struggle for Democratic Development* (Berkeley: University of California Press, 2001), 79.

14. Barry, *Mexico,* 15.

15. Ibid., 13.

16. Ibid., 17.

17. Levy and Bruhn, *Mexico: The Struggle for Democratic Development,* 105.

18. Barry, *Mexico,* 15.

19. Ibid., 13; and Levy and Bruhn, *Mexico: The Struggle for Democratic Development,* 87, 294, nn. 35, 36.

20. Levy and Bruhn, *Mexico: The Struggle for Democratic Development,* 294, n. 36.

21. Barry, *Mexico,* 15.

22. Ibid., 25.

23. Escandon, "Women's Movements, Feminism, and Mexican Politics," 207; John Warnock, *The Other Mexico: The North American Triangle Completed* (Montreal: Black Rose Books, 1995), 141.

24. Escandon, "Women's Movements, Feminism, and Mexican Politics."

25. Valencia Garcia, "The PAN in Guanajuato," 229, in Kevin J. Middlebrook, ed., *Party Politics and the Struggle for Democracy in Mexico: National and State-Level Analyses of the Partido Accion Nacional* (La Jolla, Calif.: Center for U.S.-Mexican Studies, University of California, San Diego, 2001), 209–258.

26. Levy and Bruhn, *Mexico: The Struggle for Democratic Development,* 87, 294, n. 35; Barry, *Mexico,* 29–30.

27. Levy and Bruhn, *Mexico: The Struggle for Democratic Development,* 167.

28. Escandon, "Women's Movements, Feminism, and Politics in Mexico," 212.

29. Victoria E. Rodriguez, *Women in Contemporary Mexican Politics* (Austin, University of Texas Press, 2003), 114.

30. Ibid., 116.

31. Ibid.

32. Ibid., 114–125. This section is particularly helpful on women's roles in the political parties.

33. Ibid., 119–120.

34. Ibid., 121–122.

35. Ibid.

36. Escandon, "Women's Movements, Feminism, and Mexican Politics," 214.

37. Rodriguez, *Women in Contemporary American Politics,* 118.

38. Ibid., 180.

39. Sarah Babb, *Managing Mexico: Economists from Nationalism to Neoliberalism* (Princeton, N.J.: Princeton University Press, 2001), 9.

40. Barry, *Mexico,* 3–12.

41. Ibid., 160–161.

42. Ibid., 161.

43. Ibid., 161–162.

44. Ibid., 166–170.

45. Report of the Secretaria de Hacienda y Credito Publico, Mexican Finance Ministry, 1991, cited in Levy and Bruhn, *Mexico: The Struggle for Democratic Development,* 167, n. 36.

46. UN Economic Commission for Latin America and the Caribbean (CEPAL) figures, cited in Warnock, *The Other Mexico,* 180–184.

47. Ibid., 180–181.

48. Asa Cristina Laurell, "Social Policy in Mexico," in Kevin J. Middlebrook and Eduardo Zepeda, eds., *Confronting Development: Assessing Mexico's Economic and Social Policy Changes* (Palo Alto, Calif.: Stanford University Press, 2003), 320–349.

49. Ibid., 339.

50. Ibid., 337.

51. Ibid., 325; Laurell also cites her 1997 report, "La reforma contra la salud y la seguridad social" (DF, Mexico: ERA, 1997).

52. Ibid., 337. As noted by Laurell, the new "basic package" of covered health services for the poor includes "household hygiene; family planning and Pap smears; pre-, peri- and post-natal care; child nutrition and development; immunizations and control of parasites; mobile medical care for persons with acute respiratory disease; prevention and control of t.b., hypertension, and diabetes; accident prevention and first aid, and community training for self-care."

53. Marta Lamas and Sharon Bissell, "Abortion and Politics in Mexico: 'Context is All,'" *Reproductive Health Matters* 8, 16 (November 2000) 10–23.

54. As discussed in United Nations, *Abortion Policies: A Global Review,* vol. 2, *Gabon to Norway* (New York: United Nations, Department of Economic and Social Affairs, Population Division, 2001), 135–137.

55. As defined in the 1931 Criminal Code for the Federal District, physician penalties range from one to three years' possible imprisonment for performing an abortion *with* the woman's consent, and three to six years without that consent; the potential range becomes six to eight years' imprisonment if the abortion is deemed "physical or moral violence." In addition, a doctor or midwife performing an illegal abortion may be suspended for two to five years; in 1976, the Federal Ministry of Public Health prohibited "qualified lay birth attendants from inducing an abortion." Finally, a woman who has had an illegal abortion can be subject to anywhere from six months to five years' imprisonment (United Nations, *Abortion Policies,* 136). All three countries under study have made the TAC requirement and exemptions part of the relevant jurisdiction of criminal law; the Canadian federal criminal code, state-by-state legislation in the United States, and in the Federal District and state codes in Mexico, each of which have their own criminal codes.

56. Ibid.

57. Heather L. Williams, *Social Movements and Economic Transition: Markets and Distributive Conflict in Mexico* (UK: Cambridge University Press, 2001), 28.

58. Chappell Lawson, *Building the Fourth Estate: Democratization and the Rise of a Free Press in Mexico* (Berkeley: University of California Press, 2002), 62–64.

59. Rodriguez, *Women in Contemporary Mexican Politics,* 94–95.

60. Marta Lamas et al., "Building Bridges: The Growth of Popular Feminism in Mexico," in Amrita Basu, ed., *The Challenge of Local Feminisms: Women's Movements in Global Perspective* (Boulder, Colo.: Westview Press, 1995), 324–347.

61. Rodriguez, *Women in Contemporary Mexican Politics,* 104.

62. Ibid., 105–106.

63. Barry, *Mexico,* 3–12; Rodriguez, *Women in Contemporary Mexican Politics,* 105–112.

64. Escandon, "Women's Movements, Feminism, and Mexican Politics," 209–210.

65. Ibid.

66. Ibid., 209.

67. Ibid.

68. Ibid., 108; and Lamas 1994, cited on p. 108.

69. Lamas et al., "Building Bridges," 337.

70. Rodriguez, *Women in Contemporary Mexican Politics,* 107–109.

71. Maria Luisa Tarres, "Mas alla de lo publico y lo privado: Reflexiones sobre la participacion social y politica de las mujeres de clase

media en Ciudad Satelite," in Orlandina de Oliveira, ed., *Trabajo, poder y sexualidad* (Mexico City: El Colegio de Mexico), cited in Rodriguez, *Women in Contemporary Mexican Politics,* 112.

72. Rodriguez, *Women in Contemporary Mexican Politics,* 107.

73. Escandon, "Women's Movements, Feminism, and Mexican Politics," 211.

74. Teresa Carrillo, "Women and Independent Unionism in the Garment Industry," in Joe Foweraker and Ann Craig, eds., *Popular Movements and Political Change in Mexico* (Boulder, Colo.: Lynne Rienner Publishers, 1990), 213–233; also Escandon, "Women's Movements, Feminism, and Mexican Politics, 210–211.

75. Rodriguez, *Women in Contemporary Mexican Politics,* 79.

76. Ibid., 109.

77. Population Council website, www.popcouncil.org, accessed 3/14/02.

78. Ibid., accessed 5/6/02.

79. Ibid.

80. Mexfam website, www.mexfam.org.mx, accessed 7/23/03; and Adriana Ortiz Ortega, Ana Amuchastegui, and Marta Rivas, "'Because They Were Born from Me': Negotiating Women's Rights in Mexico," in Rosalind Petchesky and Karen Judd, eds., *Negotiating Reproductive Rights: Women's Perspectives Across Countries and Cultures* (London: Zed Books, 1998), 145–179.

81. Mexfam website, "Mexfam's Perspective," www.mexfam.org.mx, accessed 7/23/02.

82. Deborah A. Billings et al., "Constructing Access to Legal Abortion Services in Mexico City," *Reproductive Health Matters,* May 17, 2002, 1–8.

83. Ibid., 1.

84. Lamas and Bissell, "Abortion and Politics in Mexico," 13.

85. "The Campaign for the Decriminalization and Legalization of Abortion in Latin America and the Caribbean," *Concentric Media,* 1999, www.concentric.org, accessed 10/2003.

86. CRLP, *Women of the World,* 145–162, esp. n. 155.

87. Inter-American Development Bank website, www.iadb.org, and World Bank website, www.worldbank.org, accessed 8/13/03.

88. Mexfam website, www.mexfam.org.mx, accessed 7/23/03.

89. For example, Kathleen Staudt, ed., *Women, International Development, and Politics: The Bureaucratic Mire,* 2nd ed. (Philadelphia: Temple University Press, 1997); Nicole Haberland and Diana Measham, eds., *Responding to Cairo* (New York: Population Council, 2002).

90. Deborah Billings et al., "Constructing Access to Legal Abortion Services in Mexico City," 2.

91 United Nations, *Abortion Policies,* 137.

92. Perez-Palacios et al., "Linking Reproductive Health Services," Mexico City, November 4, 1997, p. 2.

93. CRLP, *Women of the World,* 151.

94. Perez-Palacios et al., "Linking Reproductive Health Services," 10–30.

95. Billings et al., "Constructing Access to Legal Abortion Services in Mexico City," 4.

96. Ibid.

97. For example, Rodriguez (*Women in Contemporary Mexican Politics,* 216) notes that on March 8, 2000, International Women's Day—just three months before the presidential election—all presidential candidates held meetings with women's NGOs. "As one report put it, 'they offered everything, from roses to legalizing abortion.'"

98. Billings et al., "Constructing Access to Legal Abortion Services in Mexico City," 3; Lamas and Bissell, "Abortion and Politics in Mexico," 22, n. 6.

99. Ibid., 10.

100. Ibid.

101. Ibid., 10–12, as described in detail throughout the whole article.

102. Ibid., 19.

103. Ibid.

104. Ibid.

105. Billings et al., "Constructing Access to Legal Abortion Services in Mexico City," 4.

106. Ibid.

107. Ibid., 4–5.

108. Lamas and Bissell, "Abortion and Politics in Mexico," 17.

109. Ibid.

110. Ibid.

111. Ibid., 17–18.

112. Ibid., 19.

113. Interview with Mexfam member, July 2002.

114. Lamas and Bissell, "Abortion and Politics in Mexico," 20.

115. John Ross, "The New Mexican Inquisition," *The Texas Observer,* January 25, 1999, reprinted on www.lasamericas.com, February 2, 1999, accessed 5/2004.

116. Ibid.

117. Ibid.

118. Elena Poniatowska, "Paulina," *La Jornada,* April 2000, cited in Lamas and Bissell, "Abortion and Politics in Mexico," 15–16.

119. "Baptism Denied in Mexico," reprinted from the *New York Times,* May 26, 2000, listed on the International Planned Parenthood Federation website, www.ippf.org, accessed 5/30/00.

# 5

# The Transnational Nature of Reproductive Choice Issues

This chapter concerns the extent to which the abortion issue has become a transnational one in North America. Historically, the transnational nature of organizing on reproductive choice issues can be seen with, first, the International Planned Parenthood Federation and then later Human Life International on the other side of the question. HLI has partners in Human Life International Canada and Pro-Vida in Mexico. Although Vatican unease with demographic policies that include reproductive control has been demonstrated since the 1950s, more recently women's rights groups and the Holy See have opposed one another in a more public manner at UN conferences, particularly the Cairo International Conference on Population and Development in 1994 and the Beijing World Conference on Women in 1995. Besides the IPPF, groups that have consistently opposed the Vatican's stance on reproductive rights include the International Women's Health Coalition (an umbrella feminist women's health group based in New York City) as well as certain governments, including those of Canada, Japan, and the European Union.

We will begin with a history of UN conferences, how they are called and structured, and the role of NGOs versus official delegations. In particular, the privileged access given to the Holy See as a "state" rather than an NGO will be examined and how this has affected the formulation of UN Plans of Action at the end of population and women's conferences. The discussion will illustrate the importance of treating the UN framework as a feedback loop of influence, a contested site of power interactions between organizations such as the Holy See, international feminist organizations, and the internal politics of nation-states, all represented in state delegation submissions to the UN. Although many people are familiar with the policy of the George W. Bush administration regarding the use of funds from the U.S. Agency for International Development (USAID), it is important to know about the long-term rhetorical battles over the meaning of "development" and "North vs. South sovereignty" within the UN since the 1950s and how those debates have shaped the more recent debates over the definition of "the family," "reproductive rights," and "gender rights." When examined closely, discourse shifts can reveal the extent of power shifts between states and/or between international organizations at the UN. Similarly, knowing the ways in which power may be shifting through the UN terrain enables the public to anticipate ways in which official discourse may shift in the time before the next UN International Population Conference.

In keeping with the identification of institutional and discursive period shifts in the United States, Canada, and Mexico on abortion policy, this chapter will provide evidence on these changes regarding UN structures and program texts. Overall, there are two different policy periods that have been operative with reference to women and reproductive rights over the UN's history. The first was when the largely U.S.-based family planning industry worked to fund country-specific activities, often through the IPPF and the UN Population Fund (UNFPA), in which women were viewed as passive beneficiaries of U.S.-led development programs. The second period—touched off in large part by the emergence of the internal women's program structure in the UN and through the conferences on population and women, as well as the emergence of women's movements in most countries—in effect took back control over the framing of women's reproductive rights as issues that women knew about and had a right to decide for themselves. The second process, where the framing power was retaken from largely white male scientists and "experts" based in the United States, did not happen without a fight, as will be shown.

In assigning relevant political opportunity structure and advocacy network variables for both policy periods, at the level of international fora Sidney Tarrow's concepts of access to the state and availability of allies are clearly the most relevant. This was true for population scientists privileged in the first period by funders such as the Rockefeller Foundation that wished to bring "developed" notions to the rest of the world, including population control. It also became true for the Vatican and for women's organizations in terms of being able to structurally access the UN conferences, to have voices during the preparations and during the actual event. The argument to be made here is that the Vatican has had undue access to the UN structure, given that it is not a state. Availability of allies also became important in period two for the Vatican and pro-life groups and women's pro-choice groups, due to increased knowledge of "how to play the UN game," both in terms of representation at the New York headquarters and at the conferences. Participating in UN activities is a multilevel strategic process, one that undoubtedly both sides have learned from each other. Important allies for the Vatican have included certain Catholic states, pro-life U.S. politicians, and the North American transnationally based HLI. For pro-choice groups, key allies have included (1) "woodwork" pro-choice women, those who had spent years participating in various UN fora, including Arvonne Fraser and Nafis Sadik; (2) help from unexpected quarters such as Tim Wirth, undersecretary of state for global affairs during the Clinton administration; (3) the IPPF; and (4) globally based women's organizations, including the IWHC.

In terms of Margaret Keck and Kathryn Sikkink's strategies available to advocacy networks, the most relevant to this description are the uses of symbolism by anti-choice groups, principally but not limited to the Vatican. From the first to the second period, the symbolism shifted a bit from the Vatican trying to fan the flames of a divide between privileged Western women and those from the rest of the world (who might value large families) into attempting to resurrect the tired rhetoric that feminists and gay people are all radical and indistinguishable from one another. Pro-choice responses included the use of moral and material leverage, responding to the continued pro-life emphasis on the immorality of abortion. The discourse frame used by the pro-choice side in both policy periods has been to deny that there is a difference between women around the world in terms of their desire to control their own reproductive processes and to highlight that this type of control leads to more economic freedom for women.

## The Structure of Representation in the UN

Arvonne Fraser, former coordinator of the Office of Women in Development at USAID, and Marilyn Danguilan of the Philippines, are women who have written scholarly accounts on the issue of group representation at and through the UN, which is steeped in their own experiences as members of their official delegations to UN conferences.[1] Both note that there is a time lag, generally a few years, between the calling of an international conference by either the General Assembly or the UN Economic and Social Council (ECOSOC) and the ultimate event. As Fraser notes, once a conference topic has been decided, either a special secretariat will be established or a UN agency assigned for the conference organizing.[2] Questionnaires may be sent out to all nations to elicit their views and further information, and "all member states are officially informed and they get to work."[3] Then "extensive background chapters are prepared, and preparatory committees meet to go over and revise or prepare a draft document for submission to the conference." Similarly, background chapters are prepared for the official delegates, with "negotiations between nations" across capitals often taking place to "resolve differences on particular points." There will usually be at least three meetings of the Preparatory Commissions, or "Prep Coms" (in the UN vernacular), before the final conference.[4]

The composition of the official delegations to all UN conferences is weighted toward governmental representatives. The delegation is typically headed by top officials of either the Department of Foreign Affairs from various countries or from the U.S. Department of State. Other delegates may be drawn from relevant government agencies, academic departments, interest groups, and NGOs, but as Fraser notes, they only speak for the official government that they are representing. They are, however, also sources of information for the national government that may solicit these delegates' views on matters in advance.[5] With reference to NGOs, Fraser writes that many early actions by the UN were a result of these women who "moved back and forth between organizations and governmental institutions," transmitting the ideas back and forth. She cites the example of the Inter-American Commission on the Status of Women, begun in the 1920s, which lobbied successfully for including the equal rights provision for women in the UN Charter.[6] Similarly, she has noted that over time, "the best international conferences" are those where government and NGO delegates "confer formally and informally before, during and after the conference," where the NGOs will often "recommend . . . specific language that they want inserted into the document."[7] NGOs and states must meet the requirements of the UN Charter (which, among other things, promises nondiscrimination based on race, gender, and other grounds) to be admitted as official members.

NGOs as such did not gain their own parallel forum until they demanded it in 1992.[8] Fraser notes that these events, held at the same time as the official conference, have served many functions, from galvanizing interest across national organizations and the international media, as well as serving as a participatory forum for interested government officials who had not been included on the official delegation. She also describes the freer, less constrained structure of these conferences, especially because statements were not constrained by a government's view on the issue. Thus, they served as a "marketplace of ideas" and a venue for the exchange of information, experience and networking between individuals and groups.[9] The NGO conference is organized by interested international organizations that are recognized by the UN; the organizations then raise the money to host the event. As with the official conference's secretariat, the NGO conference organizers delegate responsibility to a director and a staff, who then establish a subcommittee to ensure that the daily newschapter is published, covering both official delegation decisions and forum discussions and decisions. During the world conferences, the "NGO forum becomes . . . a highly sophisticated lobby, aimed in the short term at influencing the conference and the world's media" and in the longer term at influencing governments, media, and public opinion around the world.[10] It is also true that those who currently or historically have opposed a particular topic may attend the NGO forum to "use the fact of the conference for their own ends." Also, an NGO may try to petition for ECOSOC accreditation, of which there are three levels. If given accreditation, the NGO can send representatives to the main conference and/or the Prep Coms (not just the parallel NGO forum). The top level of accreditation is recognition by the UN as having special competence in virtually every area; the middle level, which is attained by most NGOs, including twelve pro-life ones as well as Catholics for a Free Choice, requires that NGOs show this competence in vaguely defined specific areas; and the lowest is that of "roster" status, including Human Life International and the International Right to Life Federation. If they wish to attend the Prep Coms or the final conference, groups in this lowest rung must try to negotiate with kindred groups in the second tier to give up some of their spaces to third-tier representatives. Examples will be given later.

As Fraser sums up, for women's organizations to become effective actors in the international system, they have had to learn a lot about the UN system over decades. This includes learning about the "unique UN system which operates more by consensus than majority rule," the difference between different governmental and party system structures, "the differences in cultural and religious traditions that affect both women and governments, and the conflicts between modernization, the drive for equity and the pull of tradition."[11] One reason for the necessity of learning their way around the inside UN pathways is that the end result of a conference is a "world program of action" recommending specific actions for national or international governments or other groups. While these recommendations may become "owned" by representatives from a particular country and funds pledged to enact them, they may also simply be dependent on the goodwill of various national and international actors to implement them.[12] For example, the Program of Action adopted at the first International Women's Year Conference in Mexico City in 1975 included a recommendation that governments establish "specialized policy machinery for the advancement of women." By the end of the 1980s, 137 of the reporting countries had created such units."[13] Yet the fact that the majority of UN countries in the industrialized and nonindustrialized worlds have ratified the Convention to Eliminate Discrimination Against Women has not influenced the United States to ratify. However, if there is consistent and sustained pressure by national networks closely tied to the UN process, a country may in fact implement some of these important programs, as happened with the Philippines during the Beijing World Conference on Women in 1995, where the result of national and international women's networking in government, academic, diplomatic, and civil society group settings was the implementation of the thirty-year plan for gender and development.[14] Lacking this type of proactive networking, the UN Plan of Action has no autonomous power to force itself on nations.

## The History of the Vatican at the UN

Danguilan notes that for the Cairo Conference on Population and Development, as was true for others, Prep Coms 1 and 2, held in

March 1991 and May 1993, respectively, established the skeletal frame of what would be worked on at the final Prep Com.[15] While language is negotiated by states with NGO input at the earlier Prep Coms, it is particularly at the final Prep Com meeting where member states negotiate most of the contents of the major document of the conference. If a member state objects to certain language, that language is placed in brackets. With the UN's mode of consensus decisionmaking, one state can heavily influence the agenda for the final conference by bracketing language at the final Prep Com. That state has most often been the Vatican when it comes to the UN Conference on Population and Development and more recently the conferences on women and children as well. As Danguilan, a physician who was a member of the Philippine official delegation to the third Prep Com for the Cairo conference in 1994 and to the Beijing conference in 1995 notes, the less contested (bracketed) language after the final Prep Com, the more consensus is evident. If there are brackets in the language as it goes to the delegates for the conference, the delegates must negotiate them before beginning other work at the conference. The importance of being an actor at the final Prep Com is highlighted by Danguilan when she states that "most UN observers say that at least 60 percent of the final outcome of a UN world conference is determined during the preparatory meetings."[16] Thus, from the standpoint of a state actor feeling strongly on an issue, the strategy is to hold fast to its objections during the final Prep Com so that the document released after the Prep Com meetings becomes the basis for the "official conference" document. Another part of the strategy is to lobby the global media and opinion leaders in certain selected states to retain the bracketed language in the version of the document emanating from the World Conference on Women, so that it remains in the Plan of Action that will then influence the global framework for the next ten or twenty years. All of these strategic options were exercised by the Holy See regarding the 1994 Cairo Conference on Population and Development, as chronicled by Danguilan, who began as an official member of the Prep Com 3 delegation from the Philippines. After that meeting, due to strenuous lobbying by the Catholic Church in the Philippines, the only Catholic country in Asia, she and another prominent woman were removed from the delegation.[17] She attended the World Conference on Women as an NGO delegate.

The Holy See represents the Pope, his authority in Vatican City in Rome, and the worldwide Roman Catholic Church. It began its presence at the UN by attending meetings of the General Assembly, the World Health Organization (WHO), and the UN Educational, Scientific, and Cultural Organization. When the Holy See first inquired about potential UN membership in 1944, U.S. Secretary of State Cordell Hull responded that Vatican City did not meet the requirements. Although the Holy See—wielding its sovereign authority over Vatican City and the Catholic Church—acts as the international relations liaison for the Church in general, performing functions related to treaties and receiving of envoys, it lacked critical authority in one matter, according to Hull. "Under the UN Charter, a member state is required to commit military power in collective measures," while "Article 24 of the Lateran Pacts of 1929 binds the Holy See and Vatican City to a policy of neutrality which is regarded as incompatible with membership."[18] Thus, the definition as it has consistently stood is a requirement to be able to commit a military force to aid UN missions. In 1956, the Holy See became elected to ECOSOC and to the International Atomic Energy Agency.[19] ECOSOC is a major coordinating council within the UN system, coordinating the work of the fourteen specialized UN agencies. It issues policy recommendations to the UN system and member states, and its "purview extends to over 70% of the human and financial resources of the UN system."[20]

The Holy See became a permanent observer to the UN in 1964 simply by naming a permanent observer, based on its historical presence at the UN. Danguilan explains that the permanent observer category was begun as a matter of custom in 1946, when Switzerland named one and this was accepted by the Secretary-General. The UN Charter contains no provisions on the category.[21] Although, historically, permanent observers could attend and participate in UN meetings, they could not vote in the General Assembly. "Recently, however, General Assembly resolutions . . . have invited 'all states' to participate, and they have been able to participate with full voting rights."[22] This is an interesting case of rights being granted simply on the basis of longevity. First, based on its attendance at the UN, the Holy See was granted nonstate permanent observer status, and then it benefited when states were granted voting rights. One of the chief opposition groups to the Vatican's influence at the UN is the U.S.-based CCFC, which notes that by various common criteria, the Vatican does not enjoy state status so should not be allowed to vote as other states do.[23] Overall, the chief argument against the Holy See's participation on this basis is that it is not a state according to the UN's definition, yet it gets to exercise all the rights of states at the UN. Thus, the Holy See and Switzerland share the same curious status in the UN system.

The important relevant distinction to make is that the Holy See is the only international religious body accorded these rights; there is a significant difference between the rights of a state and of an NGO in the UN system. All other religions get to petition for (and often receive) NGO status. There are very clear ways in which status differentials between NGOs and the Holy See's ambiguous state status are found with respect to the official conferences. First, in the Prep Coms leading up to the official conferences, which often take years of negotiations, such as those leading up to the Cairo International Population and Development Conference, states have votes and are part of the official representation while NGOs do not. NGOs may monitor public plenary sessions and open sessions of "working groups" (subgroups) appointed to work out disagreements on certain issues, but they do not vote. Their influence during Prep Coms is felt in watching the official, national government-appointed delegations and lobbying those delegations in between sessions.[24] National government delegations are free to take or ignore their advice. Official state delegations at the Prep Coms are able to voice opposition at the sessions and to delay delegates' consideration of other matters.

## UN Conference History
## and Developing Discursive Conflict

### The Scientific Expert–Led Model of Development

As Danguilan and others have noted with reference to many UN conferences, disagreement between states over contraception policies has been evident since the UN entered the population and development field in the early 1950s. The period from the 1950s through the 1970s has been characterized by Danguilan and others as the "development period," in which the UN, often through UNFPA and usually affiliated with the International Planned Parenthood Federation and/or the Population Council, brought reproductive health information and care to countries in the developing world of Africa, Asia, and Latin America where no other provisions were generally being made.

The prevalence of the development period through the late 1970s can be viewed as based on a large fraction of self-interest in the United States, based both on fear that population growth in the third world would threaten the living standard in other parts of the world and the laboratories' desire to have ready-made testing grounds for their products.

The first decades of the development period belonged mainly to the scientists and UN administrators of the population fund. Even though the first World Population Conference was held in Rome in 1955, there seems to be no available record of Vatican opposition to it. This was also true for the next such conference in Belgrade, Yugoslavia, held in 1965. These two proto-conferences were held by and for the population experts and were not open to global participation. This changed for the next population conference, the first such UN World Population Conference held in Bucharest in 1974. The opening of participation to all UN member states, the fact of the momentous *Roe v. Wade* decision in the United States in 1973 and accompanying media attention, made it apparent that the UN population conferences had entered a new era of becoming the site of contestation over reproductive rights. Danguilan notes that the Plan of Action adopted at the end of the Bucharest conference added a new feature that would prove highly significant for the future. In addition to the old emphasis on population control, the newer idea was the inclusion of the factors leading up to fertility, such as governments providing "incentives and disincentives for couples to limit their family size." This warranted an integration of contraception and family planning into the traditional maternal and child health programs.[25] It also guaranteed that opposition from the Holy See over these sections would intensify.

By 1984 and the next World Population Conference in Mexico City, opposition to including family planning and contraception had clearly hardened. The Holy See was able to work in a new political opportunity structure since the 1980 presidential election of Ronald Reagan and his particular openness to Vatican lobbying.[26] The U.S. delegation was headed by pro-life former senator James Buckley and completely changed the U.S. position taken ten years earlier to favor that of the Holy See. The U.S. text for 1984 stated that the United States and other governments had previously been swayed by "extremist reactions," and that "population control programs alone cannot substitute for the economic reforms that put a society on the road toward growth and . . . slowing population increases as well."[27] This text parallels nearly verbatim Holy See and pro-life NGO objections that population control policies are based on false Malthusian assumptions that population growth outside the industrialized world is unwarranted and unmanageable. The final plan also adopted the language, revisited ten years later, of the Mexico City principle that abortion not be used as a method of family planning. This was again tied to Holy See pressure.

As with most of the positions taken in the reproductive policy area, there is a grain of truth in it, however magnified to an unrecognizable degree. The first twenty years of U.S. and UN development policy can be faulted precisely on the grounds of privileging certain populations over others and of using that policy to yield results of mixed benefit. Another problem with this policy in the eyes of many other countries was that it came tied to conditions imposed by the World Bank that finances would only be released if the countries adopted population policies.[28] However, to argue as the United States did in 1984 and the Vatican has since that any policy aimed at controlling population growth is wrong ignores women's own desire to have control over their reproductive lives. Although the earlier development policies could be argued to have helped women to a certain extent while also bypassing their wishes as to the methods of family planning, the later opposition to family planning is based precisely on the same grounds.[29] It also demonstrates a divide-and-conquer mentality on the part of the Holy See to prevent pro-choice women from working together on a global scale.

Over time, the control over UN policies affecting women's reproductive rights has shifted to a broadened issue network involving church groups on both sides of reproductive matters, national government representatives from around the world, the U.S. private family-planning organizations funded by the USAID, and activists springing from the second-wave women's movement. The latter group, according to two Population Council authors, stems from changes largely wrought by the women's movement both in the United States and globally, that "many feminists are now found in high-level policy and management positions in foundations and in family planning, health, research, and advocacy agencies" from which they can work to "further the acceptance of women's goals within their organizations and to secure funds to aid in feminist-supported activities," including in the population planning field. Similarly, until at least the 1970s in the United States and probably beyond, the women's movement in industrialized countries tended to neglect the impact of development policies upon their counterparts elsewhere until women from the other countries mobilized to teach the population scientists and women's movement actors in other countries about the pernicious effects of UN policies.[30]

There were two interesting outcomes of the 1984 conference for the purposes of this discussion. The first was the banding together of the Group of 77 (G-77) and its "Mexico Declaration" issued at the conference's conclusion that the industrialized world was the problem in terms of using up world resources and therefore that development and population policies were targeted at the wrong countries.[31] It also showed the emergence of the developing countries' bloc as a real counterforce within the UN structure that would have to be reckoned with in the future. The second major development with an eye toward the future was the final text calling for governments to "make family planning services universally available as a matter of urgency."[32] In short, the nexus of various long-term developments came together at about the time of the 1984 Mexico City World Population Conference. These included the Holy See's displeasure at language shifts in the documents, which in turn reflected equal emphasis on the "old" economic development model and the newer emphasis on family planning as both wanted by women and helpful to controlling global demographics. The rise in power of a socially conservative government headed by Ronald Reagan gave the Holy See a stronger entrée into U.S. domestic politics as reflected in the U.S. submission to the Prep Coms and final document. Another noticeable factor was the organization of the developing world into the G-77, which portended its ability to act as a cohesive bloc as a counterweight to real or perceived U.S. and European control. Finally, despite the presence of conservative, cost-cutting governments in many countries, women were stronger in the 1980s than in the 1970s due to the results of organizing. Women could thus begin to flex their muscles in the Prep Com and final preparation conferences as well, starting in Mexico City in 1984.[33]

Different conferences over time have been charged with varied mandates. For example, the 1984 Mexico population conference was charged with reviewing the Bucharest 1974 Plan of Action and to develop the recommendations for further implementation. The Cairo conference in 1994 had a mandate to investigate the relationship of sustained economic growth, sustainable development, and population.[34] Depending on their order in the conference scheduling as well as the site of the conference, alliances can shift from one to the other, resulting in different rhetoric and voting patterns. For example, the Cairo conference, which took place after the Rio de Janeiro Earth Summit, enabled the demographic planners of the UN Development Program to work with environmentalists in making their arguments. In this they were opposed by international women's networks, sufficiently sophisticated by then to point out the unequal nature of this type of argumentation. It also fostered no love from the Vatican, which saw these arguments as false Malthusian strategies. Other conferences have included the World Summit for Social Development, held in Copenhagen in 1995, with poverty and development as its theme; one in Vienna aimed at human rights; and one in Beijing, focused on action for equality, development, and peace. As noted by Danguilan, "all these conferences somehow had 'empowering women' as one of their major themes."[35]

### Women's Increasing Influence

The other set of relevant conferences includes the UN international conferences on women, with the first such conference held in 1975 in Mexico City, starting off the "UN Decade for Women" through 1985. As has been noted in the literature, the Holy See conducted a similar campaign for women's conferences as those on population, working to influence Muslim countries to oppose U.S. and Western-led delegations' emphasis on family planning and reproductive rights. Fractiousness between these groups of women, including the fact that a self-described terrorist member of the Palestine Liberation Organization was the Palestinian delegation leader, became evident at the 1985 Nairobi World Conference on Women. As was noted previously by Fraser, UN conferences, particularly recent ones, can easily be turned into media performances especially if controversy seems present. The Nairobi conference was one such event, where Muslim women publicly confronted Western women for "overemphasizing" demographic policies that hurt their countries. While this made good theater, it is also true that the women's movement in mostly non-

Muslim countries was by 1985 seasoned enough to treat the exchange as good fodder for the media.

For many, the ICPD in Cairo in 1994, the Beijing conference in 1995, and the Beijing +5 review in New York City in 2000 have been the most contentious and interesting conferences. Each conference has bested the media and NGO attendance record of the previous one. Starting with the ICPD, the structure of influence and representation was highly contested. The long-term, rather porous structure of discourse on document preparation leading up to the final UN conference may be shown in that the resolution calling for the Cairo conference on population and development happened in 1989, yet the preparations did not begin until 1991. Thereafter, five regional conferences were held, with the documents from these serving as the basis for the document of the Cairo conference's Plan of Action. During the three Prep Coms that took place between 1992 and 1994, the "agenda of that conference was set and the work program scheduled, and the document studied and filtered before given over to the official delegates of the world conference."[36]

There were two sets of issues on which the Holy See protested most strongly at the Cairo conference, having bracketed significant amounts of language throughout the Prep Coms. By the time of the official conference, the first two days had been spent in the general session solely on one section, paragraph 8.25, Chapter 8 (concerning health, morbidity, and mortality). The final draft before the conference, released on May 13, 1994, "kept the entire 8.25 section enclosed" at the request of the Holy See and Costa Rica, Honduras, El Salvador, Nicaragua, Malta, Benin, Poland, and Slovakia . . . among others."[37] Examples of the disputed language include the following:

> All governments, intergovernmental organizations and relevant NGOs are urged to deal openly and forthrightly with unsafe abortion as a major public health concern. . . . Governments are urged to assess the health and social impact of induced abortion, to address the situations that cause women to have recourse to abortion and to provide adequate medical care and counseling. Governments are urged to evaluate and review laws and policies on abortion so that they take into account the commitment to women's health and well-being . . . rather than relying on criminal codes or punitive measures.

In short, this section recognized that whether legal or illegal, abortions are sought around the world by women who cannot care for children in certain circumstances. Among other objections, the Holy See practiced the politics of divide and conquer, asserting that this was an example of how the United States "was imposing on other countries the 'right to abortion on demand.'" The Holy See consistently maintained across population conferences that it could not agree to language about safe abortion, for by its definition, abortion was never safe for the fetus.[38] Another was to the use of the term "unwanted pregnancy," because the Vatican's definition was that every pregnancy is wanted (by God). The chair of the Main Committee by this point urged the delegates "not to turn the ICPD into a conference on abortion."[39]

The EU's proposed changes to the text of paragraph 8.25 as presented at Prep Com 3 and subsequently signed on to by many countries on all continents included language that "all attempts should be made to eliminate the need for abortion" and that "in no case should abortion be promoted as a method of family planning." The latter clause had been included in the 1984 population conference in Mexico City, although the Holy See did not sign on to the ultimate document. The EU-revised paragraph also had a new ending to the effect that "any measure to provide for safe and legal abortion within the health system can only be determined at the national level through policy changes and legislative processes."[40] It was clearly hoped that this compromise would take account of most of the Holy See's objections. After that, the chair of the Main Committee proposed further revisions along the lines of the EU-sponsored changes. Yet he moved the paragraph's language so that all text followed from the beginning statement reaffirming the 1984 Mexico City principle that abortion not be used as a method of family planning and making the language about abortion policy being only open to change at the national legislative level even clearer. This revised text brought about the women's caucus objections that the Mexico City language had been applied in an overly broad fashion since 1994 to "preclude support for legal abortion counseling and services, and to prevent any discussion of the problem." However, the Holy See objected to the second compromise attempt, arguing that it could not accept any language stating that there are "circumstances in which abortion is legal" and therefore could not support the paragraph.[41] The official delegates' response was a chorus of "boos," the first time ever in the history of the UN. By this point, most Catholic states had abandoned the Vatican's position, including Ireland, Poland, and the Philippines. Only a few Latin American allies remained.

As is usually the case with contentious language, after more than two days of negotiations, the Main Committee chair referred this particular paragraph to a working group of fourteen members to report back in two days. It did not include the Holy See, whose delegation constantly worked behind closed doors, and all inquiries were referred to the press office. During the two days allotted to the working committee, the Holy See made public a statement signed by Mother Teresa, calling abortion "the greatest destroyer of peace in the world today."[42] Ultimately, the revised text authored by the working group, submitted on September 9, 1994, added some technical changes, such as going from "legal" to "not against the law" and included in a footnote the WHO's definition of unsafe abortion. This still did not satisfy the Holy See, which continued to oppose the paragraph and the chapter. It did record agreement with the majority of the draft document, for the first time at a UN population conference.

The ICPD secretariat had hoped for a noncontroversial conference that could concentrate on its main theme of environment and population. To this end, the secretariat, led by conference secretary-general Nafis Sadik, an Egyptian (woman) physician and head of the UNFPA, held thirty-five meetings to prepare and invited NGO participation. Similarly, under Sadik's leadership, "the original draft of the Plan of Action (after the Prep Coms had finished) was revised more than a dozen times." Some critics of the final product regarding demographic policy hold that the section was too "watered down" and "emphasized the individual's actions in parts of the world where the economy was declining and the religion and culture tend towards pronatalism."[43] However, many reasons have been given for why the ICPD spun out of control. One was that there were numerous fault lines among the participants, including the United States versus the Holy See, feminists versus the Holy See, feminists versus demographers, and some Muslim states (Iran, Libya) aligned with the Holy See against feminists and the United States. Both the Pope and the United States were accused of violating rules that were painstakingly worked out beforehand; for example, in April 1994, after the conclusion of Prep Com 3, Pope John Paul violated the previous agreement between the UNFPA and the Holy See in unilaterally releasing the text of his remarks after his meeting with Sadik. Part of the Pope's charges that the United States "was interested in foisting abortion rights on the world" through the UN, or as he called it the "culture of death," were unfortunately given evidence when in March 1994 the U.S. State Department also broke the rules by sending a cable to all diplomatic and consular posts stating that the "present language on abortion rights is inadequate, and that the United States believes that access to safe, legal and voluntary abortion is a fundamental right of all women."[44]

What is clear from both these governments breaking the rules is how important the abortion issue had become in international politics, seemingly never too far away from UN deliberations. Although the secretariat in the form of chair Nafis Sadik had tried to keep the abortion issue off the table, so to speak, by framing it in the section regarding public health and not gender rights, it was soon pulled from that section by Holy See rhetoric and elevated as one of the main issues. Alison McIntosh and Jason Finkle also note that in essence, the secretariat's strategy of trying to work out all possibly conflicting issues beforehand was inherently undercut by its other action of being broadly inclusive of NGOs in the preparatory process.[45] Examples of this are that NGOs for the first time had access to the conference halls and participated in the drafting of the Prep Com and final versions of the report. This seems to have formed a benchmark from which the UN cannot now retreat in its conference preparations. Other lines of opposition were seen, likely ascribed to a framework where the population "scientists" who had for so long controlled the definition of the issue were being opposed by an increasingly savvy active network of women's movement organizations.[46] Thus, women's movement organizations, for example, took the view that demographically driven programs "intended to act directly on fertility" were coercive and deprived a woman of her right to choose the timing of her children. Similarly, the feminist viewpoint has been that women's empowerment through education, job training, and "otherwise raising their status in the family and community" logically will lead to opting for smaller families.[47] Similarly, McIntosh and Finkle implicitly critique Sadik's chairing of the conference report preparations, as she "had been in contact with U.S. foundations, international women's groups especially from the U.S. and Nordic countries," and "remained firmly in control of drafting the document and did not hesitate to overrule groups whose views she did not endorse."[48] The new open and consultative approach begun by the woman secretary-general of the 1994 Cairo conference offended those who were accustomed to controlling the development and population areas through claiming to hold scientific expertise.

Some notable instances of women's groups activities to influence the document through the Prep Com process included circulating the "Women's Declaration on Population Policies," just prior to Prep Com 2, by the IWHC. This document reflected the input of twenty-four experts from five continents, stating as a goal the inclusion of a "broad range of reproductive health and development issues to be incorporated into population policies." As noted by McIntosh and Finkle, despite tension between the populationists and the IWHC at Prep Com 2, a decision was reached "to accommodate the women's demands" by including two new chapters: "Gender Equality and the Empowerment of Women" and "Reproductive Rights, Reproductive Health, and Family Planning." Similarly, language was added to reflect various possible framings of "family" and "families."[49] Needless to say, these would become the subject of Holy See disagreement at the final conference, chapters to which it ultimately did not sign on. Next, there was a campaign in the eleven months remaining until Prep 3, headed by feminists from various organizations, while "radical feminist views were sidelined by this coalition in an effort to win acceptance." As part of this lobbying strategy, feminists gave lectures, appeared on panels, lobbied the ICPD secretariat, presented briefings to State Department officials and members of Congress, participated in the Prep Coms, and "secured a number of seats on the final official delegation."[50] By Prep Com 3 in March 1994, feminists in the IWHC and the Women's Environment and Development Organization, chaired by Bella Abzug, among other things "a veteran of population conferences since Bucharest in 1974," put together a women's caucus with a membership of more than three hundred people from around the world. At Prep Com 3, the caucus held workshops and meetings, presented resolutions to delegates, acted as a transmitter of information between the caucus and floor debates, and "drafted new language on issues proving difficult."[51] Among these, of course, were issues of contraceptive and abortion rights as well as the definition of "family."

While McIntosh and Finkle seem willing to give the Holy See the benefit of sincere opposition to these ideas, they do not do the same for the women's caucus developed for Prep Com 3, stating that they "tended to close ranks in the face of Holy See opposition" and that feminists basically controlled the agenda by the end of Prep Com 3. Obviously this is an overstatement, given the evidence of argumentation that occurred during the final conference and the extreme measures taken to move beyond the abortion issue. The IPPF also notes that much of its own strategic plan of action adopted in 1992 was a strong influence on the 1994 Cairo ICPD program, firmly "moving the focus of family planning away from fertility targets and national demographic goals towards meeting the needs of individuals for family planning and reproductive and sexual health care."[52] Thus, if McIntosh and Finkle wish to blame an international feminist conspiracy for the results of the Cairo conference, they would seem to need to include the IPPF in the mix.

Overall, groups worked throughout the strong oppositional fractures and tension throughout the Cairo process to produce a Plan of Action representing some important firsts, especially for women. These included the "first mention in a UN document that abortion could be legal and safe" (not subscribed to by the Holy See), "the first time that women's interests in population matters had been broadly and seriously considered, and the unprecedented level of NGO participation" (and it should be added media coverage, especially of the NGO forum).[53] Another piece that was included for the first time was attaching long-term dollar amounts to the reproductive health and family planning aspects of the final program to link policy and implementation. Although the figures may not have been high enough, and the formula proposed redistribution of the financial responsibility from the then-practiced 25:75 ratio from recipient and donor countries to a 33:66 ratio, the Plan of Action was important for what it did address. In the intervening time, private donors such as George Soros have emerged to become important funders in this area.

Between 1975 and 1994, important discursive and real power shifts took place between women and men in the areas of development and global population policies. Danguilan has noted that prior to 1975, in the international development period, "women were considered to be passive beneficiaries of development aid and 'targets'

of population planning." The UN Decade for Women raised the con-
sciousness of women and of (some) population experts who saw
women as essential contributors to development.[54] Similarly,
Danguilan notes that the Cairo conference placed women at the center of population policies and called for "investments in improving
reproductive health presence in teaching programs" and general
improvements aimed at facilitating women's education, to lighten
their workloads and in "widening their employment opportunities."[55] Although some in the population establishment clearly dis-
agree with this emphasis on general educational, social, and employment empowerment as a means to raise girls' and women's
self-esteem and power to make choices, including in reproductive
rights, it highlights an important shift in UN text and understand-
ings. In addition to mentioning the safety of abortion and its importance for the first time, the Cairo Plan of Action discussed for the
first time women's right to sexual health, meaning "their right to
have control over and decide freely and responsibly on matters related to their sexuality."[56]

New issue framings by the Holy See at Cairo and again at
Beijing and New York have included the ideas that all feminists are
radical and that pro-choice ones wish to foster a culture of death
around the world. The culture of death rhetoric is found in most current HLI materials and on their website. Similarly, the Holy See
argues against the UN as a "world government," which if left to its
own devices would force all countries to adopt liberal initiatives.
This is puzzling, given the Vatican's own privileged representational
status within the UN and actions it has taken there and elsewhere to
lobby national governments against abortion. For example, even as
the Holy See railed against "world government by international
organizations" at Cairo, it quietly was trying to push through an
international conscience clause into the Plan of Action to elevate to
the international level laws adopted in some countries, including the
United States, where pro-life medical practitioners can opt out of
providing abortion procedures. Similarly, one study has shown that
since the formation of the EU, the Vatican has lobbied both the
European Parliament and the Council of Europe, having had more
success at the latter, which ironically has no legislative powers. Like
the UN, however, the council's authority derives from its moral
stances and persuasive powers on that basis, including on international organizations. For instance, the UN solicited the Council of

Europe Parliamentary Assembly's delegates during its Cairo preparations. A coalition of "stalwart Vatican allies and Christian Democrats strategically shifted the tone of the assembly's ensuing report to the UN" on reproductive rights issues.[57] Examples are that the assembly's original language, stressing that "all population policies must be based on freedom of choice," was amended by adding "in the belief that the choice of responsible procreation is an inalienable right of all couples." Similarly, in a sentence reading that "this freedom can only be exercised in a context of human dignity," the Christian Democrats added "based on the values of life and the family" after the word "freedom."[58] Across the Cairo and Beijing time frames, the Holy See consistently punched out two points throughout the international media: that reproductive choice equaled abortion and that changing definitions of family meant only giving rights to gays and lesbians. On the latter front, the Holy See expended much energy during 1994, the UN International Year of the Family, in defeating pro–civil union legislation both in the European Parliament and at the national legislative level in Italy.[59]

With regard to Holy See lobbying activity between the 1994 Cairo and 1995 Beijing conferences, Danguilan notes that all the language the Holy See had bracketed prior to Cairo was bracketed before the 1995 conference. This effectively ensured that the process start over again, to the effect that of "the 362 paragraphs in the draft document that went on to Beijing, 438 sets of brackets remained around disputed text in about 171 paragraphs"; others have noted the figure as at about 40 percent of the proposed Beijing document.[60] These were not due to the Holy See alone but included the "usual suspects" such as Islamic countries and Benin, Honduras, Costa Rica, Guatemala, Ecuador, Malta, and other Latin American countries.

However, many were surprised that after rebracketing most of the text that had been adopted at Cairo and was to be considered at Beijing, the Holy See also stated just before Beijing that it intended "not to reopen issues that had been decided to the satisfaction of many nations in Cairo." Many observers attributed this as an attempt to regain the stature lost by its intransigence at Cairo.[61] Another extremely savvy tactic was in naming one of the best and most prominent women law professors in the United States, Mary Ann Glendon of Harvard, as the head of the Holy See delegation to Beijing to counter the impression that only men were pro-life. The delegation itself was majority female. Another interesting shift practiced both by the Holy See and developed nations' delegations at Beijing was their decision to sit at the back of the plenary hall and let the delegations from the G-77 countries in effect run the show.

Ultimately, the Holy See found itself waging a mostly losing battle at Beijing, because the provisions on abortion and women's sexual rights were retained (although the latter was moved down ninety sections to one of the last paragraphs) and a new concept, that of gender, was added. This fueled the Holy See's attempt to define "gender" as "removing any distinctions between women and men in the law" and thus ultimately condoning homosexuality. Delegates were not buying the argument, however. The Holy See did not sign on to the health section of the document. In addition to the Program of Action containing the wording that women have the "sexual right" to say no to sexual intercourse, other firsts were evident in the document. Regarding abortion, which took time to negotiate but generated little of the heat evident at Cairo, the new phrasing at Cairo, enshrining women's rights to "quality health care and related information," survived the Beijing negotiations. The Holy See's action of attaching an international conscience clause to this phrasing, undertaken in the Beijing Prep Coms, was overruled in the final document. Another new abortion-related clause added in Beijing was to have governments "consider reviewing laws containing punitive measures against women who have undergone illegal abortions." A compromise with the Holy See was reached to add language from the Mexico City population conference in 1984 that "abortion should not be promoted as a method of family planning."[62] Another extremely important first in the Beijing Plan of Action was the inclusion of asking each head of state or chief delegate to list "country-specific actions that their nation would take to empower women within their borders."[63] About half of the 187 member states represented there complied. In short, an enforcement mechanism of sorts was built into the Plan of Action for the first time, enabling successive reviews of it to measure success such as happened at the Beijing +5 conference in New York in 2000.

Overall, the negotiations took even longer to conduct than at Cairo; agreement was not secured on the final Plan of Action until 5 A.M. on the last scheduled day.

## Important NGO Actors
## in the Transnational Framework

The International Planned Parenthood Federation, founded in Bombay, India, in 1952, and the International Women's Health Coalition have been overt but not the only actors working to preserve text concerning women's reproductive rights in UN Plans of Action and in national laws. Another chief actor in this coalition has been the U.S.-based CCFC, with branches in Canada and Mexico and a key representative for Catholic women wanting a broader range of reproductive choice options than permitted by the Vatican. CCFC recently celebrated its twenty-fifth anniversary and has included many different endeavors in its strategic repertoire. For example, it observes the activities of the Vatican constantly and informs its membership via newsletters and publications. Other recent CCFC campaigns include the "See Change" campaign in the 1990s, lobbying the UN Secretary-General to revoke the Holy See's special status in that the Holy See does not conform to the definition of a state by accepted measures, it does not represent women because women do not live in Vatican City, and it works against the reproductive rights of women. So far, CCFC has not been successful in changing the UN's mind, but it has been a high-profile campaign that has garnered much media interest. Other prominent campaigns currently include "Bishop Watch," to inform women around the world which Catholic bishops are lobbying most strongly against reproductive choice in various media, and "Condoms4Choice," arguing against the Catholic Church's prohibition in this matter. Within North America, the IPPF and CCFC are active in opposing attempts to limit women's reproductive rights, while CCFC usually confines itself to commentary on Church-linked actions. Another transnational actor is the National Abortion Federation, which includes as members NARAL from the United States and CARAL from Canada.

One of the more recent campaigns undertaken by the IPPF is devoting a link to its website entitled "Held to Ransom," in which it describes the impact of the global gag rule, based on the 1984 Mexico City policy from the population conference reinstated by President Bush in January 2001. Planned Parenthood has decided not to comply with the rule, stating that a member organization receiving USAID funds cannot "promote abortion." It thus states that its revenue loss from this policy decision has been $18 million since 2001, and "an estimated further 75 million has been lost with respect to grants and commodities" promised during the first five years of the millennium.[64] Another press piece on the website states that the estimated loss is about $8 million per year, "about 8 percent of the IPPF's total income." Other governments, notably those of the Netherlands, Sweden, the EU, and Japan, which also fund the UN Population Fund, have "stepped into" the breach to fund IPPF, as has the Bill and Melinda Gates Foundation, which has not completely replaced the $8 million per year but pledged the $8 million over five years.[65] Similarly, the Soros Foundation has been funding research and delivery projects for the Population Council since the end of the 1990s. Although all funds may not have been replaced, it appears that at least a good portion have. On its website, IPPF notes that currently, only about .05–.07 percent of its income goes toward abortion-related activities, and that most of it has been spent on counseling and post-abortion care.[66]

The results that IPPF draws from the loss of USAID funding include less money available for reproductive health education and contraceptives, which will violate the "ICPD 1994 Programme of Action pledge to make available universal access to a full range of high-quality reproductive health services, including for family planning and sexual health, by 2015."[67] However, the IPPF also focuses on the complicating factor of donor countries not meeting their 1994 ICPD funding commitments, combined with the fact of increasing demand for contraception.

Contraceptive use was only about 10 percent in the G-77 countries in the 1960s; today it is at about 40 percent. The IPPF claims that the lag in funding both through the UNFPA and the denial of USAID funding, at the level of each $1 million, could lead to "360,000 more unintended pregnancies, 150,000 more induced abortions, 800,000 additional maternal deaths, 110,000 additional infant deaths, and 140,000 additional deaths of children under 5."[68] Thus, IPPF's current strategy is to strongly emphasize the detrimental effects of withdrawal of USAID funding under the Mexico City policy/global gag rule reinstatement, and the shortfalls in member contributions to the UNFPA, as both immediately harmful but in direct violation of the 1994 Cairo Plan of Action, which the majority of 187 UN member nations signed.

One of the chief opponents of women's reproductive rights

active both in North America and UN Conferences is Human Life International, claiming to hold the status of the world's largest pro-life organization, its Canadian affiliate, Human Life International Canada, and two groups active in Mexico, Vida Humana based in Miami and Pro-Vida in Mexico.[69] In one recent high-profile campaign, HLI and HLIC members went to Chiapas, Mexico, and mounted loud public protests to rescind that legislature's amendments to its abortion law. They were successful in that the law was put on hold status, which is still in effect.

HLI was founded in Washington, D.C., in 1981 and claims sixty chapters in the United States and affiliates in eighty-nine countries. Its assets were valued at $12 million in 2001, with a reported annual income of $7.4 million. The organization was founded by a Catholic priest, Father Paul Marx, and experienced a "protracted internal struggle for control and allegations of impropriety by his successor," Father Thomas Euteneuer.[70] The group is well connected to the Vatican, always invited to participate in Vatican-sponsored conferences on sexuality and reproduction. HLI has a record of being extremist in its statements, such as using anti-Semitism and approving of doctors' murders in its statements. For these reasons, it was denied the coveted NGO consultative status with ECOSOC, which it sought in 1990. Among other reasons given for its denial was that HLI's stance was "against the purposes of the UN" and intolerant.[71] As noted by Francis Kissling and Jon O'Brien, such status is essential in the age of increased civil society importance, if a group is to have an impact at the UN. The Canadian affiliate, HLIC, ran into political problems of its own under director Theresa Bell, when Revenue Canada revoked its charity status due to its political activities. The response of HLI and HLIC was to begin a new organization to get around these barriers by incorporating in upstate New York in 1997 as the Catholic Family and Human Rights Institute (CAFHRI).[72] While it was formed to try to gain consultative status to ECOSOC, it has not yet done so and is still linked overtly to HLI, the United States, and Canada, especially through gaining funding. HLI holds the lowest roster status.

Given the organization's inability to gain this status, Austin Ruse, the recent director of CAFHRI and the founder of numerous anti-feminist, anti-reproductive rights organizations, has set up an office with a UN Plaza address and conducts lobbying at the UN and to national governments. The rather interesting position in which he finds himself is speaking out publicly against the UN as a body out to "rule the world" (which it cannot do, not having the power to overrule national policies) and run by "radicals," including feminists. At the same time, he has tried to get CAFHRI to become an NGO with consultative status. As noted by CCFC, the fact that CAFHRI overtly speaks out against the UN should disqualify it from ever receiving such recognition, as consultative status is only granted to organizations supporting the goals of the UN. CCFC has gained such status. Thus, CAFHRI is theoretically limited in its avenues to directly lobby the UN, but it has adopted strategies to advance its influence. Among them are its "Friday Fax," which "draws back the curtain on the UN activities and airs its dirty laundry." As Kissling and O'Brien have noted, CAFHRI takes advantage of the flexible UN procedures as to accreditation for conferences and the opportunity to speak, under its inclusive environment.[73] Thus, this group which only holds roster status with regard to ECOSOC, actively violates the rules of U.S. lobbying in accepting money from its Canadian affiliate (evidence of foreign influence on U.S. politics) yet locates its office on the UN Plaza and has registered at the recent UN conferences. CAFHRI has publicly admitted to taking money from HLI, the Homeland Foundation (a church-affiliated group located in New York City, headed by a priest), as well as from Brigham Young University Law School.[74]

One particularly aggressive way in which HLI and HLIC have participated under the CAFHRI umbrella at UN conferences was at the World Conference on Women in Beijing in 1995 and during the Prep Com process for the Beijing +5 review held in New York City in 2000. The varied tactics to this end included Austin Ruse, CAFHRI president, sending "urgent" e-mails to mobilize anti-feminist and pro-life groups to participate in the Prep Com process and hopefully the final conference so as to counteract the "radical feminist agenda" adopted in the 1995 Beijing Plan of Action, purportedly one of the "most radical and dangerous documents you can imagine."[75] Another strategy as detailed by CCFC is that of over-registration at UN conferences, where pro-life groups work to register despite their lack of accredited ECOSOC consultative status. As noted by CCFC, based on Ruse's organizing, many roster groups were able to take advantage of the lack of clear UN guidelines and arrange to pack the meetings.[76] They included REAL Women of Canada and the Campaign Life Coalition (the other two most prominent Canadian anti-choice groups that have existed since the 1980s), the International Right to Life Federation, the U.S. National Right to Life Committee, and the Society for Protection of Unborn Children, among others. Three hundred and fifty individuals from these groups managed to gain individual accreditation to attend the final conference, including the fact that half of the sixty REAL Women accredited delegates were members of the Franciscan Friars of Renewal, established in New York in 1987. This would seemingly duplicate the official representation given to the Holy See in abundance at all levels of the process. During the Prep Coms, CAFHRI worked with the twelve accredited pro-life groups to gain admittance to the Prep Coms. In addition to the previously mentioned groups attending the final conference, U.S.-based groups such as Eagle Forum, Alliance for Life, and Concerned Women for America and Family Life International got accreditation for the Prep Coms. The outcome of these strategies was that the Catholic Church was able to have a disproportionate number of representatives present covering every aspect of the preparatory meetings and conference than any other world religion.

In the final analysis, while not wishing to understate the impact these groups had on the final text of the 2000 Beijing +5 review, it is probably true that similar to the Holy See at the Cairo population conference in 1994 and the Beijing women's conference in 1995, their influences were procedural largely by tying the consultative procedures in knots and slowing down the process, as was their goal. However, the Holy See's presence as a nonmember state with voting status and its impact on the Cairo and Beijing texts must not be ignored either.

## Conclusion

What this analysis shows is that the site of contestation over women's sexuality and reproductive rights has moved increasingly to the international and transnational levels, as has indeed happened with trade agreements across the world and the consequent new political and social frameworks. Therefore, as analysts of attempts to curtail women's reproductive rights, we must be "smarter" about the variety of options available within different opportunity structures and the different tactics and types of rhetoric that may be employed.

While the Holy See and affiliated NGOs (such as HLI) and countries have found ways to work the UN system largely by attending Prep Coms, bracketing language, and withholding agreement so as to significantly reduce the amount of ground covered at the conference, other groups work to minimize their final effect on Plans of Action and on national laws. These groups include the IPPF and CCFC at the international level, as well as NAF and CCFC at the transnational level. The movement across the two policy periods in UN and transnational organizing history has not been without problems, both inside the UN and outside of it. To the extent that women's organizations across the world can now work together more strongly and have a better awareness of the existence of globally tied NGOs and the workings of the UN structure, the news for the future can be positive.

The parts of the political opportunity structure that were shown to matter most in policy periods one and two were access to the state and availability of allies, respectively. These factors have been found to be important in the country-based chapters, particularly moving into the later policy periods when different sides of the question display strategic learning from each other. Access to the state first, by the Vatican and then by women's NGOs at the parallel fora, got the groups into the same arena, during which time they sometimes talked to each other, at other times past each other. Similarly, availability of allies was crucial to both sides of the abortion struggle in getting their message out during conferences as well as in the intervening years. This worked for the Vatican in convincing certain countries (i.e., United States and Philippines) to change their country's official position on abortion or contraception in between conferences. Similarly, allies of the pro-choice side worked to get those arguments covered in the global media during conferences, especially the Beijing one, as well as negotiating with teams from other countries during the Prep Coms to carry over some of the gains won at the Cairo conference to Beijing.

Leverage politics, material and moral, have been used by both sides of the abortion issue. This was seen, for example, in the Vatican's claim that pro-choice groups have been using a world government, the UN, to further a pro-choice agenda, even while doing so itself at the Beijing conference in (unsuccessfully) trying to get a global conscience clause inserted in the Plan of Action. A sort of material politics was seen by the CCFC See Change strategy in attempting to have the Vatican removed from its status as a privileged voting nonstate member. The material argument came in through the CCFC and other groups' demonstration that the Vatican was having access to power structures and benefits such as office space and press contacts that no other advocacy group could obtain. Whether UN women's conferences are continued due to the controversy engendered by the Vatican and religious right groups worldwide is in doubt. However, it is quite likely that the future holds much more rhetoric of a material and moral nature being shot around the globe on the issue of abortion.

## Notes

1. Marilen J. Danguilan, *Women in Brackets: A Chronicle of Vatican Power and Control* (Manila: Philippine Center for Investigative Journalism, 1997); Arvonne Fraser, *The U.N. Decade for Women: Documents and Dialogue* (Boulder, Colo.: Westview Press, 1987).
2. Fraser, *The U.N. Decade for Women,* 10.
3. Danguilan, *Women in Brackets,* 3.
4. Fraser, *The U.N. Decade for Women,* 10–11; Danguilan, *Women in Brackets,* 25–38.
5. Fraser, *The U.N. Decade for Women,* 10–11.
6. Ibid., 6.
7. Ibid., 11.
8. Danguilan, *Women in Brackets,* 91, n. 1.
9. Fraser, *The U.N. Decade for Women,* 12–13.
10. Ibid.
11. Ibid., 14–15.
12. Ibid., 10–11.
13. Marian Sawer, "Femocrats and Ecorats: Women's Policy Machinery in Australia, Canada and New Zealand," in Carol Miller and Shahra Razavi, eds., *Missionaries and Mandarins: Feminist Engagement with Development Institutions* (London: Intermediate Technology Publications/United Nations Research Institute for Social Development, 1998), 112.
14. Danguilan, *Women in Brackets,* 202.
15. Ibid., 25–26. As Danguilan notes, the March 1991 first Prep Com for Cairo identified the six clusters of priority issues for the conference as population growth, distribution, structure, migration, environment, and development. While she notes that these initially concentrated mainly on demography, later attempts were made to "link these demographic factors with environmental effects." The second Prep Com in May 1993 worked to formulate the draft document, containing the demographic-environmental links as well as "using as comprehensive an approach to population as possible."

16. Danguilan, *Women in Brackets,* 3.

17. Ibid., 61–62.

18. Ibid., 18.

19. Ibid. As Danguilan points out, "the Holy See consists of the Pope, the College of Cardinals and the central departments that govern the Church. The Holy See has long been active in the UN and maintains full diplomatic relations with 157 countries."

20. UN website, www.un.org, ECOSOC link, accessed 8/20/03.

21. Danguilan, *Women in Brackets,* 18.

22. Ibid., 19.

23. Ibid., 20–21, nn. 1–3. Another point in this argument from the CRLP in New York is that according to the Montevideo Convention on the Rights and Duties of States (ratified December 1933 by Latin America and the United States), which provided an international legal definition of statehood, four criteria must be met: permanent population, a defined territory, government, and the capacity to enter into relations with other states. The CRLP argues that the Holy See fails to meet the first two criteria.

24. Ibid., 25–38.

25. Ibid., 10–11.

26. Ibid., 13, n. 7. Carl Bernstein, cited in research conducted by CCFC, stated that "Pio Laghi, a Vatican diplomat, went around the State Department . . . in at least six secret meetings at the White House" (concerning Reagan's anti-Communist agenda in Poland) and that "in response to concerns of the Vatican, the Reagan administration agreed to alter its foreign aid program to comply with the Church's teaching on birth control."

27. Ibid., 13.

28. Ibid., 9.

29. Ibid., 15. Danguilan cites Paul Demeny, "Bucharest, Mexico City, and Beyond," *Population and Development Review* 11, no. 1 (March 1985), who wrote that in six months alone in India in 1976, over six million people were sterilized.

30. C. Alison McIntosh and Jason L. Finkle, "The Cairo Conference on Population and Development: A New Period?" *Population and Development Review* 21, no. 2 (June 1995): 232–260.

31. Fraser, *The U.N. Decade for Women.*

32. Danguilan, *Women in Brackets,* 14.

33. McIntosh and Finkle, "The Cairo Conference on Population and Development."

34. Ibid., 228.

35. Danguilan, *Women in Brackets,* 187.

36. Ibid., 2–3. As Danguilan notes, the regional discussions for the Cairo conference were structured as follows: Asia/Pacific, Africa, Europe/North America, Arab States, and Latin America/Caribbean.

37. Ibid., 93.

38. Ibid., 94.

39. Ibid., 95.

40. Ibid.

41. Ibid., 96–97.
42. Ibid., 98.
43. McIntosh and Finkle, "The Cairo Conference on Population and Development," 230.
44. Ibid., 245–246.
45. Ibid., 227, 235–245.
46. Ibid., 225–250. McIntosh and Finkle adopt a critical tone toward the international women's movement for altering the framework that demographers had used for the better part of thirty-five to forty years.
47. Ibid., 227.
48. Ibid., 230.
49. Ibid., 238.
50. Ibid., 239.
51. Ibid.
52. IPPF, "The Need for Family Planning: Remaining Challenges," www.ippf.org, accessed 10/2003.
53. McIntosh and Finkle, "The Cairo Conference on Population and Development, 249–250.
54. Danguilan, *Women in Brackets,* 11.
55. Ibid., 14.
56. Ibid., 192.
57. Gordon Urquhart, "Conservative Catholic Influence in Europe: The Vatican and Family Politics," CCFC, 1997, 10–13.
58. Ibid., 11.
59. Ibid., 13.
60. Ibid., 158, 189; Jeanette H. Johnson and Wendy Turnbull, "The Women's Conference: Where Aspirations and Realities Met," *International Family Planning Perspectives* 21, no. 4 (December 1995): 155–159.
61. Johnson and Turnbull, "The Women's Conference," 156.
62. Ibid., 156–157.
63. Ibid., 159.
64. IPPF website, www.ippf.org, link to "Held to Ransom" website, www.heldtoransom.org, accessed 10/2003.
65. IPPF, "The Gates Foundation and the International Planned Parenthood Announce," press release, December 11, 2000; IPPF, "Donor Governments and DAC [Development Assistance Committee]: Snapshot of Donor Contributions," *DAC Watch* 3 (December 2000), accessed at www.ippf.org, 10/2003.
66. IPPF, *Newsletter for Donors* 3, no. 1 (February 2001), accessed at wwwippf.org, 10/2003.
67. IPPF website, "The Need for Family Planning," www.ippf.org, accessed 10/2003.
68. IPPF website, *European Network's DAC* [Development Assistance Committee] *Watch* 3 (2000), accessed at www.ippf.org, 10/2003.
69. Frances Kissling and Jon O'Brien, Catholics for a Free Choice, "Bad Faith at the UN; Drawing Back the Curtain on the Catholic Family and Human Rights Institute," 2001, 7.

70. Ibid.
71. Ibid., 7–8. Kissling and O'Brien cite Front Lines Research, April 1995.
72. Ibid., 6–9.
73. Ibid., 17–18.
74. Ibid., 15.
75. Ibid., 19–20.
76. Ibid.

# 6

## Looking to the Future: New Challenges to Legal and Social Rights

Many interesting threads can be drawn from the preceding discussion concerning the status of reproductive rights in the three countries under study and regarding the strength of pro- and anti-choice movements within North America. Although the news is not all discouraging, many discouraging trends have arisen at the same time as the opening of UN conferences to NGOs and women, namely that anti-choice movement groups have learned to function quite effectively within the UN structure and have, as in the 1994 International Conference on Population and Development (Cairo), strongly affected both the proceedings and final Plan of Action.

By using different criteria, the triad of nations in this study may be grouped in two ways. First, if changes to the state-society relationship are examined, Canada and Mexico would be grouped more closely together, both having undergone significant change since the 1980s. Canada underwent a strong shift regarding its traditional Westminster model of parliamentary supremacy with the enactment of the 1982 Charter of Rights and Freedoms as part of its overall constitutional reframing project. The result was that the Canadian Supreme Court acquired newly found power and an early example of it was to use Section 7 of the Charter, protecting the rights to "life, liberty and security of the person" to overturn the hospital-based, therapeutic abortion committee system in place since Parliament's enactment in 1969. Mexico started to see cracks in its legitimating facade of pseudo-democracy in the 1980s, due to pressures both from outside (global economy, UN conferences, and global public opinion) and inside (party shifts, abdication of corporate representatives from the PRI to the PAN, media opening away from governmental control, and ultimately legitimation of increased civil society participation). This resulted in opposition parties gaining control for the first time in state legislatures and, even more important, for the mayor of Mexico City and the city council. It also resulted in a push for greater inclusion of women in electoral seats, campaign themes, and more women-friendly public policies, including the Robles law of 2000.

Along the more current axis of where the countries are today, Canada and the United States would be grouped more closely together, with Mexico the outlier. This grouping acknowledges the vast difference between constitutional rights to privacy and liberty—in the United States as enshrined in *Roe v. Wade* (1973) and *Morgentaler* (1988) in Canada—and that in both societies, the need for abortion services has remained virtually constant while the availability of facilities to provide surgical abortions has declined. In these two countries, abortion is paradoxically legal but less available than ten years ago. Mexico retains abortion as a federal crime, with the universal exemption for rape and incest, which is not always allowed as has been seen. Both the United States and Canada had intervening abortion policy periods of federal accountability and oversight (the United States from 1973 until the 1980s and Canada from 1969 until 1988) between the first stage of abortion policymaking and the current third stage. While the two federal governments have been only too willing to get out of the business of abortion, instead turning much of the responsibility for rights implementation (United States) and access to insured health care (Canada) back to the states and provinces, the fact that the second period existed in each country and not yet in Mexico is quite important. In the United States, women still have the core of *Roe* to draw on in terms of the right to privacy in the first trimester, as acknowledged by *Casey* author Justice Sandra Day O'Connor, even as their access to such abortion procedures has been greatly diminished. In Canada, the 1988 *Morgentaler* decision is the legal footing for women's pro-choice rights, enshrined in the language of "liberty and security of the person." This decision overturned the inconsistent access women had to the only legal abortions previously available, in hospitals. However, the shrinking availability of health-care dollars and facilities has accomplished in Canada what the pro-life movement in the United States has achieved, which is to shrink access to legal, safe abortion.

The difference between these two countries and Mexico is that there is still a relatively consistent framework in which safe, legal abortions may be accessed. This does not exist in Mexico and will not unless and until the federal government takes on the willingness to oversee the implementation of a pro-choice framework. Mexico will be caught in its second period of abortion policymaking, analogous to the first in the United States and Mexico, until the PAN government leaves federal office. Without such an intervention, access to abortion within constitutionally prescribed grounds will not happen for Mexican women. It is true that rural women and those of limited means have been especially hard hit by the decreasing availability of abortion access and medical dollars in the United States and Canada. This is true for any type of state program, where women constitute the highest percentage dependent on the program and statistically the most hurt when it is withdrawn. In Mexico, even the constitutionally prescribed exemptions to the national illegality do not get implemented under the current climate, as seen in the Baja case of *Paulina* in 1999. It is even more true in Mexico than in the United States and Canada that women's access to abortion and reproductive health care generally is inconsistent and largely unavailable outside major cities in a few states. Similarly, the same difference between women who have health-care coverage or independent means to access a legal abortion in Canada or the United States and an illegal one is magnified in Mexico. Finally, because all three countries are federations and legal politics are often enshrined within political and regional rivalries, it remains the case that where a woman lives determines her fate in terms of abortion and health-care access. The disparity is worst in Mexico, where illegal abortion is one of the highest causes of maternal death.

## Status of Abortion Politics Within the Three Countries

The most helpful approach from the wide-ranging comparative social movement literature has been to combine the "political opportunity structure" model of Sidney Tarrow and the advocacy network strategies theorized by Margaret Keck and Kathryn Sikkink. We have combined the knowledge of political opportunity structural shifts across abortion policy periods in Canada, the United States, and Mexico to postulate what the next period might bring. Similarly, the network strategies of the transnational pro-choice and pro-life movements have been shown as changing with policy period changes in the three countries and in certain instances helping to force those changes.

Starting with the United States, three policy periods and political opportunity structure shifts were identified. The first period stretched from the mid-nineteenth century until the 1960s. This was a period where physicians basically secretly provided abortions although they were illegal nationally, with some groups, notably mainstream Protestant churches and some health providers (often nurses) working to lobby physicians directly for increased access, not legislators.

The political opportunity structure was more or less closed to influence from civil society actors. Access to the state in the form of finding state legislatures willing to pass laws concerning the conditions under which abortion was to be performed was helpful to physicians. In this way, as the medical profession organized itself, it also organized its turf and was able to get penalties established for nonphysicians performing abortions. Just as important to physicians was access to the state during the second period when they found themselves hurt by the laws they had earlier worked to pass and began lobbying for national legal reform. The need for this reform was ultimately precluded by the 1973 *Roe* decision. The framing strategies used by the medical network, in Keck and Sikkink's terminology, were basically for doctors to use moral leverage mainly on state legislators and such other members of the public who were interested. They mainly stated that it was good for the United States that they be the ones to perform reproductive services, for only they could ensure the country's health.

The second period in the United States was led off by the Supreme Court's rather unanticipated *Roe v. Wade* decision. Unlike the first period, in which the consensus of the medical experts and legislators was that the appropriate location for action on abortion policy was at the state level and that the relevant discourse was to allow the "experts" to decide when abortion was indicated, the second period was one where doctors and the newly formed second-wave women's movement worked as allies to shift the main locus of abortion policy activity to the national level. They were aided and essentially preempted in this by the *Roe* decision, after having worked for a few years toward the end of nationalizing the policy debate in the late 1960s. All three elements of the political opportunity structure appear to have been quite important in enabling the shift to the second period. These elements included a change in political alignments to favor more civil society action and public questioning in the wake of the Vietnam war, the availability of women's movement actors to help doctors in their nationalizing quest, and access to the state in terms of a sympathetic Supreme Court. The advocacy network types of argumentation used were moral leverage, where doctors worked to persuade state legislators that the previously enacted penalties were being enforced too vigorously, and women's movement claims about autonomy of women and equal rights. Women's movement groups, such as NARAL and NOW, began to use the strategy of accountability politics toward the end of the second period, as they became more comfortable using the Washington-insider strategies of lobbying and campaign contributions.

The start of the third period in U.S. abortion policy history was definitively set off by the Supreme Court's 1989 *Webster* decision, which offered legitimation for some state restrictions on abortion (such as use of public medical facilities, counseling requirements, and conscience clauses). It was soon followed by the 1992 *Casey* decision upholding more state restrictions, such as twenty-four-hour waiting periods, viability testing, and most important, removed the *Roe* trimester framework as the benchmark of balancing women's rights to privacy versus the "compelling" state's interest to intervene. *Casey* thus rolled back both the time clock of women's pregnancy and that of national politics in suggesting that the state could have a compelling interest to intervene as early as the first trimester, which had to be balanced with its interest in "protecting potential life."

The outcomes in these two cases at this time showed the cumulatively greater strength of the pro-life movement, which had quickly begun organizing directly after the *Roe* decision. The movement worked at two levels. The first level was working to pass state legislation that would conflict with *Roe*'s definition enough to send abortion back to the Supreme Court for a second look, which happened in *Webster* in 1989. The second level was to work through Congress, which also was fruitful in that the Hyde Amendment, forbidding federal Medicaid funds and passed within a year of *Roe,* was soon followed by a majority of the states passing similar legislation, upheld as constitutional.

The most important piece of the political opportunity structure in enabling the third period to start was the notion of changing political alignments, seen as sweeping electoral victory for the Republican Party at the presidential and Senate levels in 1980 and the beginning of President Ronald Reagan's "new federalism" model of devolving administrative and financial responsibility back to the states. This is very similar to what has happened in the Canadian situation since the late 1980s. In this third period of U.S. abortion policy, the prevailing view of the governmental majority is that restrictions on abortion by the states are allowable and will be tolerated, as are inequalities in access based on where a woman lives or her financial status. These inequalities are exacerbated by the current financial situation of states (and provinces), which are concurrently more strapped for money and responsible for funding more health services than in the past.

It is also clear that the change in political alignments to a Republican majority, favoring pro-life views, in the third period provided access to the state for pro-life groups where the opposite had been true in the previous nationalized period. Some examples have been the repeated attempts to pass "partial birth abortion" legislation in Congress and the sequential implementation of global gag orders on USAID funds by succeeding presidential administrations. Therefore, since the late 1980s, when most of the UN women's conferences have taken place, the pro-life position has been in a more privileged position in terms of support at the highest levels of government and funding to attend conferences than was true in the 1970s. The advocacy network strategies among pro-choice groups such as NAF and NARAL have been to hold politicians accountable by holding press conferences and giving or withholding campaign funds (also viewed as material leverage). They have also strongly alluded to the symbolism inherent in *Roe* and the women's movement of the 1970s not to let the status of women's equality and right to choose be vitiated. The pro-life groups, especially the Christian Coalition and Human Life Institute, have been equally adept at tailoring their rhetoric across the second and third policy periods, from "fetal rights" to the global "culture of death," the latter echoing the Vatican's statements at UN conferences. As has also been shown, in the third period in both the United States and Canada, pro-choice and pro-life groups have displayed the results of having learned rhetorical twists and strategic options from each other. Also, for the sake of survival, both sides have become truly transnational, the kinds of advocacy networks envisioned by Keck and Sikkink.

The third period is still in place in the United States today, where state autonomy to restrict abortion is almost as wide as it was up until 1973. While states cannot outlaw abortion outright, as they previously could, they also have the freedom to enact new and creative restrictions not even imaginable in the late 1960s. The third period also has seen the introduction of violent anti-abortion groups such as Randall Terry's Operation Rescue and Joseph Scheidler's Pro-Life Action League and an escalation in physician and clinic staff murders and attacks. It is somewhat ironic that the radical fringe would escalate on the abortion issue precisely during the time when the pro-life side has been seen as very successful in rolling back the post-*Roe* clock of state abortion availability in the legislatures.

The Canadian evolution across the three policy periods of abortion policy has been quite similar to that of the United States in certain respects, a surprising trajectory because the two political systems are so very different. Indeed, it is hard to imagine three more different political systems than the ones chosen for this study. The central concepts that Canada shares with the United States over the three historical periods include (1) the fact that the first and second policy periods were largely structured around doctors' needs and initiatives (combined with the presence of women's movement actors in the coalition during the second period); (2) the political opportunity structure criterion of the importance of shifting political alignments in bringing about both the second period and the third, evidenced by a strong party shift in government (which has also been of crucial importance to Mexico during its second period); and (3) the national governments' display of surprisingly little concern in the third period that women still die or are left infertile as in the 1950s and 1960s and currently in Mexico, due to the unequal access to abortion under the "constitutionally legal" framework.

As in the United States, the first Canadian period centered around the organization of the medical profession and its desire to enshrine control over the performance of abortion and contraception services. Unlike the United States, where criminal law is chiefly promulgated by the states, the Canadian situation is one where the federal government occupies this field, and so the first abortion restrictions were put into the federal criminal code by the twentieth century. Also as in the United States previously and currently in Mexico, this framework left some wiggle room for doctors to perform abortions if they so wished; it did not prevent them from being prosecuted, which was the main catalyst for lobbying toward greater national regulation, thus bringing about the second period with the 1969 Criminal Code of Canada revisions in the omnibus amendments. As in the United States, physicians enjoyed a near monopoly of access to federal members of Parliament during the first period on Canadian abortion policy, and they used much the same moral leverage as their U.S. counterparts, that having doctors hold a monopoly on abortion provision was a good thing for the country.

The move toward the second period, in which the key early event was the 1969 decriminalization of abortion, brought about a shifting political alignment in which the national Liberal government of Prime Minister Pierre Trudeau was re-elected in 1968 with a clear majority that his previous government had not possessed. Therefore, he was willing to act on revisions to the Criminal Code of Canada, including those on abortion, after this election. Similarly, physicians still had access to the state and were able to lobby the federal government to more or less enact the bill that they wished to see happen. Because most parts of the second-wave women's movement were as yet unformed or nascent, these groups became an important set of available allies as the second period—in which abortion was believed to be a national policy best conducted at the national level—progressed. In the early part of the second period, the moral leverage and accountability used by the doctors was similar to those of the first period, but as women became organized into groups in the 1970s, two distinct pro-choice themes were heard. The first was the liberal democratic "women's autonomy" used by CARAL and NAC; the second was the more radical "women must have complete control over production and reproduction" used by OCAC and other groups centered in Toronto.

Another key event in the political opportunity structure taking place during the second period but ultimately underlying the event that set off the third period was that of the Charter entrenchment in 1982. After this, women's groups began to advocate in even stronger terms for women's constitutional equality as promised in the Charter, helped along by newly formed legal groups such as LEAF. The pro-life side was much weaker at that point than it became in the 1990s, such that arguments for including fetal life as protected in the Charter, which went unheeded, were given by very small groups such as Campaign Life.

The 1988 *Morgentaler* decision by the Canadian Supreme Court was a turning point from the second to third policy periods in different ways, constituting at first a positive opening in the political opportunity structure for pro-choice groups and now perhaps a negative one. The potential negative assessment is formed on the same basis as that in the United States: that turning a thorny policy over to the subnational governments that probably have less will to enforce it than the federal government is in itself a de facto defeat for the pro-choice side. This is coupled with the North American neoliberal policy shift apparent in Canada since the 1980s, where the federal contribution to health care and insurance has declined, while requiring more of the provinces. The *Morgentaler* decision allowed increased civil society input into the process in the media as court interveners. This court decision can be identified as one of the most important examples in Canadian democracy of showing that the old Westminster model, if not dead, at least was declining due to the need of Parliament to move over and make room for the judicial branch. Moreover, it was also true that *Morgentaler* retained a clause for parliamentary action that *Roe* did not. The political opportunity structural shift that just preceded the third period was the large Conservative victory nationally in 1984. Although the Conservatives were called upon to try to reinstate a national framework after two 1989 Supreme Court cases threatened the post-*Morgentaler* framework, splits within the party were such that no compromise was ultimately possible.

The ways in which the post-*Morgentaler* framework have not been kind to the pro-choice movement are that provinces are still free to restrict their funding of insurance coverage for abortion services, to either not have it at all (PEI) or to restrict it to hospitals (Saskatchewan). Again, the same checkerboard system of access that was in place prior to *Morgentaler* remains in place, the only difference being that clinics are now legal but not necessarily funded.

As in the United States, it is not clear whether the country's evolution to the third stage of the abortion policy period is positive or negative. Although constitutional equality on abortion matters does exist, the process of accessing an abortion in a large country with unevenly dispersed facilities and funding schemes does not appear to be very easy. The nature of shifting abortion policy funding almost completely to the provinces is similar to the U.S. devolutionary process in the third period, yet the political opportunity structure in

Canada has not granted access to the state at the subnational level to the pro-life movement as it has in the United States. This is largely because of the difference in the constitutional division of powers, where provincial legislatures have not been given the authority to affect the conditions surrounding abortion other than licensing of facilities and funding them. In terms of framing strategies, both pro-choice and pro-life options demonstrate what they have learned over the years as well as the fact that both sides have learned from their counterparts in the United States and at UN conferences. Thus, the Canadian pro-choice movement continues to advocate to keep women's rights as strongly entrenched as the day the Charter was enacted, calling upon the national government to use its penalty of fining provinces that do not fund "medically necessary services," as detailed in health legislation. Pro-life groups continue to talk about the "selfishness" of the women's movement and the "culture of death" that surrounds a government that does not protect fetal life on the same order as the rights of the person.

In Mexico, the two policy periods discussed were those of nearly unlimited federal control over public debate and policy until the 1980s and how civil society has been opening since that time. Thus, states began to legislate some limited exceptions to the national prohibition on abortion in the 1980s. Since then, however, most of the parties have talked about abortion as a potential policy for liberalization, except the Christian Democratic PAN, the national ruling party since 2000.

Currently, it seems that the Mexican situation is best described by placing it in the second period, that of increasing federal attention to abortion policy, although it is not yet widely agreed by politicians or the public that the federal government is the best lobbying focus. Yet because abortion is still nationally illegal, Mexico retains elements of the first and third policy periods as seen in the United States and Canada, namely, that doctors have organized rather self-protective schemes in which they can work around the system, as in the first period. In the third period, where abortion is putatively legal in Mexico, it is at the state level—with widely varying access to such services—and is tolerated by the Mexican government as well as by third-period U.S. and Canadian national governments.

With regard to the political opportunity structure, changing political alignments toward the end of the first period in the 1980s, such that the PRI was broken in half internally and could no longer retain its absolute monopoly on Congress, the presidency and state governments gave access to a newly revitalized civil society. At the same time, the availability of allies across civil society was key, including labor groups and women's groups that traditionally did not align themselves with feminism. On another dimension, the first period in the UN system on abortion rights, the "development" period, gave international donors such as Planned Parenthood (Mexfam) a foothold into Mexico to first distribute contraceptives and information on a sub rosa basis and then later with the approval of the federal Health Ministry. Similarly, newer transnational actors such as IPAS and the Soros Foundation have been instrumental in providing equipment for abortion training and completion of procedures at hospitals, which is usually allowable by law. To the extent that U.S.-based actors, including Planned Parenthood and the HLI (Pro-Vida) have been active in Mexico longer than in Canada, the transnational linkage has provided access to the state for both sides of the abortion question. Similarly, the presence of a strong ally in the Catholic Church for the pro-life organizations has been helpful to their efforts.

Issue framings by the pro-choice groups such as GIRE, Mexfam, and IPAS in the second period since the late 1980s have included moral and material leverage, namely, that Mexican women and Mexico in general would be better off if women had complete control over their reproductive lives. However, they have been countered by Pro-Vida's traditionalist claims, bolstered by the current Christian Democratic government of President Vicente Fox, that women's traditional roles must be followed, which include having many children.

If there is any key theme to come from the U.S.-Mexico-Canada comparison, it is this: that under these three divergent constitutional and health-care frameworks, women who have the advantages of time, money, providers, and geographical location are still "okay" under the current framework, while those lacking one or more of these crucial resources will either opt for an unsafe abortion, running a one-in-three risk of dying, as in Mexico, or perhaps opting out of having an abortion altogether.

## Appendix: Cases on Abortion Policy in the United States, Canada, and Mexico Across the Policy Periods

| Case | Year | Issues | Disposition |
|------|------|--------|-------------|
| | | U.S. Cases | |

First Policy Period, 1860–1973:
Subnational Control of Abortion Policy and Public Contestation

| Case | Year | Issues | Disposition |
|------|------|--------|-------------|
| *Griswold* | 1965 | "Right to privacy" for married couples regarding contraception upheld | Pro-contraception |
| *Belous* | 1969 | Prosecution of California doctor for "procuring" abortions | Anti-choice |

Second Policy Period, 1973–1989:
Nationalization of Abortion Policy and Discourse

| Case | Year | Issues | Disposition |
|------|------|--------|-------------|
| *Roe* | 1973 | Abortion ban | Pro-choice |
| *Doe* | 1973 | Hospital and doctor restrictions, residency requirement | Pro-choice |
| *Bigelow* | 1975 | State law prohibiting newspaper ads for abortion services | Pro-choice |
| *Danforth* | 1976 | Parental and spousal consent, saline abortions, record keeping and reporting | Pro-choice |
| *Beal* | 1977 | Medicaid funding limits and the Social Security Act | Pro-choice |
| *Maher* | 1977 | Medicaid funding limits and equal protection | Pro-choice |
| *Poelker* | 1977 | Abortion in public hospitals | Pro-choice |
| *Colautti* | 1979 | Physician's duty to fetus | Pro-choice |
| *Belotti* | 1979 | Parental and judicial bypass procedure | Pro-choice |

*continues*

| Case | Year | Issues | Disposition |
|------|------|--------|-------------|
| *Harris* | 1980 | Constitutionality of Hyde Amendment | Anti-choice |
| *Matheson* | 1981 | Parental notice | Anti-choice |
| *City of Akron* | 1983 | Second-trimester hospitalization, parental consent, waiting period, informed consent lecture | Pro-choice |
| *Planned Parenthood (Kansas City)* | 1983 | Second-trimester abortions in hospital pathology report, second doctor after viability, parental consent with judicial bypass | Pro-choice |
| *Simopoulos* | 1983 | Second-trimester abortions only in state-licensed facilities | Anti-choice |
| *Thornburgh* | 1986 | Informed consent lecture, waiting period, physician's duty to fetus, record keeping and reporting, second physician requirement | Pro-choice |
| *Zbaraz* | 1987 | Parental notification, waiting period | Pro-choice |

Third Policy Period, 1989 Onward:
A Return to Subnational Abortion Politics

| Case | Year | Issues | Disposition |
|------|------|--------|-------------|
| *Webster* | 1989 | Preamble defining life, restrictions on public facilities and funding, fetal viability testing | Anti-choice |
| *Hodgson* | 1990 | Two-parent notice and judicial bypass procedure | Anti-choice |
| *Akron Center* | 1990 | Parental notice and judicial bypass procedure | Anti-choice |

*continues*

| Case | Year | Issues | Disposition |
|------|------|--------|-------------|
| *Rust* | 1990 | First Amendment challenge to executive branch regulation against abortion counseling by agency getting federal family planning grants | Pro-choice |
| *Casey* | 1992 | Informed consent lecture, waiting period, spousal notice, parental consent, record keeping and reporting, definition of medical emergency | Anti-choice |
| *Bray* | 1993 | Use of 1871 Civil Rights Act to enjoin protestors from blocking abortion clinics as conspiracy to violate civil rights | Anti-choice |
| *NOW* | 1994 | Abortion clinics can use the federal racketeer–influenced and *Corrupt Organizations Act* to sue anti-abortion protest groups for damages | Pro-choice |
| *Madsen* | 1994 | First Amendment challenge to Florida state court injunction creating a buffer zone between abortion clinic and protestors. | Pro-choice |
| *Lambert* | 1997 | Parental notice and judicial bypass procedure | Anti-choice |
| *Carhart* | 2000 | Late-term abortions; upholds requirement of women's health exemption | Pro-choice |

*continues*

| Case | Year | Issues | Disposition |
|------|------|--------|-------------|

**Canadian Cases**

Second Policy Period, 1969–1988:
Nationalization of Abortion Law and Medical Insurance Funding

| | | | |
|------|------|--------|-------------|
| *Morgentaler* | 1988 | Strikes down the therapeutic abortion committee requirement in the 1969 criminal code amendments based on Charter, Section 7, "Life, Liberty and Security of the Person" | Pro-choice |

Third Policy Period, 1988 Onward:
Returning Abortion and Funding Administration Primarily to Provinces

| | | | |
|------|------|--------|-------------|
| *Borowski* | 1989 | Attempt to have Supreme Court protect fetal life in Charter, Section 7 | Pro-choice |
| *Daigle* | 1989 | Boyfriend's Quebec injunction against girlfriend's abortion overturned | Pro-choice |

**Mexican Case**

Second Policy Period, 1988 Onward:
The Opening to Civil Society Participation

| | | | |
|------|------|--------|-------------|
| *Paulina* | 1999 | Abortion denied to minor in Baja California in defiance of the legal rape exemption | Anti-choice |

# Acronyms

| | |
|---|---|
| ACLU | American Civil Liberties Union |
| ALI | American Law Institute |
| AMA | American Medical Association |
| ASA | Association for the Study of Abortion |
| AUL | Americans United for Life |
| BC | British Columbia |
| CAFHRI | Catholic Family and Human Rights Institute |
| CARAL | Canadian Abortion Rights Action League |
| CCF | Cooperative Commonwealth Federation |
| CCFC | Catolicas por el Derecho a Decidir (Catholics for a Free Choice) |
| CIHI | Canadian Institute for Health Information |
| CMA | Canadian Medical Association |
| CNC | National Peasant Confederation |
| CNOP | National Confederation of Popular Organizations |
| CONAMUP | Coordinadora Nacional del Movimiento Urbano Popular (National Coordinating Committee of Urban Popular Movements) |
| CRLP | Center for Reproductive Law and Policy |
| CRM | Consejo Regional de Mujeres (Women's Regional Council) |
| CTM | Confederation of Mexican Workers |
| DF | Distrito Federal (Federal District) |
| ECOSOC | Economic and Social Council |
| ERA | Equal rights amendment |
| FDA | Food and Drug Administration |

| | |
|---|---|
| FFQ | Fédération des femmes du Quebec (Federation of the Women of Quebec) |
| FNALDM | Frente Nacional por la Libertad y los Derechos de las Mujeres (National Front for Women's Rights and Liberty) |
| GEM | Grupo de Educacion Popular con Mujeres (Group for Women's Popular Education) |
| GDP | Gross domestic product |
| GIRE | Grupo de Informacion en Reproduccion Elegida (Group for Information on Reproductive Choice) |
| G-77 | Group of 77 |
| HLI | Human Life International |
| HLIC | Human Life International Canada |
| ICPD | International Conference on Population and Development |
| IMF | International Monetary Fund |
| IMSS | Mexican Social Security Institute |
| IPAS | (a nonprofit organization that protects women's reproductive health and rights in the United States and abroad) |
| IPPF | International Planned Parenthood Federation |
| IWHC | International Women's Health Coalition |
| LEAF | Women's Legal Education and Action Fund |
| MP | Members of Parliament |
| NAC | National Action Committee on Status of Women |
| NAF | National Abortion Federation |
| NAFTA | North American Free Trade Agreement |
| NARAL | National Association for Repeal of Abortion Laws (renamed in 1997 the National Abortion and Reproductive Rights Action League) |
| NAWL | National Association of Women and the Law |
| NDP | New Democratic Party |
| NGOs | Nongovernmental organizations |
| NOW | National Organization for Women |
| NRLC | National Right to Life Committee |
| OCAC | Ontario Coalition for Abortion Clinics |
| PAC | Political action committee |
| PAN | National Action Party |
| PEI | Prince Edward Island |
| PM | Prime Minister |

| | |
|---|---|
| PMR | Party of the Mexican Revolution |
| PNR | Party of the National Revolution |
| PPM | Promocion Politica de la Mujer (Women's Policy Bureau) |
| PR | Proportional representation |
| PRD | Partido de la Revolucion Democratica (Party of the Democratic Revolution) |
| PRI | Institutional Revolutionary Party |
| RCAR | Religious Coalition for Abortion Rights |
| RHPF | Reproductive Health and Family Planning Program |
| SHA | Society for Humane Abortion |
| TAC | Therapeutic abortion committee |
| UN | United Nations |
| UNFPA | UN Population Fund |
| USAID | U.S. Agency for International Development |
| WHO | World Health Organization |

# Selected Bibliography

Antrobus, Peggy. *The Global Women's Movement: Issues and Strategies for the New Century.* Black Point, NS: Fernwood, 2004.

Armstrong, Pat, and Hugh Armstrong. *Wasting Away: The Undermining of Canadian Health Care.* Toronto: Oxford University Press, 1996.

Author's interview with Marilyn Wilson, executive director, Canadian Abortion Rights Action League, Ottawa, July 24, 2001.

Babb, Sarah. *Managing Mexico: From Nationalism to Neoliberalism.* Princeton, N.J.: Princeton University Press, 2001.

Barry, Tom, ed. *Mexico: A Country Guide.* Albuquerque, N.M.: Inter-Hemispheric Education Resource Center, 1992.

Bashevkin, Sylvia. *Women on the Defensive: Living Through Conservative Times.* Toronto: University of Toronto Press, 2003.

Brodbeck, Tom. "Hope Government Pays: Morgentaler Applauds Class Action," *Winnipeg Sun,* July 28, 2001.

Brodie, Janine. "Choice and No Choice in the House." In Janine Brodie, Shelley Gavigan, and Jane Jenson, ed., *The Politics of Abortion.* Toronto: Oxford University Press, 1992.

Canadian Medical Association, Masterfile, January 2001.

Canadians for Choice. Press release. "Women's Health Endangered by Provinces Refusing Funding for Abortion Care," May 4, 2001.

CARAL (Canadian Abortion Rights Action League). "Executive Summary of Brief to Legislative Committee on Bill C-43," 1969.

———. Information sheet. "Abortion in Canada Today: Province-by-Province Status," Spring 2001.

———. "Reciprocal Billing Agreements for Abortion Services Under the Canada Health Act," 1999.

CARAL website and Pro-Choice Action Network. "Abortion History—Chronology of Events." Available at www.caral.ca. Accessed 2001, 2002, and 2003.

Castells, Manuel. *The Power of Identity.* Oxford, UK: Blackwell, 1999.

Center for Reproductive Law and Policy (CRLP) and Grupo de Informacion en Reproduccion Elegida (GIRE). *Women of the World: Issues and Policies Affecting Their Reproductive Lives, Latin America, and the Caribbean.* 1st ed. New York: CRLP, November 1997.

————. "Women's Reproductive Rights in Mexico: A Shadow Report," New York, December 1997.

Chappell, Louise A. *Gendering Government: Feminist Engagement with the State and Australia and Canada.* Vancouver: University of British Columbia Press, 2002.

Dahl, Robert. *Who Governs?* New Haven, Conn.: Yale University Press, 1961.

de Valk, Alphonse. *Morality and Law in Canadian Politics: The Abortion Controversy.* Dorval, Quebec: Palm, 1974.

Dobrowolsky, Alexandra. *The Politics of Pragmatism: Women, Representation and Constitutionalism in Canada.* Toronto: Oxford University Press, 2000.

Dunphy, Catherine. *Morgentaler: A Difficult Hero.* Toronto: Random House, 1997.

Dunsmuir, Mollie. *Abortion: Constitutional and Legal Developments.* Ottawa: Library of Parliament, Parliamentary Research Branch, Paper Number 89-10E, August 1998.

Garrow, David J. *Liberty and Sexuality: The Right to Privacy and the Making of* Roe v. Wade. New York: Macmillan, 1994.

Gonzalez, Lucero M. "La penalizacion del aborto en Mexico," *Mujeres y Politica* (Universidad Autonoma Metropolitana, Xochimilco, Mexico), No. 1 (Autumn 1992).

Gorney, Cynthia. *Articles of Faith: A Frontline History of the Abortion Wars.* New York: Simon and Schuster, 1998.

Haussman, Melissa. "Of Rights and Power: Canada's Federal Abortion Policy, 1969–1991." In Dorothy McBride Stetson, ed., *Abortion Politics, Women's Movements, and the Democratic State.* Oxford, UK: Oxford University Press, 2001.

Health Canada. "Canada's Health Care System." Available at www.hc-sc.gc.ca. Accessed 2004.

IPPF (International Planned Parenthood Federation) website, www.ippf.org. Accessed 2003.

Jenson, Jane. "Getting to *Morgentaler*: From One Representation to Another." In Janine Brodie, Shelley Gavigan, and Jane Jenson, eds., *The Politics of Abortion.* Toronto: Oxford University Press, 1992.

Keck, Margaret E., and Kathryn Sikkink. *Activists Beyond Borders: Advocacy Networks in International Politics.* Ithaca: Cornell University Press, 1998.

Kellough, Gail. *Aborting Law: An Exploration of the Politics of Motherhood and Medicine.* Toronto: University of Toronto Press, 1996.

Kettl, Donald. *The Global Management Revolution.* Washington, D.C.: Brookings Institution, 2000.

Lamas, Marta. "De la A a la Z: A Feminist Alliance Experience." In Victoria

E. Rodriguez, ed., *Women's Participation in Mexican Political Life.* Boulder, Colo.: Westview, 1998.

Lee, Judy. Report in Statistic Canada's *The Daily.* Available at www.statscan.ca. Accessed 12/18/00.

Levy, Daniel C., and Kathleen Bruhn. *Mexico: The Struggle for Democratic Development.* Berkeley: University of California Press, 2001.

Morton, F. L. *Morgentaler v. Borowski: Abortion, the Charter, and the Courts.* Toronto: McClelland and Stewart, 1992.

NAF (National Abortion Federation) website, www.prochoice.org. Accessed 1/14/04 and 1/19/04.

NARAL website. "Fact Sheets: Access to Abortion," "Proactive Policy Institute," "State Legislation," and "Medicaid: Discriminatory Funding for Abortion." Available at www.naral.org. Accessed 1/3/02, 1/31/02, 1/14/04, 1/15/04, and 1/19/04.

Naylor, David. *Private Practice, Public Payment.* Montreal: McGill-Queen's University Press, 1986.

Ortiz, Adriana Ortega, Ana Amuchastegui, and Marta Rivas. "Because They Were Born from Me: Negotiating Women's Rights in Mexico." In Rosalind Petchesky and Karen Judd, eds., *Negotiating Reproductive Rights: Women's Perspectives Across Countries and Cultures.* London: Zed Books, 1998.

Petchesky, Rosalind Pollack. *Abortion and Women's Choice: The State, Sexuality, and Reproductive Freedom.* Boston: Northeastern University Press, 1985.

Rankin, Pauline, and Jill Vickers. "Locating Women's Politics." In Manon Tremblay and Caroline Andrew, eds., *Women and Political Representation in Canada.* Ottawa: University of Ottawa Press, 1998.

Risse-Kappen, Thomas, ed. *Bringing Transnational Relations Back In: Non-State Actors, Domestic Structures and International Institutions.* Cambridge: Cambridge University Press, 1999.

Rodriguez, Victoria E. *Women in Contemporary Mexican Politics.* Austin: University of Texas Press, 2003.

Schattschneider, E. E. *The Semisovereign People: A Realist's View of Democracy in America.* New York: Holt, Rinehart and Winston, 1960.

Smith, T. Alexander. *The Comparative Policy Process.* Santa Barbara: ABC-Clio, 1975.

Stetson, Dorothy McBride. "Abortion Politics: Public Policy in Cross-Cultural Perspective." In Marianne Githens and Dorothy McBride Stetson, eds., *Abortion Politics: Public Policy in a Cross-Cultural Perspective.* New York: Routledge, 1996.

Studlar, Donley, and Raymond Tatalovich. "Abortion Policy in the United States and Canada: Do Institutions Matter?" In Marianne Githens and Dorothy McBride Stetson, eds., *Abortion Politics: Public Policy in a Cross-Cultural Perspective.* New York: Routledge, 1996.

Tarrow, Sidney. *Power in Movement,* 2nd ed. Ithaca: Cornell University Press, 1998.

————. "States and Opportunities: The Political Structuring of Social Movements." In Doug McAdam, John D. McCarthy, and Mayer Zald, eds., *Comparative Perspectives on Social Movements*. New York: Cambridge University Press, 1996.

Tatalovich, Raymond. *The Politics of Abortion in the United States and Canada: A Comparative Study*. Armonk, N.Y.: M.E. Sharpe, 1997.

Taylor, Malcolm. "Health Insurance: The Roller Coaster in Federal-Provincial Relations." In David P. Shugarman and Reg Whitaker, eds., *Federalism and Political Community*. Peterborough, Ontario: Broadview Press, 1989.

Tuohy, Carolyn. *Accidental Logics: The Dynamics of Change in the Health Care Arena in the United States, Britain, and Canada*. New York: Oxford University Press, 1999.

United Nations. *Abortion Policies: A Global Review*. Vol. 2, *Gabon to Norway*. New York: United Nations, Department of Economic and Social Affairs, Population Division, 2001.

# Index

# About the Book

Despite legal affirmations of women's rights to abortion, actual access to the procedure in North America is increasingly curtailed. Melissa Haussman analyzes this disturbing disparity between official policies and daily realities in the United States, Canada, and Mexico.

Haussman examines the successes of U.S. anti-choice groups—groups that have extended their reach to effectively contest the rights of women throughout North America—as well as the efforts of pro-choice groups fighting to keep abortion available in Canada and the United States and to legalize it in Mexico. Her sobering conclusion is that basic reproductive rights are at risk of becoming meaningful only to the wealthy.

**Melissa Haussman** is associate professor of government at Suffolk University.